I0561052

William Jay

Prayers for the use of families

The domestic minister's assistant

William Jay

Prayers for the use of families
The domestic minister's assistant

ISBN/EAN: 9783337284015

Printed in Europe, USA, Canada, Australia, Japan

Cover: Foto ©Lupo / pixelio.de

More available books at **www.hansebooks.com**

PRAYERS

FOR THE

USE OF FAMILIES:

OR, THE

DOMESTIC

Minister's Assistant.

BY WILLIAM JAY,

AUTHOR OF SERMONS, DISCOURSES, &c. &c.

Hartford,

PUBLISHED BY SILAS ANDRUS.

1829.

PREFACE.

If, in the title of this volume, the author has used the word " minister," in rather an unusual latitude ; its adjective will serve to explain, and restrict it. The " domestic" minister, intends, not the pastor, or preacher : not the servant of the Most High God, who officially shows unto men the way of salvation—but he, who adopts the resolution of Joshua—" As for *me* and my *house, we* will serve the Lord."

The preservation and spread of religion should not depend, exclusively, on a particular order of men, however important their functions may be. *All* christians, in their respective stations, ought to co-operate with those, who are, by designation, workers together with God.

It ought to be a matter of thankfulness, that the number of ministers, properly so called, who enter into the spirit of their office, and preach the truth as it is in Jesus, is exceedingly increased. But compared with the field, and the vastness of the work, the labourers are yet few. And few they would be found, if multiplied a thousand fold ; and we should *still* need, the property, the talents, the influence, the example, the exertions, and the prayers, of *all* the subjects of divine grace.

And can their services be dispensed with—*now?*

God is not the God of confusion, but of peace : and He has said, " Let every thing be done decently and in order." It is his providence that determine the bounds of our habitation, and furnishes the several stations we occupy : and into *these* we are to look for our duties and opportunities. Men are often led out of their own proper sphere of action, in order to be useful; but it is ignorance, if not discontent, and pride, that tempts them astray.

As the stream of a river is most lovely and beneficial, when it patiently steals along its own channel, though it makes not so much noise, and excites not so much notice, as when it breaks over its banks, and roars and rolls as a flood ; so good men are most acceptable, and useful in their appointed course. Wisdom will estimate every man, by what he is, not out of his place and calling, but in them. *There* we naturally look after him ; there we unavoidably compare- him with his obligations ; there we see him habitually—and there he gains a character, or goes without one.

It is to be feared, that some, even of the stricter professors of religion, have a zeal of God, but not according to knowledge. It blazes at a distance · but it burns dim at home. In a day like the present, there will be many *occasional* calls of public *duty;* but it will be a sad exclamation to make at a dying hour, " My own vineyard have I not kept." In the spiritual, still more than in the temporal neglect, " He that provideth not for his own, especially those of his own house, hath denied the faith, and is worse than an infidel."

" You wish to serve your generation ?" It is well that it is in your heart; but let it be according to the will of God. And how does this require you to proceed ? From public relation into private, or from private into public ? Does it order you to waste time and strength, to go to a *distance;* and begin labouring, where difficulties will be too great, and means too few, to allow of your improving the waste, back to your own door ? Or, to begin *near ;* to cultivate onward ; to clear and fertilize the ground as you advance ; so as to feel every acquisition already made, converted into a resource to encourage, support, and assist you, in your future toil ?

" You long to be useful ?" And why are you not ?
Can you want either opportunity, or materials—
you, who are placed at the head of families ; *you*,
who are required to rule well your own households ;
to dwell with your wives according to knowledge ;
to train up your children in the nurture and admonition of the Lord ; to behave towards your servants, as remembering that you also have a master
in heaven.—Behold, O man of God, a congregation,
endeared and attentive, committed to thy trust.
Behold, a flock whom you may feed with knowledge and understanding ; and before whom you
may walk as an example in word, in conversation,
in charity, in spirit, in faith, in purity. Behold a
church in thy house. Behold an altar on which to
offer the morning and evening sacrifice of **prayer**
and of praise.

Here, observe these things without preferring
one before another ; here teach and exhort, and reprove with all long suffering and patience ; here
officiate—and " ye shall be named the PRIESTS of
the Lord ; men shall call you the MINISTERS of our
God."

The remark of Baxter is worthy our regard—" If
family religion was duly attended to, and properly
discharged, I think the preaching of the word,
would not be the common instrument of conversion." And Gurnal says—" The family is the nursery of the church. If the nursery be neglected,
what in time will become of the gardens, and the
orchards."

The author will not endeavour to establish the
duty of domestic worship. Many excellent things
have been written upon this subject : and what he,
himself, could offer in support of the practice, is
already before the public."*

It is futile to allege, as some have done, that
there is no positive and express command for it

* See the Introduction to the author's four volumes of Short Discourses for the use of families.

1*

in the Scripture ; when nothing would be more easy, than to prove the will of God—from the simplest deductions, from the fairest reasonings, and from the most generally acknowledged principles.

The examples of the faithful; the commendations which God has bestowed upon them in his word ; his promises and threatenings ; the obvious and numberless advantages resulting from domestic devotion, as to personal religion, and relative government—with regard to those that preside in the family ; and as to instruction, restraints, and motives—with regard to relations, children, and servants : all this must surely be enough to induce any man, capable of conviction, to terminate with a broken heart, the mischiefs of neglect ; and to swear unto the Lord, and vow unto the Mighty God of Jacob—" Surely, I will not come into the tabernacle of my house, nor go up into my bed, I will not give sleep to mine eyes, nor slumber to mine eyelids, until I find out a place for the Lord, an habitation for the Mighty God of Jacob."

As to objections arising from—shame—a want of time—the unfashionableness of the usage—or its interfering with visits or dissipations ; all this, in a being, who yet owns himself to be a moral and an accountable creature, is unworthy of argument, and would be too much honoured, by the attempt of refutation.

There is one thing however, which deserves notice. It is the apprehension of inability to perform this duty. With respect to some, if not many, it is no breach of charity to conclude, that this is an *excuse*, rather than a *reason*. It is disinclination, or at least, the want of a more powerful conviction, that hinders them from adopting this salutary usage, rather than incapacity. There are few cases in which the old adage is not to be verified : " Where there is a will, there is a way." You feel little difficulty in making known your distresses or wishes to a fellow creature : and the Lord look-eth, not to the excellency of the language, but to the heart. The facility would be increased by practice, and the divine blessing.

And I cannot but earnestly recommend the use of free and extemporaneous prayer, where it is practicable. There is in it, a freshness, a particularity, an appropriateness, an immediate adoption, and use of circumstances and events, which cannot be found in the best composed forms.

Yet there are those, who have only a slender degree of religious knowledge ; or discover a natural slowness and hesitancy of utterance ; or feel a bashfulness of temper, so that they cannot gain confidence enough even to make a proper trial. And this diffidence is often found, even with persons of education and understanding—Indeed, such are more likely to feel difficulty, than the vulgar and illiterate, whose ignorance is friendly to fluency, and whose confidence is not perplexed by modes of expression, or embarrassed by the influence of reputation.

Now in cases of inability, or extreme difficulty, surely the greatest zealot for free prayer, would recommend forms in preference to neglect.

Besides, there are others—many in the establishment, and no few out of it ; who, deem a form more eligible : and it is needless to remark, that they have a right to their opinion : and as their practice will of course be regulated by it ; it is desirable to aid them in their own way.

And surely in this case, as well as in many others, where we see so much talent, and religion, and even devotional taste, in the opposing advocates ; candour requires, and compels the concession, that all the arguments, all the advantages, cannot be on *one* side of the question.

Bigotry delights in exclusion ; but the meekness of wisdom is satisfied with preference ; and freely says, " Let every one be fully persuaded in his own mind." The amiable Dr. Watts observes—" Many a holy soul has found his inward powers awaken-ed, and excited to lively religion, in the use of a form, where the wants and wishes of the heart have been happily expressed ; and considering the various infirmities that surround human nature, even the wisest and best of men, may be glad of such assistances, at some seasons.''

Several books of prayers have issued from the press ; and it is not necessary to undervalue, or conceal them, in order to excuse or even justify, another effort in the same cause. The great ex-cellency of some of these composures is well known.

Yet it must be confessed, that such works, com-pared with other religious publications, are still very few ; and that the far greater part of what we possess, is more for personal and private use, than domestic. Even in the deservedly popular volume of Jenks, there are only *family* prayers for *one week* ; the rest for all *individual* service.

But whatever might have been the author's own opinion of the expediency, or necessity of such a work as this—in order to furnish a greater abund-ance—or to accommodate a difference of tastes—or to excite attention by newness—or to edify more by brevity and simplicity ; he can truly aver, that he was principally induced to undertake it at the request of many, urged, for years, with im-portunity.

In complying with their desires, he still fears he shall not satisfy their wishes. He unquestionably has not satisfied his own. In the want of that lei-sure, which allows a man to throw his whole soul into the composition of this work ; and then to employ all his skill in correcting and completing it, he has done, at the intervals of much public duty, and interruption, for a few months, what he could ; and such as it is, should it obtain accep-tance, he shall consider it the greatest honour that could have been conferred upon him, that while living and when dead, the service of God should ever be performed in words which he has furnished, so imperfectly.

He can reckon on some esteemed connexions, whose partiality, as it has often admitted him into their circles as a friend, and employed him at their domestic altar as an expositor and intercessor, will retain him as an assistant, in this volume ; and thus while absent in body, he will be present in spirit. He is also blessed with children, who will not neglect a practice, to which, in the order of a happy family, they were so early accustomed, and which was never rendered irksome by tediousness ; and they will—he knows they will—train up their children in the same holy and lovely usage ; and should relationship and endearment, serve to render the book the more valued and useful as a sacred bequest to his descendants ; this alone would keep him from thinking he had laboured in vain.

PERCY-PLACE, April 1820.

Advertisement.

THE author begs leave to offer a few words, on the execution of the work itself, here submitted to public attention.

Family prayers ought to be short, especially, where reading the Scriptures makes a part of the service—and it ought always to make a part. Hence the prayers for the week-days, may be read in five or six minutes : those for the sabbath are commonly a little longer, as families have then more leisure, and are more united : those for particular occasions, as they rarely return, and the events are remarkable, are the longest of all.

A prayer is distinguishable from the repetition of a creed; or the annunciation of a system of theology ; how much more from the sparring and reflections of controversy! A tincture of the author's own particular sentiments, was hardly avoidable : but he has sought after nothing, that would be offensive to christians, who differ from him. And as religious persons accord much more when kneeling, than sitting ; he ventures to think, no one will be unable to join in these forms, who believes in the fall of man, the redemption of the cross, justification by faith, the necessity of divine influence, and of that holiness, without which we cannot see the Lord. The author braves the suspicion of those, who are illiberal enough to guage a man's orthodoxy, by the use of an invariable doxology ; in the words too, which man's wisdom teacheth. Not that he thinks it wrong to close a prayer with a Scriptural meaning in human terms ; but he prefers the words which the Holy Ghost useth ; and where they afford a diversity, why should he be afraid to avail himself of it ? In this respect, the sacred writers would not bear the ordeal of some system-critics.

The author thinks no one can blame him, for using so much of the language of the Scriptures : there is a sacredness in it ; and it is well known : much of it too has been used ,evotionally : and contains the adorations, confessions, supplications, and thanksgivings uttered by men of God before us, while kneeling at a throne of grace.

Besides being Scriptural in the diction, he has endeavoured to be very plain and simple. There is a great difference between addressing men, and addressing God. The least artificial mode of uttering our thoughts in prayer is the best. Prayer admits of no brilliancies : every studied ornament it rejects with disdain. He who feels interested in prayer, will forget all critical and elaborate phraseology. And it is an infelicity to be deplored, rather than an excellency to be admired, when ingenuity of thought, or surprisingness of expression, catches and keeps off the attention from devotion. There are young divines, who not only err in preaching—by substituting finery for elegance, and the affectation of art for the eloquence of feeling ; but in their devotional exercises too— showing off their tawdrinesses, even in the presence of God, and praying in a strained, inflated style, unintelligible to the ignorant, lamented by the pious, and contemned by the wise. The greatest men have always been distinguished by the plainness and simplicity of their devotional language. What a difference is there between the other compositions of Johnson, and his prayers ? No hard word, no elaborate sentence, no classical, no metaphorical allusion is to be found in any of the few forms of devotion which he has left us. The same excellency pervades the liturgy. And it is worthy of remark, that in no prayer recorded in the Bible, is any figure employed, unless as familiar as the literal expression.

This, however, does not forbid the use of sentences not *directly* of the nature of petition. Prayer is designed, not only as a homage to God, but as a moral exercise to affect ourselves: and to accomplish this' purpose, we must be informed, or reminded. What, therefore, tends to make us *feel* the things we implore, is not to be considered, as some call it, a preaching or talking in prayer. Read all the prayers given us in the Scriptures; there is not one of them which does not contain expressions of enlargement, not immediately petitionary—yet conducive to the design.

With regard to appropriateness, Jenks has observed, "That we may as well expect to find a shoe that will fit every foot, as a form of prayer to suit every purpose." Family prayers must be necessarily general, or adapted to the state of a household, *devoid of its peculiarities.* No form can be made to include every particular circumstance, or occurrence; the very things that would render it suitable to one family, would even hinder the use of it by another. The author fears, whether in two or three instances, he has not forgotten this.

Yet events and circumstances are perpetually arising, and it is of great importance to notice them *devotionally.* Almost every prayer in the Scriptures arose out of particular occurrences, and was designed to improve them. Here is a difficulty which there is only one way of removing. It is by adding some short addresses, applicable to certain events and circumstances; and which the reader may insert, in their proper place, in the prayer; or use at the end of it. Many of these, therefore, the author has supplied in the close of the volume. Many more might have been added, had the prayers been designed for *personal* and *private* use.

In *seventy* forms of the same kind, it was not easy to maintain so much diversity as some would wish. Family devotion in itself, admits of less variety, than either private or public worship But though similarity will be sometimes found, sameness, he believes, with a few very trifling exceptions, has been avoided. This does not extend however to the repetition of the same *Scripture* sentences.

The author has felt what a difference there is between offering, and writing a prayer: but he endeavoured, as much as possible, when he retired to compose, to place himself by thought, in the situation of performance: and followed the same mode in writing, which he has always found the best, in praying, to exclude formality, and to gain variety, viz. to yield to the *present* feeling of the mind, whether it leads to indulge *principally* in confession, or in thanksgiving, petition, or intercession.

Some things must be *always* expressed; others can be admitted only *occasionally.* Yet these should not be forgotten. Cases of affliction ; the state of public affairs ; the nation ; the cause of God in the world ; these and other things, though not particularized in every exercise, must be noticed so frequently, as to keep the mind alive to them.

With regard to the prayers for particular occasions—such as pertain to days of mourning, fasting or thanksgiving ; and those which respect the beginning and end of the year, will draw forth no objection. But as to those which regard religious *festivals*, some will probably condemn the author on the ground of consistency. On that ground he is willing to be tried. Consistency refers to professed principles; and he avows principles, which raise him above any particular body of christians, while yet he deems it his honour to belong to one of them in preference to all others.

But his attachment to his regiment, does not make him an enemy to the army of which it is a part. Let every one of us, says the Apostle, please his neighbour, for his good to edification. Why should not the author wish to be serviceable to members of other communions, as well as to those of his own?

Dr. Watts, though a firm Pedobaptist, has yet composed and inserted in his excellent book, several hymns, adapted to the convictions of those, who practise adult baptism, by immersion only.

And the late Mr. Newton, though an Episcopalian, made no scruple, when desired, to draw up a plan for a dissenting academy.

Let us stand in the liberty wherewith Christ has made us free. Let not him that eateth, despise him that eateth not; and let not him that eateth not, judge him that eateth, for God hath received him. Who art thou that judgest another man's servant? to his own master he standeth or falleth. One man esteemeth one day above another, another esteemeth every day alike. Let every man be fully persuaded in his own mind. He that regardeth the day, regardeth it unto the Lord; and he that regardeth not the day to the Lord, he doth not regard it. Here every thing non-essential is left, where it ought to be left, to individual *conviction* and *candour*.

Upon these principles, the author thinks, a dissenter, without superstition, may use these forms, on these *very days:* especially as he is under no compulsion, and he has nothing to do with the day, but as a season of leisure, and as reminding him of some important truth.

A christian, although he disregards the seasons, must love the *subjects* connected with them: and at some time or other, he may wish more *expressly* to notice them; and this he can do, by means of these forms, with the omission of a few words.

It is comparatively easy to be long and diffuse, but to be select, and yet full, brief, and yet comprehensive—this is the trial.

The author could have composed a single
prayer, far superior to any of these ; but the difficulty lay in the number ; and the work must be
judged of as a whole.

It is hardly necessary to observe, that with a
slight alteration, and the substitution of the singu-
lar number for the plural, most of these prayers
will serve for the closet, as well as the family.

FAMILY PRAYERS

——:o:——

First Week.

——:o:——

SUNDAY MORNING.

O COME let us worship and fall down, let us kneel before the Lord our Maker, for he is our God, and we are the people of his pasture and the sheep of his hand.

Yes, O Lord, we are thine ; and Thee we are bound to serve. We grieve to think, how many of our fellow creatures live without Thee in the world ; and confess with shame, that other lords have had dominion over *us:* but henceforth, by Thee only, will we make mention of thy name. We hope Thou hast subdued the insensibility and indifference towards Thyself, so awfully natural to us; and awakened in us the inquiry, " Where is God my Maker that giveth songs in the night ?" We hope we are disposed to acknowledge Thee in all our ways ; but we feel our need of the exercises of devotion. We trust we hold communion with Thee every day ; but we find week days, to be worldly days ; and our allowed intercourse with secular concerns, tends to reduce our heavenly impressions, and to make us forgetful of our work, and our rest. We therefore bless Thee for the return of a day, sacred to our souls and eternity ; a time of refreshing from the presence of the Lord ; in which, by waiting upon Thee, our hearts are enlarged, and our strength is renewed ; so that we can mount up with wings as eagles, run and not be weary, and walk and not faint.

2*

This is the day which the Lord hath made, we will rejoice and be glad in it. O let our minds be withdrawn from the world, as well as our bodies. Let our retirement be devout. Let our meditation be sweet. Let our conversation be edifying. Let our reading be pious. Let our hearing be profitable ; and on Thee may we wait all the day.

Afford us the supply of the spirit of Jesus Christ. None can need thy succours more than we. Thou knowest our infirmities : let thy strength be made perfect in our weakness. Our duties are far above our own power : let thy grace be sufficient for us. Our dangers are numberless, and we are utterly unable to keep ourselves from falling ; hold Thou us up, and we shall be safe. The burdens we feel would press our lives down to the ground ; lay underneath us thine everlasting arms. Fears alarm us ; cares corrode us ; losses impoverish us ; our very affections are the sources of our afflictions—surely man walketh in a vain show—surely we are disquieted in vain ; all, all is vanity and vexation of spirit. While in the world we have tribulation ; in Thee may we have peace : and in the multitude of our thoughts within us, may thy comforts delight our souls.

Yet, O Lord, we would remember, that gratitude becomes us much more than complaint. Our afflictions have been light, compared with our guilt ; and few, compared with the sufferings of others. They have all been attended with numberless alleviations : they have all been needful : all founded in a regard to our welfare : all designed to work together for our good. We bless Thee for what is past, and trust Thee for what is to come : and cast all our care upon Thee, knowing that Thou carest for us.

Thou hast commanded us to pray for all men, that we may be bound by our very devotions, as we have opportunity to do good unto all men, especially unto them that are of the household of

faith. May we always cherish and display benevolent dispositions towards our dependents, forgiving dispositions towards our enemies, peaceable
dispositions towards our neighbours, and candid
dispositions towards our fellow christians. May
we be able to say with our Lord and Saviour,
whosoever shall do the will of my Father that is in
heaven, the same is my brother, and sister, and
mother. And pray with Paul, grace be with *all*
them that love our Lord Jesus Christ in sincerity.
May the goings of our God and King be seen, this
day, in every Christian sanctuary. Go with *us* to
thy house, and give testimony to the word of thy
grace. May it have free course and be glorified
in the hearts and lives of those who shall hear it.
May it enlighten the ignorant, awaken the careless,
reclaim the wandering, establish the weak, comfort
the feeble minded, and make ready a people prepared for the Lord.

Remember those who are, this day, denied our
advantages. Be a little sanctuary to them in the
midst of their privations, and let them know that
Thou are not confined to temples made with hands.
And O forget not those who never enjoyed our
privileges; never smiled when a sabbath appeared; never heard of the name of a Saviour—and let
thy way be known on earth, thy saving health
among all nations. Our Father, who art in
heaven, hallowed be thy name. Thy kingdom
come. Thy will be done in earth, as it is in
heaven. Give us this day our daily bread. And
forgive us our trespasses, as we forgive them that
trespass against us. And lead us not into temptation; but deliver us from evil : for thine is the
kingdom, and the power, and the glory, for ever
and ever. Amen.

SUNDAY EVENING.

Who is like unto Thee, O Lord, among the
gods ? Who is like Thee, glorious in holiness,
fearful in praises, doing wonders ? May we approach Thee with the humility which is due to
thy greatness, and the hope that becomes thy
goodness. For though Thou art high, yet hast
Thou respect unto the lowly; and though continually adored by thrones and dominions, principalities and powers, yet Thou despisest not the
prayer of the destitute, but wilt hear their prayer.
Our fathers cried unto Thee and were delivered.
They trusted in Thee and were not confounded.
And Thou never saidst to the seed of Jacob, seek
ye me in vain.

Behold a company of sinners at thy footstool,
earnestly praying to be remembered with the favour Thou bearest unto thy people, and to be visited with thy salvation. We would not overlook
the blessings of the life that now is. If we have
food and raiment, and agreeable connexions, and
ease, and health, and safe abode, we would bless
Thee ; for we have no claim to these bounties,
and our present condition renders them valuable.
But they are not our God.

> "Give what Thou canst, without Thee we are poor,
> And with Thee rich, take what Thou wilt away."

Thou art the strength of our hearts, and our
portion for ever. Whom have we in heaven but
Thee ; and there is none upon earth that we desire
beside Thee ?

And praise waiteth for Thee, O God, in Zion.
We long to be able, with unshaken confidence, to
apply the promises of thy grace to ourselves; and
to say, Thou shalt guide *me* with thy counsel, and
afterwards receive me to glory. O say 'o our souls,
in language our consciences can understand, I am

thy salvation : and give us a token for good, that we may rejoice in Thee.

Yet, O God, we would not rest satisfied with a conviction of our relation to Thee, while we are regardless of improving it. May we walk worthy of the Lord, unto all pleasing, being fruitful in every good work, and increasing in the knowledge of God ; strengthened with all might according to his gracious power, unto all patience and long suffering with joyfulness ; giving thanks unto the Father who hath made us meet to be partakers of the inheritance of the saints in light. We can never discharge the obligations thy abundant mercy has laid us under ; but may we ever show that we are sensible of them ; and that our impressed hearts are asking, " *what* shall I render unto the Lord for all his benefits towards me ?" While we hear Thee saying, O do not that abominable thing which I hate, may we be effectually deterred from sin, and induced to watch and pray, lest we enter into temptation. May the love be shed abroad in our hearts, that none of thy commandments may be grievous. May thy glory be dear to us ; may we inquire after thy will with impartiality, and conform ourselves to it with diligence. Uphold us by thy free spirit ; and let the words of our mouths and the meditations of our hearts be acceptable in thy sight, O Lord, our strength and our Redeemer.

Hitherto we have been compelled to exclaim, my leanness, my leanness. We have been no better in religion, than a bruised reed, or smoking flax. But it is our mercy that Thou dost not despise the day of small things ; and our encouragement, that Thou givest more grace ; that Thou hast promised to perfect that which concerneth us ; and commanded us to ask and receive, that our joy may be full. May we, therefore, not only be humble but active ; may we not only shake off sloth but despondency ; may we be strong in the Lord

and in the power of his might ; and increase with
all the increase of God, till we are filled with
all the fullness of God.

Thou knowest what is in man, and what is necessary to him. Thou art not only addressing us
continually by the voice of creation, and the varying events of thy providence, but Thou hast
given us thy word and thine ordinances. We
behold our sabbaths, our eyes see our teachers,
and our ears hear the joyful sound of salvation
by the cross, and the grace of our Lord Jesus.
Prophets and righteous men desired to see the
things that we see, and did not see them ; and to
hear the things that we hear, and did not hear
them. But blessed are our eyes for they see, and
our ears for they hear. Yet we would remember,
that our responsibility will be answerable to our
talents ; that our chief danger results from our
greatest privileges ; and, that our very blessings
may be converted into a curse. We would therefore fear, lest a promise being left us of entering
into thy rest, any of us should seem to come
short of it.

Bless this family. May those of us who are at
the head of it, walk within our house with a perfect heart, and set no wicked thing before our
eyes. May we have a testimony in the bosoms
of those who have the best opportunities of ob-
serving us, that in simplicity and godly sincerity,
not with fleshly wisdom, but by thy grace we
have our conversation in the world, and more especially with them. May we conduct ourselves
towards those who serve us, as knowing that we
have a Master in heaven, and that there is no respect of persons with God ; and may our servants,
in fulfilling the duties of their station, serve the
Lord Christ. May we train up our children in the
nurture and admonition of the Lord ; and have
the inexpressible satisfaction of seeing them walk
in the truth. We ask not great things for them

of a worldly nature; only give them health of body and soundness of mind, and food and raiment convenient and sufficient for them; but, O bless them with all spiritual blessings, and number them with thy saints in glory everlasting. Pity those parents whose hearts are bleeding over children of disobedience; and hear all the pious, whose irreligious relations are forcing them often to exclaim, "How shall I endure to see the destruction of my kindred?"

Hast not Thou made of one blood, all the nations of men that dwell upon the face of all the earth? Remember the work of thy hands. Have respect unto thy holy covenant; and let the world know, that Thou hast so loved *it*, as to give thy only begotten Son, that whosoever believeth in Him should not perish, but have everlasting life.

Hearken favourably unto the prayers that have this day been offered up unto Thee for our beloved country, and for those who have been entrusted with the government thereof.

Thou hast given us a pleasant land to dwell in: Thou hast made us to rejoice in the many and great things thou hast done for us.

May we never be ungrateful for the privileges we enjoy, nor provoke Thee by our sins to remove them.

May they be continued to the latest posterity; and be sanctified to us, and to our children. As Thou hast given us such a distinguished rank among the nations, may we be for a name and a praise unto Thee, in the whole earth; and as we have been the objects of thy loving kindness, may we ever be the instruments in thy hands of good to others; and from us may the word of the Lord sound out into every land.

Now, unto Him that is able to do exceeding abundantly above all that we ask or think, according to the power that worketh in us, unto Him be glory in the church, by Christ Jesus, throughout all ages, world without end. Amen.

MONDAY MORNING.

O THOU God of all grace ; the Father of mercies, the hope of Israel, the Saviour thereof in the time of trouble : why hast Thou revealed Thyself in such lovely characters, and endearing relations, but to meet our dejections, to remove our fears, and induce us to say, it is good for me to draw nigh to God.

We come to Thee as criminals to be pardoned, as beggars to obtain relief, and as friends to enjoy communion with the God of love. We bow with submission and gratitude, to the method which Thou hast appointed and made known for all intercourse between Thee and us. We approach Thee, through him in whom Thou hast proclaimed Thyself well pleased, pleading the propitiation of his blood, and making mention of his righteousness, and of his only.

But we can have access to Thee through him only—by one Spirit—that Spirit, the residue of which is with Thee, and which has actuated the souls of thy people, in all ages. O give thy Holy Spirit to them that now ask Thee. May He open the eyes of our understanding, and convince us of sin. May He humble the pride of our self-righteous hearts, and expel us from every refuge of lies. May He glorify Christ in our wants, desires, dependence, and application, and take of the things of Christ, and show them to us. May we be enabled to receive the Lord Jesus in all his blessings and treasures ; and though now we see Him not, yet believing, may we rejoice with joy unspeakable and full of glory. In all the distresses of conscience, in all the afflictions of life, and in all the dissatisfactions necessarily experienced in creature-enjoyments, may we repair, weary and heavy laden to *Him*, who has promised to give us rest. May the vanity of the world wean us from its pursuits; and may the tribulation of the world endear the peace which no storm can prevent or destroy.

May we arise and depart hence; may we confess ourselves to be only strangers and pilgrims upon earth; and declare plainly, too plainly to be misunderstood, that we seek a better country, even an heavenly. Prepare us for all the allotments of this short, and changing, and uncertain life. May we have a safe passage out of it, and a comfortable passage through it; and be useful while we are in it. May we continually illustrate in our character and conduct, the representations Thou hast given of thy people, as the dew of heaven, the salt of the earth, the light of the world. May we never deem it enough to be blameless and harmless; but may our light so shine before men, that they may see our good works, and glorify our Father which is in heaven. May we never be ashamed of Jesus or of his words; never be deterred from the prosecution of a known duty by the fear of man; and never be discouraged from attempting it, by a consciousness of our own weakness. Having thy sanction and presence, may we be strong and courageous; and be steadfast, and unmoveable; always abounding in the work of the Lord.

What we know not, teach Thou us. Lead us into all truth. May we see divine things in a divine light, that while they inform our judgment they may sanctify the heart, and consecrate the whole life to the service and glory of God. Who can understand his errors? Cleanse Thou us from secret faults. Search us, O God, and know our hearts, try us and know our thoughts, and see if there be any wicked way in us, and lead us in the way everlasting.

Accept of our united thanksgivings for the preservation and refreshment of the past night; and take us under thy guiding and guardian care this day ; and whether we eat or drink, or whatever we do, may we do all to the glory of God, through our Lord and Saviour. Amen.

MONDAY EVENING

WE have heard that to the Lord our God belong mercies and forgiveness, though we have rebelled against him. Hence, we are encouraged to approach Thee. For we are verily guilty, we are deeply guilty. If our depravity has not always broken forth into action, our hearts have been deceitful above all things, and desperately wicked ; and if our transgressions have not been so gross as those of many of our fellow-creatures, they have been more aggravated, because committed against goodness the most astonishing, light the most clear, and advantages the most distinguishing. And Thou hast seen all, and abhorred all, and couldst easily and righteously have punished us for all. But Thou hast not executed upon us the fierceness of thine anger, because Thou art God and not man. Neither hast Thou treated us with neglect ; but Thou hast remembered us in our low estate ; and not only without our desert, but, without our desire, Thou wast pleased to devise means for our restoration to thy favour, and image, and presence.

We bless Thee for a purpose of grace given us in Christ Jesus before the world began. We rejoice that in the fulness of time he assumed our nature, and became obedient unto death, even the death of the cross ; and that as he was delivered for our offences, so he was raised again for our justification, and ascending up on high, entered into the holy place, as a proof of the sufficiency and acceptance of the sacrifice he offered. We rejoice that he has received the whole dispensation

of the Spirit, and that in Him all fulness dwells.
And we bless Thee for the proclamations of the
gospel, which hold him forth to our view in all his
grace and glory, and unsearchable riches, that we
through patience and comfort of the Scripture
might have hope.

O Thou God of hope, fill us with all joy and
peace in believing thy promises and invitations,
that we may abound in hope through the power
of the Holy Ghost. May we esteem all things but
loss for the excellency of the knowledge of Christ
Jesus our Lord ; and may we supremely desire to
win Christ, knowing that he who hath the Son of
God hath life, and shall never come into condemnation. May we prove that we are joined to
the Lord, by being one spirit with him ; may our
sentiments, tempers, and conduct, be formed after
the example which he left us ; and may we never
consider ourselves Christians, but as we long to be
like him, and the life also of Jesus is made ma-
nifest in our mortal body. May we never love a
world that crucified the Lord of glory ; nor suffer
those sins to live that caused him to die. May his
grace, in becoming poor, that we through his
poverty might be rich, make us ashamed of our
selfishness ; and may his unexampled love, in
giving his life a ransom for us, so constrain us, as
to render any services or sacrifices, for his sake,
our delight.

May He never be wounded in the house of his
professed friends ; may we rather die than bring
a reproach upon his cause. May all his followers
be dear to us. May we recommend him to those
that know him not, that they may seek him, with
us. Let the number of those who love his salvation, daily increase ; and let the accessions include
every member of our household, and all our absent friends. And hasten, O Lord, the blessed
hour, when all kings shall fall down before him,
and all nations shall serve him—and blessed be

his glorious name for ever! And let the whole earth be filled with his glory.

We praise Thee as the length of our days and the God of our mercy. In the morning we committed ourselves to thy care, and Thou hast been with us in our going out and our coming in ; and hast kept us in all our ways. Pardon whatever Thou hast seen amiss in us through another period of our time. Accept the charge of us through the approaching night ; and grant us the sleep which Thou givest thy beloved ; as we hope we desire it, not only as creatures, but as Christians ; not only to gratify our feelings, but to renew our strength for thy service, and to fit us to glorify Thee in our bodies as well as in our spirits, through our adorable Redeemer. Amen.

TUESDAY MORNING.

O Thou omnipresent and omniscient Jehovah. Thou art about our path, and our lying down ; and Thou art acquainted with all our ways. There is not a word in our tongue, but lo! O Lord, Thou knowest it altogether. Thou understandest our very thoughts afar off. Yea, the darkness hideth not from Thee, but the night shineth as the day : the darkness and the light are both alike to Thee.

Known, therefore, to thee are our sins with every aggravation ; and our necessities with all their circumstances ; and, yet, Thou requirest us to confess our guilt, and to spread our wants before Thee, in order that we ourselves may be suitably affected with them, and be prepared for the promised displays of thy goodness. Every view we take of ourselves, convinces us that we lie entirely at thy mercy, and that it is only because thy compassions fail not, we are not consumed. We know not the evil there is in one sin, and our

iniquities are more in number than the hairs upon
our head. Thou art our Creator; but of the
rock that begat us we are unmindful, and have
forgotten the God that formed us. Thou hast
nourished and brought up children; but we have
rebelled against Thee. Thou hast given us laws,
founded in a regard to our welfare as well as thine
own glory; but we have said with our lives, if
not with our lips, Who is the Lord that we should
obey his voice? Thou art the perfection of beauty,
the centre of excellency, the source of all blessedness; and Thee we ought to have loved supremely; but we have loved and served the creature more than the Creator; we have loved idols,
and after them we have gone. Instead of praying, Lord, lift Thou up the light of thy counte
nance upon us, we have asked with the multitude,
Who will show us any good? Departing from
Thee, we have made flesh our arm. We have
leaned on broken reeds, and though they have disappointed our hopes, and pierced us through with
many sorrows, we have often returned to the same
wretched dependence. Thou hast raised up for
us a Saviour; and the gospel has presented to our
view a plan of redemption and renovation, which
the angels desire to look into. But we have crowned all our guilt, by neglecting so great salvation,
and turning away from Him that speaketh from
heaven; and we deserve to be for ever excluded
from all the blessings of the cross.

O deal not with us after our desert, but according to our necessity; and where sin has abounded,
may grace much more abound. Over all our unworthiness may grace reign through righteousness
unto eternal life by Jesus Christ our Lord. It is
thy pleasure that we seek Thee. The desires
we feel are of thine own producing. We are
willing to be saved in thy own way. We love thy
salvation—we love it as it is free, and secures to
thyself the undivided glory: and we love it as it
3*

is holy, and designed to save us from the power as well as the penalty of sin. O visit us with thy salvation. Shine into our hearts, and give us the light of the knowledge of thy glory in the face of Jesus Christ. Enable us by faith to embrace thy unspeakable gift. May we sit at his feet. May we glory in his cross. May we imbibe his spirit. May we follow his example; and whatever we do, in word or deed, may we do all in the name of the Lord Jesus.

We extend our wishes beyond the little circle now kneeling in thy presence. We have various absent connexions endeared to our hearts; O place them under thy agency, as the God of grace; and keep them under thy care as the God of providence.

We would remember them that are in bonds, as bound with them, and those that suffer adversity as being ourselves also in the body. Address to the hearts of the afflicted the promise, I will be with thee in trouble; thy shoes shall be iron and brass, and as thy days, so shall thy strength be. Let glory dwell in our land, and upon all the glory may there be a defence. Do good in thy good pleasure unto Zion; build thou the walls of Jerusalem. Make bare thine arm in the sight of all the nations; and let all the ends of the earth see the salvation of our God.

May the grace of our Lord Jesus Christ, and the love of God, and the communion of the Holy Ghost, be with us all, now and for evermore. Amen.

TUESDAY EVENING.

O THOU who wast, and art, and art to come, the Almighty. With Thee is the fountain of life. In thy presence there is fullness of joy, and at thy right-hand there are pleasures for evermore. It is our privilege as well as our duty, to draw near to Thee. It is the prerogative of our nature, that of all creatures in this lower world, we alone are made capable of knowing, resembling, serving, and enjoying Thee. All our degradations and misery have been produced by our alienation and absence from Thee; and all our happiness and perfection depend upon our re-union and intercourse with Thee. We, therefore, bless Thee for the revelation Thou hast given us, and by which we learn, that thy thoughts towards us are thoughts of peace, and not of evil. We rejoice in a new and living way into the holiest, by the blood of Jesus, who has once suffered for sins, the just for the unjust, that he might bring us unto God. We pray that the grand design of this sacrifice may be accomplished in each of us. May we feel that we are brought back from the dreadful distance to which sin had conveyed us, and that we are one with God again; and henceforth, may the life that we lead in the flesh, be a life of communion with the Father of our spirits, and of devotedness to him. May thy service be the employment of our days, and the enjoyment of our hearts. May we love thy commands, and acquiesce in thy dispensations; and then we are at the gate of heaven.

We lament that this has been so little the case with us, since we have known Thee, or rather have been known of Thee. We ought to be ashamed to think, that after all the instructions of thy word, the ordinances of thy house, and the discipline of thy family, our ears are still so dull of hearing, and our hearts so slow to believe; that our souls so cleave unto the dust; that we live so much under the influence of things seen and temporal; and feel so little of the powers of a world to come. How obscure is our knowledge; how weak our faith; how low our hope; how wavering our obedience ; how lifeless our worship. O Lord clothe us with humility ; and in this attire help us to present Thee the sacrifice of a broken heart and a contrite spirit, which Thou wilt not despise.

And since Thou art the God of all grace, and hast commanded us to ask and receive, that our joy may be full ;—afford us more of the supply of the spirit of Jesus Christ, to give more decision to our character, and more earnestness to our zeal ;—that with enlarged hearts in the way of thy commandments we may run, and not be weary, and walk and not faint. May we always realize thy presence ; and may the thought, that thine eye is upon us, operate as a check to sin, an excitement to duty, and a source of consolation. May we bear with firmness and submission the various trials of life and religion, and derive from them, all the advantage which they are designed to afford. May we glorify the Lord in the fires, and may every day of trouble afford us an opportunity to prove the truth of thy promise, the tenderness of thy care, and the supports of thy grace. May tribulation work patience, and patience experience, and experience hope.

But how few, how limited, and how light are the afflictions with which we are exercised. How much more reason have we to be thankful than to complain. Bless the Lord, O our souls, and all that is within us bless his holy name. Bless the Lord, O our souls, and forget not all his benefits ; who forgiveth all our iniquities ; who healeth all our diseases ; who redeemeth our lives from destruction ; who crowneth us with loving kindness and tender mercies.

We praise Thee for the protection, the supplies and the comforts of another day. Take us under thy care for the night on which we have entered. May no evil befall us, nor any plague come nigh our dwelling. Refresh our bodies, and

renew our strength, by needful repose ; and when
we awake, may we be still with God, and rise
to love Thee more, and serve Thee better, than we
ever have done ; through our Lord and Saviour,
to whom be glory for ever and ever. Amen.

WEDNESDAY MORNING.

AGAIN we lift up our eyes unto the hills from
whence cometh our help : our help is in the name
of the Lord God, who made heaven and earth.

Thou art the Author of all existence, and the
source of all blessedness. We adore Thee for making us capable of knowing Thee ; for possessing us
with reason, and conscience ; and for leading us to
inquire where is God my Maker that giveth
songs in the night. We praise Thee for all the
information with which we are favoured, to bring
us to thyself ; especially the revelation of the gospel. Here we look into thy very heart, and see
that it is the dwelling place of pity. Here we
see thy thoughts towards us, and find that they
are thoughts of peace and not of evil. Here we
see Thee waiting to be gracious, and exalted to
have mercy. Here Thou hast told our consciences how the guilty can be pardoned, the unholy can be sanctified, and the poor furnished
with unsearchable riches.

May we be found in the number of those who
not only hear, but know the joyful sound, that
we may walk in the light of thy countenance, in
thy name rejoice all the day, and in thy righteousness be exalted. May we take Thee, the God of
truth, at thy word ; and believe the record, that
Thou hast given to us eternal life and that this
life is in thy Son. And since it is not only a faithful saying but worthy of all acceptance, that He
came into the world to save sinners to Him may

we look alone for salvation, and with all the earnestness, the infinite importance of the case requires.

And to Him may we *immediately* repair, remembering how short and uncertain our time is ; and
filled with holy horror at the thought of closing a
life of precious, but neglected privileges, with the
exclamation. The harvest is past, the summer is
ended, and we are not saved. We long for the
experience of a present salvation, not only in the
comforts, but in the renewings of the Holy Ghost.
We desire to have nothing more to do with sin ;
and pray as sincerely to be restored to thy image,
as to be reinstated in thy favour. We implore
spiritual graces, as well as spiritual blessings ; and
pray that we may always value religious duties,
as religious privileges. Deliver us from the disposition of the slave, and uphold us, in all our goings, by thy free Spirit ; and enable us to run in the
way of thy commandments with freedom and delight.

May we cherish simplicity and godly sincerity
of character ; may we be in reality before God,
what we are in appearance before men ;—Israelites indeed, in whom is no guile. May we *be*
religious, before we *profess* religion, and leave the
world, before we enter the church ; that we may
not be looking back after its forbidden follies and
vanities, but, with our affection set on things that
are above, walk worthy of Him who has called us
to His kingdom and glory.

And while we are the partakers of thy grace,
may we be also the dispensers too. Freely having
received may we freely give. May we feel it to
be the sublimest of all satisfactions, and count it
the greatest of all rewards, to save a soul from
death, and to hide a multitude of sins. And while
endeavouring to do good, may we be prepared to
bear evil. May we consider Him who endured
the contradiction of sinners against himself ; and

if reviled revile not again ; or if opposed or slighted, never grow weary in well doing.

But, we bless Thee, that the lines are fallen to us in pleasant places : we are strangers to the sufferings of those who have gone before us ; and can, not only sit ourselves, but call every man his neighbour, under the vine and under the fig-tree. May we avail ourselves of our opportunities ; and invite those around us to taste and see that the Lord is good, while it is called to-day, knowing how soon the night cometh where in no man can work.

O God count us worthy of this calling, and fulfil all the good pleasure of thy goodness, and the work of faith with power : that the name of our Lord Jesus Christ may be glorified in us, and we in Him, according to the grace of our God, and the Lord Jesus Christ. Amen.

WEDNESDAY EVENING.

O THOU that hearest prayer—Through him who is the great Intercessor, let our prayer come before Thee as incense, and the lifting up of our hands as the evening sacrifice. We bless Thee as our Creator, the framer of our bodies, and the former of our souls within us. We praise Thee for the blessings of thy providence, which encompass us on every side, and are continued to us notwithstanding our unworthiness. Thou hast not only given us life and favour, but thy visitation hath preserved our spirit, and secured our personal and relative comforts.

But above all, we thank Thee for thine unspeakable gift. Herein is love, not that we loved God, but that he loved us, and sent his Son to be the propitiation for our sins. Here our hopes find anchorage ; here believing we enter into rest ; here all our woes and wants find redress and supplies.

O may our souls be united to this Saviour by a divine faith ; he the head and we the members ; he
the vine and we the branches.   May we be his disciples and learn of him ; his soldiers, and war under his banner ; his beneficiaries, and live upon his
fullness.   When we think of our transgressions of
thy law, may we remember *him* who is the end of
the law for righteousness.   When we feel our sin,
may we think of *him* whose blood cleanseth from
all sin ; and when, viewing our trials and duties,
our weakness makes us despond, may we hear the
voice that cries *My* grace is sufficient for thee.

May we be followers of him who was meek and
lowly in heart, who pleased not himself, who went
about doing good, who said my meat is to do the
will of him that sent me, and to finish his work.
Subdue in us the selfishness that is so common to
our depraved hearts, and excite in us a disposition
to seek after the welfare of others.   May sentiments of benevolence and kindness, mingle with all
our thoughts, words and actions ; may they become
more natural, more powerful, more impartial ; may
we be good to the unthankful and the unworthy,
that we may be the children of our Father who is
in heaven, for he maketh his sun to shine on the
evil and on the good, and sendeth rain on the just
and the unjust.

Yet may we especially do good unto them that
are of the household of faith.   May all who do the
will of our heavenly Father, be dear to our hearts.
May we prefer Jerusalem above our chief joy.
Peace be within her walls, and prosperity within
her palaces.   Let her become a praise in the whole
earth.   And from the rising of the sun to the going
down of the same, may thy name be great among
the Gentiles, and in every place may incense be
offered unto Thee, and a pure offering in righteousness.   The harvest truly is great, but the labourers
are few ; command their increase ; and abundantly bless those who are already employed.

And may the sincerity of our prayers appear in our exertions and sacrifices. May we honour the Lord with our substance. In our respective stations may we adorn the doctrine of God our Saviour in all things. By every kind of consistent co-operation with our ministers, may we become helpers to the truth; and carrying the effects of the sermons we hear, and dispensing them among those who refuse to hear, win them without the word. May we never hide it in a napkin, because we have only one talent; but use what we have, that more may be given; and be concerned to obtain from the Judge of all, the approving sentence, of our having done what we could. And may we never despise the day of small things; never grow weary in well doing; but cherish with patience, as well as with diligence, every serious conviction, every pious tendency, every godly impression.

And let us not labour in vain, nor spend our strength for nought. May we be the honoured instruments of saving some soul from death; and of producing joy, in the presence of the angels of God, over one sinner that repenteth.

Above all, render us successful among those who are more fully under our instruction, influence and authority. May we rule well our own house; and have the pleasure to see all the members of our family, fellow citizens with the saints, and of the household of God. Of whom, and through whom, and to whom, are all things. To whom be glory for ever and ever. Amen.

THURSDAY MORNING.

O LORD, Thou art good, and Thou doest good, Thou hast revealed thyself as nigh unto all that call upon Thee, to all that call upon Thee, in truth. May we who now address Thee, be found the heirs of this promise ; nor suffer us, to incur the reproach of drawing near to Thee, with the mouth, and honouring Thee with our lips, while our hearts are far from Thee.   Unite our hearts to fear thy name ; and grant that we may worship Thee, in the spirit, and rejoice in Christ Jesus, and have no confidence in the flesh.   We remember that we are sinners, and acknowledge the multitude and aggravations of our offences.   Conscious not only of the reality, but the greatness of our guilt, we could indulge no hope, hadst not Thou exhibited thy infinite benevolence, and revealed a Mediator, in whom Thou art reconciling the world unto thyself, not imputing their tresspasses unto them.

Thou hast not left thyself without witness, in that Thou hast been doing us good, and giving us rain from heaven, and fruitful seasons, filling our hearts with food and gladness.   But herein is love, not that we loved God, but that he loved us, and sent his Son to be the propitiation for our sins.   Blessed be thy name, we have all the certainty we could desire, that with Thee there is mercy.   *That* mercy the publican sought, and found ; *that* mercy— has never disappointed any that trusted in it ; *that* mercy—at this very moment, cries to us—Ask and it shall be given *you*, seek and *ye* shall find.   O Lord, we avail ourselves of thy invitation, and plead thy promise.   According to the multitude of thy tender mercies, blot out our transgressions. Create in us, also, a clean heart, and renew a right spirit within us.

We hope we are convinced, that while many things are desirable, and some useful, *one* thing is needful ; and that instead of the inquiry, what shall I eat, and what shall I drink, and wherewithal shall I be clothed, the supreme anxiousness of the soul is, what must I do to be saved? O visit us with thy salvation : in the illumination of the mind, and the sanctification of the life : in all the com-

forts of the Holy Ghost, and in all the fruits of the
spirit. May we willingly obey all thy commands,
and cheerfully submit to all thy appointments. In
the annihilation of self-will, and in the temper of
implicit devotedness, may we, as to every duty,
say, Lord, what wilt thou have me to do? And
as to every event, here I am, let Him do what
seemeth Him good. Grant us piety and wisdom
to accommodate ourselves to the allotments of life ;
and enable us to maintain a christian temper and
behaviour in all the changing scenes of providence, that all things may work together, if not
for our gratification, yet for our good.

May we disengage ourselves from the present
evil world, and be received and acknowledged as
the sons and daughters of the Lord Almighty.
May the righteous be our attractions and delight ;
and though few in number, and despised by the
foolish and wicked, may we go with *them*, because
God is with them : and like Moses may we choose
rather to suffer affliction with the people of God,
than enjoy the pleasures of sin for a season.

May we walk by faith, and not by sight. May
we weigh both worlds, and may the future and the
eternal, preponderate ; and may this be our growing experience as well as profession—as for me,
I will behold thy face in righteousness, I shall be
satisfied when I awake with thy likeness.

By thy mercies we renew this morning the con-
secration of ourselves to thy service. Go forth
with us into the concerns of the day. Keep us in
all our ways. Innumerable are our dangers ; but
the greatest of all is sin. Uphold our goings
therefore in thy word, and let no iniquity have
dominion over us. May we abstain from all appearance of evil ; and the very God of peace sanctify us wholly ; and may our whole spirit, and
soul, and body, be preserved blameless unto the
coming of our Lord Jesus Christ

And to God only wise, the Father, the Son, and
the Holy Ghost, be ascribed all honour and praise,
for ever and ever.   Amen.

THURSDAY EVENING.

O -God, thy greatness is unsearchable.   Thy
name is most excellent in all the earth.   Thou
hast set thy glory above the heavens.   Thousands
minister unto Thee, and ten thousand times ten
thousand stand before Thee.   We feel ourselves
in thine awful presence to be nothing, less than
nothing and vanity: nor do we presume to approach Thee, because we are deserving of thy notice—for we have sinned—we have incurred thy
righteous displeasure—we acknowledge, that Thou
art justified when Thou speakest, and clear when
Thou judgest.

But our necessities compel us; and thy promises encourage us.   Thou art nigh unto them that
are of a broken heart, and savest such as be of a
contrite spirit.   Thou hast provided and revealed
a Mediator, who has not only obeyed, but magnified the law, and made it honourable; and Thou
hast made us accepted in the beloved.   And we
behold an innumerable multitude returning from
thy throne, successful, rejoicing, and encouraging
us to go forward.   They were not, though all
guilt and indigence, refused, or upbraided; but
freely obtained pardon, and holiness, and righteousness, and strength, and were blessed with all
spiritual blessings in heavenly places in Christ.

O look Thou upon us, and be merciful unto us,
as thou usest to do unto those that love thy name.
Convince us of sin in its penalty, and in its pollution; and may we mourn over it with a godly sorrow.   Give us that faith by which we shall be
enabled to believe on the Lord Jesus Christ; and
believing, have life through his name.

And may we not only have life, but have it
more abundantly. We often question the reality
of our grace ; but the imperfections of our religion
are too obvious, not to be acknowledged, and too
great, not to be deplored. Our souls cleave unto
the dust ; quicken Thou us according to thy word.
Strengthen in us the things that are ready to die.
May we not only live in the spirit, but walk in the
spirit. By holy resemblances, may we put on the
Lord Jesus Christ ; may the same mind be in us
which was also in Him ; and may we feel it to be
our dignity and delight to go about doing good.

And as He suffered for us, leaving us an example, that we should tread in his steps, may we learn
to suffer like Him. When reviled, may we revile
not again, but commit ourselves to Him that judgeth righteously. Whoever may be the instrument
of our grief, may we never lose sight of an over-
ruling agency, in preparing and presenting it ; but
be able to say, The cup which my Father giveth
me shall I not drink it ? In our patience may we
possess our souls, that we may be calm to inquire,
wherefore Thou contendest with us ; that weeping may not hinder sowing, nor sorrow duty.

We live in a world of changes, and have here no
continuing city ; may we seek one to come, and
have our minds kept in perfect peace, being staid
upon God. Be with us to the end of our journey ;
and after honouring Thee, by the life we have
lived, may we glorify Thee, by the death we
shall die. When heart and flesh fail, be Thou
the strength of our heart, and our portion for ever ;
at death may we fall asleep in Jesus, and in the
morning of the resurrection may He change our
vile body, that it may be fashioned like his own
glorious body, and so may we be for ever with
the Lord.

Who can understand his errors ? Forgive, O
God, the sins of the past day, in thought, word
and deed, against thy divine majesty. We bless

'Thee for our preservation, in our going out and our coming in, and in all our ways—and we bless Thee for all the supplies and indulgences, which thy good providence has afforded us.

And now, O Thou keeper of Israel, we commit our souls and our bodies to thy all-sufficient care. Suffer no evil to befall our persons, and no plague to come nigh our dwelling. May our sleep be sweet—or if Thou holdest our eyes waking, may we remember Thee, upon our bed, and meditate on thee, in the night watches.

And with the innumerable company, who never slumber nor sleep, and who rest not day and night, we would join in ascribing blessing, and honour, and glory, and power, unto Him that sitteth upon the throne, and unto the Lamb, for ever and ever. Amen.

FRIDAY MORNING.

O THOU, whose name alone is Jehovah, the most high over all the earth. When we consider thy majesty and thy purity, and reflect upon our meanness and guilt, how shall we come before the Lord, or bow before the high God? We are unworthy of thy notice, and have rendered ourselves justly obnoxious to the curse of thy holy law—and wert Thou to judge us according to our desert—the most innocent periods of our life, and the devoutest services in which we have ever been engaged, would make us shrink back with dread and despair from thy presence. But we are encouraged to approach Thee, by the revelation Thou hast given us of thyself as the Lord God gracious and merciful, the invitations and promises of thy word, and the meditation of thy dear Son. We rejoice that He put away sin, by the sacrifice of Himself, and being raised from the dead entered into the holy place, there to appear in the presence of God for us. We rejoice that we have now an Advocate with the Father to plead our cause, and a great High Priest over the house of God, to introduce our persons and our services.

May we therefore draw near in full assurance of faith, believing that all things are now ready ; that we are as welcome, as we are needy ; and that the blessings we implore, are as gracious, as they are great. Yea, Thou delightest in mercy, and hast not only permitted, but commanded us to ask, and receive, that our joy may be full. O let us not refuse to be comforted ; let us not reject the counsel of God against ourselves. Suffer us not after provoking Thee, by our rebellion, to offend Thee, still more by our unbelief. May we honour thy goodness, by our confidence in thy veracity, and come and take of the water of life freely. May we wait for no qualifications, to entitle us to those provisions, which must be bought without money, and without price ; but may we come as we are—guilty *to be* justified, unholy *to be* renewed, blind *to be* enlightened, weak *to be* strengthened, and indigent *to be* relieved and enriched. As Thou are presenting to us, in the offers of the gospel, thy unspeakable gift, may we receive Christ Jesus the Lord. May we receive Him immediately without delay, cordially without reluctance, and impartially without exception—feeling our need of, and acquiescing in all his offices, relations, influences, and blessings.

As Thou art well pleased *in* thy beloved Son, may it appear that we are well pleased *with* Him ; may we love his salvation, and glory in his cross ; may we admire his character and pant after his likeness. May we judge of our union with Him, by our being new creatures, and of our freedom from all condemnation, by our walking not after the flesh, but after the Spirit. May we try our principles by our practice, and our faith by our

works.   May the origin and certainty of our hope,
appear in its tendency—may it purify us from sin,
wean us from the world, and cause us to live with
our conversation in heaven.

And blessed with a well founded persuasion,
that when He, who is our life, shall appear, we
shall also appear with him in glory ; may we bear
with patience, the trials attached to this present
time ; and weep as if we wept not.   And knowing our obligations to thy grace, which has delivered our souls from the lowest hell, and is in-
fallibly conducting us to such a vastness of felicity,
may we be principally concerned to walk before
the Lord in the land of the living, and to show
forth all His praise·   Whether therefore we eat
or drink, or whatever we do, may we do all to the
glory of God.

But we cannot trust in our own hearts ; we dare
not rely upon our convictions and purposes—they
have often betrayed us.   We can only serve thee
in thy own strength.   We can walk no farther than
Thou leadest us; we can stand no longer than
Thou holdest us.   We therefore renounce self-
dependence ; and desire to be strong in the Lord,
and in the power of his might.   Let thy grace be
sufficient for us in the duties and events of the
day, into which we have entered.   May we abide
with God in our respective callings.   Whether we
are alone, or in company, may we be anxious to
gain good, and to do good.   May we be serious
without gloom, and cheerful without levity.·

And, now unto Him that is able to keep us from
falling, and to present us faultless before the presence of his glory with exceeding joy ; to the only
wise God our Saviour, be glory and majesty, dominion and power. both now and ever.   Amen.

FRIDAY EVENING

O GOD, the day is thine, the night also is thine.
Thou makest the outgoings of the morning and
evening to rejoice. The heavens declare thy
glory—the earth is full of thy riches, and so is the
great and wide sea. Thou art the maker, and
sustainer, and proprietor of all things. We are
the creatures of thy power, and the beneficiaries
of thy bounty. But we have sinned against heaven
and before Thee, and not worthy of the least of
all the mercies, and of all the truth which Thou
hast showed us. We are of those that rebel
against the light ; for we have resisted the dic-
tates of our consciences, the demands of thy law,
the admonitions of thy providence, and the calls
of the gospel of peace. We have made light of
those things which angels desire to look into; we
have neglected thy great salvation, and we deserve that thy wrath should come upon us, as the
children of disobedience.

But we are in the land of the living, and under
a dispensation of hope. We flee for refuge to that
dear Saviour, who said, 'deliver him from going
down into the pit, I have found a ransom, and who
himself bore our sin in his own body on the tree.
O that we may be found in him, and know the
power of his resurrection, and the fellowship of
his sufferings, being made conformable unto his
death. May we not only be justified by his blood,
and saved from wrath through Him ; but may we
derive from him an influence, that shall subdue
our iniquities, and change us into his own image,
from glory to glory, as by the Spirit of the
Lord.

Deliver us we pray Thee, from the views and
dispositions, of men of the world, who have their
portion in this life. May we never look for that
on earth, which can only be found in heaven.

Born from above, and bound for glory, may we feel the heart of a stranger, and pass the time of our sojourning here in fear. Reminded—and, O, how often are we reminded? that here we have no continuing city, may we seek one to come; and in all the changing scenes of time, know in ourselves, that in heaven, we have a better and an enduring substance.

In our journeyings through a vale of tears, cast us not away from thy presence, and take not thy Holy Spirit from us. Be Thou always within sight, or within call; for how often shall we have to address Thee? To thy wisdom we must repair for direction, or we shall every moment go astray. Thy power is our only safety. O Thou that savest by thy right hand, them that put their trust in Thee, from those that rise up against them, keep us as the apple of the eye, and hide us under the shadow of thy wing. Be Thou our strength in weakness, and our victory in conflict. We dare not say, we never *will* deny Thee; but O grant that we never may. Establish our hearts with grace, and deliver our feet from falling; and may we be sincere and without offence, until the day of Christ.

These are great blessings for us to ask; but we are undone for ever without them, and Thou hast encouraged us to hope. We plead thy command and thy promises. Ask and it shall be given you, seek and ye shall find, knock and it shall be opened unto you. No suppliant, however unworthy, or guilty, was ever rejected, or insulted at thy footstool; and we come in the name of Him who made intercession for the transgression. Him, Thou hearest always, and to Him, with the Father, and the Holy Spirit, be praises for ever and ever. Amen

O God, Thou art great, and greatly to be feared. And Thou art, also, merciful and gracious, long-suffering and abundant in goodness and in truth. May we so feel our sinfulness, as to be humbled in the dust before Thee, and filled with self-condemnation and self-despair; but let us not shrink back from thy presence, and be afraid to place our faith and hope in God. Help us to remember, that if we have no claim, on the footing of desert, we can plead thy promise, and invitation; and that if the blessings we want are infinitely great, they are dispensed as gifts, where freeness delights in the unworthiness of the receiver.

We, therefore, would neither deny, nor palliate our guilt. We know there is evil enough in one sin to plunge us into perdition; but our offences are more in number than the sand; and they have been attended with every aggravation, derivable from light and love, means and mercies. Thou hast called, and we have refused; Thou hast stretched out thy hand and we have not regarded. How often hast Thou wooed and awed, blessed and chastised us; and yet we refused to return. O Lord, pardon our iniquity, for it is great. Let the free gift be of many offences unto justification of life; and where sin has abounded, grace may much more abound.

And as we cannot serve or enjoy Thee, unless our nature be changed, as well as our state, O save us by the washing of regeneration, and by the renewing of the Holy Ghost. Deliver us from the dominion, as well as the course of sin; and from the love of it, as well as the dominion. May we reckon ourselves to be dead indeed unto sin, but alive unto God through Jesus Christ our Lord. May we view holiness as the beauty and the dignity of the soul, and long after greater degrees of

conformity to the will and the image of God.
May our hope purify us, and our religious comforts stimulate, as well as relieve. May we never
slumber, and lose our roll ; never sleep, and like
Saul be robbed of our spear and our cruse. May
we watch and pray, lest we enter into temptation.
When we grow indolent and careless, awaken us
by lively apprehensions of thy presence, and of
the eternal world, on the borders of which we
perpetually move ; may we feel the infinite importance of improving the few transient periods,
intervening between us and death ; may we daily
and hourly answer some of the grand purposes of
life and religion. May every place and every
company be the better for us. May we diffuse
knowledge and happiness by our conversation,
example, and influence ; and like our Lord and
Saviour go about doing good.

Whatever advantages we possess, may we
never forget, that this is not our rest. May we
arise and depart hence, not by quitting our sta
tions, or undervaluing the duties attached to them,
but by rising above the world, as our portion, seting our affections on things above, and having our
conversation in heaven. Expecting a succession
of encounters in passing through an enemy's land,
may we take to us the whole armour of God ; and
looking for thorns and briars in our marchings
through a wilderness, may our feet be shod with
the preparation of the gospel of peace.

Fit for every changing scene ; and in all the
events that would alarm or perplex us, may our
minds be stayed upon God, and our thoughts be
established. May we remember that trials from
thy hand are blessings in disguise, and that when
they come to be unveiled, and we can view them
in their designs and effects, they will draw forth
our gratitude and praise. Till we can walk by
sight, enable us to walk by faith , and may nothing
weaken our persuasion, that all thy ways are mer-

cy and truth to thy people; and that all things work together for good to them that love Thee.

We would not forget those who are in affliction—Do not Thou, O God forget them. Whatever be their losses or distress, help them to say, Yet the Lord thinking upon me : and may they know, that thy thoughts towards them are thoughts of peace, and not of evil, to bring them to an expected end, though it may be by a painful passage. Comfort those who are on beds of languishing. Enter the house of mourning. Be the father of the fatherless, and the husband of the widow, and the friend, and helper of the poor and needy—and have mercy upon all men.

Our Father, &c.

SATURDAY EVENING.

O God—Thou art glorious in holiness, fearful in praises, continually doing wonders. And it is not one of the least of thy wonderful works, that we are yet on this side an awful eternity, and not reaping the due reward of our deeds. We look on each other this evening with astonishment, and exclaim, it is the Lord's mercies that we are not consumed. Our whole life has been a scene of provocation against thy divine majesty; and if we with all our ignorance and self-love, can see so much depravity in ourselves, what must have presented itself to *thy* view—O Thou who knowest all things, in whose sight the very heavens are not clean, and who seest more pollution, even in our duties, than we ever found in our sins! There is no health in us. We have no works or worthiness to excite thy regard; and if ever we are saved, it must be according to thy own purpose and grace, given us in Christ Jesus, before the world began.

We come to Thee in the dear name of Him who loved us, and gave himself for us ; who magnified the law and made it honourable ; who put away sin by the sacrifice of Himself; and now ever liveth to make intercession for us.   This foundation, Thou thyself hast laid in Zion, and thy word assures us, that whosoever believeth on Him, shall not be confounded.   We hope our dependence upon Him is not a vain reliance, because we love his service as well as his sacrifice, and long to wear his image, as well as to be justified by his blood.   We hope we are willing to deny ourselves, and take up our cross and follow Him— in the regeneration—and whithersoever He goeth.

O make us partakers of that salvation which is designed to deliver us from our sins, and to bring us into the glorious liberty of the children of God. Put thy laws into our minds, and write them in our hearts, and render our obedience to thy will holily natural, and delightful to us.   Rectify all our principles, and give us clear and consistent, and influential views of divine truth.   May we never undervalue or neglect any part of thy revealed will ; but regard the practice the gospel enjoins, as well as the doctrine it exhibits ; prize its commands as well as its promises ; and cultivate such a disposition, as will render every religious duty a spiritual privilege.

Sanctify us in every relation, office, transaction, and condition in life.   Keep us, if we prosper, from being exalted above measure ; and if exercised with adversity, suffer us not to be swallowed up of over-much sorrow.   May divine grace preserve the balance of the mind in all our varying circumstances, and teach us, in whatsoever state we are, not only to be content, but to glorify God, and be an edifying example to those around us.

May we always be principally concerned for soul-prosperity, and be willing to submit to any means, however trying, that thy wisdom shall judge necessary, to promote and secure it.   May we so pass through things temporal, as not to miss those that are eternal, at last, or to lose sight of them, for a moment, now. Too long have our feet and our hands been in the mire ; O disengage us, purify us, elevate us ; our souls cleave unto the dust, quicken Thou us according to thy word. May none of our mercies be lost upon us ; but may they prove the means of exciting our gratitude, warming our devotion, and encouraging our confidence. May none of our trials be unimproved—may they all embitter sin, wean us from the world, and endear to us the Scriptures, the throne of grace, and the sympathy of that Almighty friend who is touched with the feeling of our infirmities.

May none of our religious opportunities be unsanctified. May we be thankful for the frequency of their recurrence ; may we gladly avail ourselves of them ; and instead of resting in the mere outward performance, may we be concerned to worship Thee, in spirit and in truth, and to obtain from thy word, all the benefits it is intended and adapted to afford.

For this purpose, we implore thy blessing on the solemnities of the Sabbath, which is so soon to open upon us. May we in the morning awake with Thee, and begin, go through, and end the day in thy faith, fear, and love. May we have satisfactory evidence in our own minds, that we do not wait upon Thee in vain ; and may our profiting appear unto all men.

And thus by all the discipline of thy family, and the ordinances of thy house, may we grow in grace, and in our meetness for the inheritance of the saints in light. And when the evening of life itself shall arrive, and we are called to retreat from every mortal care, and we close the period of toil and trouble, by falling asleep in Jesus—and open our eyes upon the rest that remains for the people of God, and enter the temple above, to go no more out And may the grace of. &c. Amen.

SUNDAY MORNING.

O Thou King eternal, and immortal, invisible, dwelling in the light which no man can approach unto, and whom no man hath seen, or can see. Thou art incomprehensible, and the highest arch-angel cannot find Thee out unto perfection. Yet Thou hast been pleased to reveal thyself; and by means of thy word, we behold Thee in every character and relation that can suit our necessities, or encourage our hope. Thy throne is in the heavens, and thy kingdom ruleth over all; and all nations before Thee are as nothing; yet thou condescendest to regard the things that are done in the earth; and despisest not the prayer even of the destitute. Thou art exalted above all blessing and praise: our goodness extendeth not to Thee—but unless thine be extended to us, we are undone for ever. Without Thee we can do nothing; we *are* nothing. In Thee we live, and move, and have our being. The way of man is not in himself; it is not in man that walketh to direct his steps. We are universally indigent and dependent; but as Thou art able, so thou art willing, to take the charge of us; and here we are, the living to praise Thee; and to acknowledge that goodness and mercy have followed us all the days of our lives.

We bless Thee, that Thou hast regarded our souls, as well as our bodies; and no less provided for our future interests, than our present. When there was no eye to pity us, Thou didst remember us in our low estate ; and when there was no arm to rescue, Thou wast pleased to lay help on one that is mighty ; and thou hast sent thy own Son into the world, not to condemn the world, but that the world through Him might be saved. To Him may we turn our believing regards, and find in Him the wisdom, righteousness, sanctification, and redemption, which, as perishing sinners, we need. In all our approaches to Thee, may we have boldness, and access, with confidence, by the faith of Him. May we know that He has borne our grief, and carried our sorrow ; and be able to rejoice in him as our sacrifice, our sympathising friend, our almighty helper, and our lovely example. May we drink into his spirit. May we transcribe the excellencies of his character into our own. May we place our feet in the very prints of his steps ; and follow Him in the regeneration, till we shall be perfectly like Him, and see Him as He is.

We desire to acknowledge Thee in the dispensations of thy providence ; and to own thy agency in all the events that befall us, whether pleasing or painful. Thou hast a right to govern us ; and Thou knowest what will best advance our welfare. May we commit our way unto the Lord, and be able to say at thy footstool, in unfeigned submission, Here I am, let Him do what seemeth Him good. If darkness veils thy dealings with us, may we trust and not be afraid ; believing, that what we know not now, we shall know hereafter ; and that the developement of thy conduct will issue in perfect satisfaction and praise.

We bless Thee for the institutions of religion, in the use of which Thou hast promised to draw near to those that draw near to Thee. We rejoice in another of the days of the Son of man ; may we call off our minds from the cares of the world, and attend upon the Lord without distraction. Quicken and elevate our souls, that rising above the formality of devotion, we may come even to thy seat, and enjoy a little of the blessedness of those that have entered thy temple above, and are singing the song of Moses and the Lamb. We are going to assemble in the house of prayer—pour upon us the spirit of grace and of supplication ; and rank us in the number of those who hunger and thirst after righteousness. We are going to the house of 'praise—awaken in us every grateful and cheerful emotion, and may we speak to ourselves in psalms, and hymns, and spiritual songs, singing and making melody in our hearts unto the Lord. We are repairing to the house of instruction—enable us to receive the kingdom of God as a little child. Teach us of thy ways. Lead us into all truth. And let us be neither barren nor unfruitful in the knowledge of our Lord and Saviour Jesus Christ.

For this purpose, let thy presence go with us ; and let thy word come to us ; not in word only, but in power, and in the Holy Ghost, and in much assurance. Bless all the churches of the faithful ; and the ministers of the everlasting gospel, of every name, and of every nation. Clothe the priests with salvation ; and let thy saints shout aloud for joy. May our country prosper in all her lawful interests both domestic and foreign. Bless the chief magistrate of our nation, and all that are in authority ; may they rule in thy fear, and be guided by thy counsel ; and may the people lead quiet and peaceable lives in all godliness and honesty. Make us glad according to the days wherein Thou hast afflicted us, and the years wherein we have seen evil. Let thy work appear unto thy servants, and thy glory unto their children, and let the beauty of the Lord our God be upon us ; establish Thou the work of our hand upon us, yea, the work of our hand, establish Thou it.

Our Father, &c.

SUNDAY EVENING.

WHEN we consider the heavens the work of thy fingers, and the moon and the stars which Thou hast ordained, Lord, what is man, that Thou art mindful of him, or the son of man that Thou visitest him. In thy sight the heavens are not clean; and Thou chargest thine angels with folly—With what truth therefore *may* we, and with what humiliation *ought* we, to exclaim, behold we are vile!

And yet, we believe—help Thou our unbelief, that Thou waitest to be gracious unto us ; and art exalted to have mercy upon us. And Christ also has once suffered for sins, the just for the unjust, that He might bring us unto God. Through his obedience unto death, even the death of the cross, it is honourable in Thee, to save all that come unto Thee by Him and Thou art faithful and just, as well as gracious and merciful, in forgiving us our sins, and in cleansing us from all unrighteousness.

We bless thy holy name, for a foundation on which the guilty, the depraved and the helpless, can build, a hope that maketh not ashamed ; for a refuge from the curse of a broken law ; for a fountain opened for sin, and uncleanness ; and for a fulness, from which we can receive, and grace for grace We want to appropriate and realize, all the representations given of the Saviour in thy word ; and to find it to be, in our own experience, what thy people have found him to be, in all ages of the world. May our persons and our services be accepted in the beloved. May we be justified freely by thy grace, through the redemption that is in Christ Jesus. May we be saved by the washing of regeneration, and the renewing of the Holy Ghost. We are weary and heavy laden, give us rest. We are depraved in all our pow-

ers—work in us to will and to do of thy good
pleasure. We are ignorant—fill us with knowledge of thy will, in all wisdom and spiritual understanding, that we may approve things that are
excellent, and be sincere and without offence, till
the day of Christ.

Many eyes are upon us—lead us in a plain path
because of our enemies. Many watch for our
halting ; but, may we put to silence the ignorance
of foolish men, and constrain them by our good
works, which they behold to glorify God, in the
day of visitation.

Some did run well, but are hindered : they began in the spirit, but are now walking in the flesh.
We tremble for them—and we tremble for ourselves : we pray for them, and we pray for ourselves. Recover and restore them, and keep us,
by thy power, through faith unto salvation. May
we never draw back ; never turn aside to the right
hand or to the left ; never stand still ; never look
back ; never seem to come short through unbelief,
but be always abounding in the work of the Lord—
and so much the more as we see the day approaching.

Though we are ignorant of the future, and know
not what a day may bring forth, keep us from
being of a doubtful mind. May we be careful for
nothing May we go on our way rejoicing, persuaded that all thy dispensations are designed and
adapted to prove, that Thou carest for us.

We can even now, see much of thy wisdom,
righteousness, and kindness, in events, that once
perplexed us, and alarmed ; and what we know
not now, we shall know hereafter. Soon the mystery of providence will be completed and explain-
ed. Soon shall we have passed these dark and
mournful regions ; and then our sun shall no more
go down, nor our moon withdraw herself ; for God
shall be our everlasting light, and the days of our
mourning shall be ended.

And till we arrive at heaven, our home, may we gratefully avail ourselves of all the advantages afforded us in our journey. We bless Thee for wilderness privileges ; for the manna ; the streams of the smitten rock ; the fiery cloudy pillar ; the tabernacle and the ark. We bless Thee for the sabbath, the sanctuary, and the ministry of the word. We bless Thee for the opportunities we have, this day, enjoyed in waiting upon Thee. Many who love thy salvation, have passed the sacred hours, in solitude. Many have had no means of grace to invite their attendance. And many who have been assembled together, have not heard the gospel of the grace of God, in truth. O, let not our privileges increase our guilt, and aggravate our condemnation, so that it shall be more tolerable for Sodom and Gomorrah, in the day of judgment, than for us. Let not the truths we have been hearing, visit us only as weekly guests ; but may they be residents in our hearts. May the word of Christ dwell in us richly, in all wisdom. And though the exercises in which we have been engaged are transient, may the effects produced by them be deep and durable ; may the sabbath pervade the week, and the spirit of devotion actuate us in the absence of its forms : whether we eat, or drink, or whatever we do, may we do all to the glory of God.

Bless, O bless the rising generation, the sources of future families and communities. When the clods of the valley shall be sweet about us, may they be found a seed to serve Thee. Many of them have had the advantage of religious education ; they have seen pious examples ; they early kneeled at the domestic altar ; from infancy they knew the holy Scriptures, and have often been alarmed, often melted under the word preached ; and frequently have they been ready to subscribe with their own hand, and surname themselves by the name of Israel. O let not these promising appearances and beginnings be destroyed. O, let not the wild beast out of the wood, carry off the lambs of the flock ; but may the Shepherd of Israel gather them with his arm, and carry them in his bosom.

Regard all thy professing churches. Bless them with soundness of doctrine ; purity and liberality of discipline ; and sanctity and amiableness of character, in their members : and the Lord add to his people, how many soever they be, an hundred fold. Yea, let a little one become a thousand, and a small one a strong nation ; and all the families of the earth be blessed in *Him*—who is all our salvation, and all our desire—to whom be glory and dominion, for ever and ever. Amen.

MONDAY MORNING.

O Thou King eternal, immortal, and invisible— we would adore Thee, and take shame to ourselves : and though allowed to approach thy divine majesty, we would never forget the sentiments of humiliation and contrition, which become such creatures as we are. Father! we have sinned against heaven and in thy sight, and are not worthy to be called thy children : we are not worthy of the least of all thy mercies. Yea, we have merited thy displeasure : and thy righteousness would be completely acquitted in our destruction.

O, for hearts of flesh! Lord, produce in us that sensibility of soul, which will lead us to feel our vileness, to deplore our guilt, and to cast ourselves at thy feet, abhorring ourselves, and repenting in dust and ashes. And impart to us that faith, which will enable us, to hope in thy word, and derive strong consolation from the invitations and promises of the gospel. We are come to implore the greatest blessings the God of love can give ; but our application is not presumption : we are come to call Thee, Abba Father, to enter thy house, to sit down at thy table, to lean on thy arm, to walk with God; but we are not come unbidden or uncalled: Thou hast called us by thy grace; and it is thy commandment that we should believe on the name of thy Son, Jesus Christ. Lord, we assent, we submit, we depend, we apply. Since He came into the world to save sinners, we take Him as *our* Saviour; and glory in Him, as made of Thee, to us wisdom and righteousness, sanctification and redemption.

And, O, may our minds be fixed and filled with admiring thoughts of his person and offices; may our hearts be inflamed with a sense of his boundless compassion and love. By the new and living way which he has not only revealed but consecrated for us, may we come to Thee; and enjoy all the advantages of a state of reconcileation and friendship with God. May the most open and familiar intercourse, be maintained, between Thee and our souls. To Thee may we commit our way and our works; and in every thing by prayer and supplication make known our requests unto God; and be Thou always near, to guide us and to defend; to relieve us in trouble, and to help us in duty. And may we walk humbly with our God; wondering at the condescension, that deigns to regard our mean affairs; the patience, that bears with our manners; and the kindness, that employs so many means to advance our everlasting welfare.

We grieve to think, that a world so full of thy bounty, should be so empty of thy praise. O, that men would praise the Lord for his goodness, and for his wonderful works to the children of men. Bless the Lord, all his works, in all places of his dominion, bless the Lord, O my soul.

Again thy visitation hath preserved our spirits. Through the dark and silent watches of the night, Thou hast suffered no evil to befall us, nor any plague to come nigh our dwelling. And we are

not only the living to praise Thee, this morning :
but the distinguished, and the indulged. Many
who have seen the light of the day, as well as ourselves, are encompassed with want, and pain, and
wretchedness ; but we have all things richly to
enjoy.

Thou takest pleasure in the prosperity of thy
servants ; may we always take pleasure in the ad-
vancement of thy glory. Thou art never weary
in doing us good ; may we never grow weary in
well doing. Thy mercies are new every morning ;
every morning, by thy mercies, may we present
our bodies a living sacrifice, holy, and acceptable,
which is our reasonable service.

And to the God of our salvation, the Father,
the Son, and the Holy Spirit, be ascribed, the
kingdom, the power, and the glory, for ever and
ever. Amen.

MONDAY EVENING.

O THOU, in whose presence angels bow, and
arch-angels veil their faces, enable us to serve
Thee, with reverence and godly fear. O Thou,
who art a Spirit, and requirest truth in the inward
parts, help us to worship Thee in spirit and in
truth. O righteous Father, we would not come to
Thee harbouring the love of any sin in our bosoms :
for thou hast assured us, that if we regard inquity
in our hearts, Thou wilt not hear us. We must
address thee as sinners ; but we acknowledge our
trangression, and our sin is ever before us ; we desire to have nothing more to do with idols ; we
hate every false way ; and long to be Israelites indeed, in whom is no guile.

Nor would we, O God, appear in thy presence,
indulging a worldly temper, and seeking after an
abundance of those things, that afford no satisfac-

tion in the possession, and perish in the using.
After all these things do the Gentiles seek, and
our heavenly Father, knoweth what things we
have need of, before we ask him; and will ad-
minister them as our wants and welfare may require. We are hastening towards an hour, which
will show us the vanity of all earthly pursuits and
possessions. When a few more suns have rolled
over us, it will be a matter of indifference, whether
we have been rich or poor; successful in our enterprises, or disappointed; admired of our fellow-
creatures, or despised : but it will be of eternal
moment to us, that we have mourned for sin ; that
we have hungered and thirsted after righteousness ;
that we have loved the Lord Jesus Christ in sincerity, and gloried in his cross.

May these objects, therefore, however despised
of men, engross our chief solicitude. May we labour for that meat, which endureth unto everlasting
life ; may we lay up treasure in heaven ; may we
seek the honour that cometh from God only. O,
remember us with the favour thou bearest unto
thy people, and visit us with thy salvation. Deliver us from the condemnation of the law, and the
bondage of corruption, and bring us into the glorious liberty of the children of God. Justify us
freely from all things, and renew us in the spirit of
our minds. Produce in us those principles and
dispositions, which will render thy service perfect
freedom ; and make it our meat to do the will of
our heavenly Father, and to finish his work.

Expel from our minds all sinful fear and shame,
and with firmness and courage may we confess the
Redeemer before men, and go forth to Him without the camp, bearing his reproach. And may
our zeal be according to knowledge. Fill us with
all wisdom and spiritual understanding. May we
walk circumspectly. May we never take a wrong
course, or a wrong step. May we venture on
nothing, without asking counsel of God. Without

prejudice, may we repair to the Scriptures, and kneeling before the divine oracles, ask, Lord, what wilt Thou have me to do? May we faithfully study our conditions and connexions in life, and observe every dispensation of thy providence, that we may see how we can honour Thee in our body and spirit, and serve our generation according to the will of God.

Thou hast commanded us to be pitiful, and to pray for all men. We would remember, that every moment of pleasure to us, is a moment of anguish to some ; and that while our health and our relative comforts are continued, many are confined to beds of languishing, or sighing. Lover and friend hast thou put from me, and mine acquaintance into darkness. In the multitude of their thoughts within them, may thy comforts delight their souls ; and if not in the suffering, yet in the review of their trials, may they be able to say, " It is good for me that I have been afflicted." Let not the prosperity of the successful destroy them : or the table of the indulged, prove a snare. In every state may the voice be heard and obeyed, arise and depart hence, for this is not your rest.

We know not what a day may bring forth ; yet we would not be anxious in prospect of the future, nor perplex ourselves with that care about events, which, it is our duty and privilege, to cast upon Him, who careth for us. We would keep our minds in perfect peace, being stayed upon Thee. Assure us, that nothing can befall us without thy permission, appointment, and administration ; assure us that Thou hast engaged to make all things work together for our good—say to our hearts, I will never leave thee nor forsake thee.

> Grant us thy counsels for our guide ;
> And then receive us to thy bliss ;
> All our desires and hopes beside,
> Are faint and cold compared with this.

Amen.

TUESDAY MORNING.

O THOU God of Abraham, of Isaac, and of Jacob; the God of all the righteous, and of all that hunger and thirst after righteousness : blessed are the people that are in such a case, yea, happy is the people whose God is the Lord. May we be fellow heirs, and of the same body, and partakers of thy promise, in Christ, by the gospel.

We hope in thy word. There we see thee, not on a throne of judgment, whose term would make us afraid, but on a throne of grace, waiting to be gracious, and exalted to have mercy. There we hear Thee saying, not—" depart ye cursed into everlasting fire, prepared for the devil and his angels," but—" look unto me and be ye saved, all the ends of the earth, for I am God and there is none else." They that know thy name, will put their trust in thee, for thou Lord hast not forsaken them that seek thee. How many glorified in heaven, and what numbers now living on earth, are thy witnesses, O God, exemplifying in their recovery from the ruins of the fall, the freeness, and riches, and efficacy, of thy grace. All that were ever saved, were saved by thee, and will through eternity, exclaim, Not unto us, O Lord, not unto us, but to thy name give glory, for thy mercy and for thy truth's sake. And after all thy communications, thou art the same Lord, over all, and rich unto all, that call upon thee. Thou hast the same ear to hear, the same heart to pity. the same hand to deliver.

But thou hast chosen to transact all thy concerns with us through a Mediator. In Him, it hath pleased thee, that all fulness should dwell. Him thou hast exalted at thy own right hand, to be a Prince and a Saviour, to give repentance unto Israel and remission of sins.

To Him therefore may we look ; on Him may we entirely depend : and in Him, with all the seed of Israel, may we be justified and glorified. May we know how to derive relief from his sufferings, without losing any of our abhorrence of sin, or longing after holiness. May we feel the double efficiency of his blood, in tranquillizing our consciences and cleansing them : may we delight in his service as well as his sacrifice ; and under the constrainings of a love that passeth knowledge ; may we live, not to ourselves, but to Him that died for us and rose again.

In all our approaches to thee, may we have boldness and access, with confidence, by the faith of Him. Give us much of the spirit of grace and of supplication. By a constant readiness for the duty, and a frequent performance of it, may we pray without ceasing ; and by guarding against every discouragement, may we pray, and not faint.

May we cherish a grateful and cheerful disposition ; not murmuring and repining, because all our wishes are not indulged, or because some trials are blended with our enjoyments ; but sensible of our desert, and impressed with the number and greatness of thy benefits, may we bless the Lord at all times, and may his praise continually be in our mouth. And may our gratitude be real and practical, and increasing with our obligations. Enable us to inquire, Lord what wilt thou have me to do ? Enable us to resolve, I will walk before the Lord in the land of the living ; enable us to pray—

Make me to walk in thy commands,
'Tis a delightful road ;
Nor let my head, or heart, or hands,
Offend against my God.

We commend to thy pity, and thy power, all those who are any way afflicted in mind, body, or estate. May the young find it good to bear the yoke in their youth ; may they that know thee not, be chosen in the furnace of affliction ; and may thy own people find thee a very present help in trouble. Smile upon our country. Enlighten the understandings of those who are at the head of pub-

lic affairs, and enable them to instruct the people
what to do. May our magistrates be men fearing
God and hating covetousness ; make our officers
peace, and our exactors righteousness. Let not
oppression be ever seen on the side of judgment,
nor a perverse spirit be mingled in the midst of
the people. Let glory dwell in our land, and upon
all the glory may there be a defence. May the
grace of, &c. Amen.

TUESDAY EVENING.

O THOU, that hearest prayer, unto Thee shall
all flesh come. Lord teach us to pray. We have
reason to fear, that the language of our lips, and
the feelings of our hearts, in our religious exercises, have not always agreed. We have frequently taken carelessly upon our tongues, a name
never pronounced above, without the deepest reverence and humility. We have often desired
things which would have proved our injury ; and
we have deprecated things which have proved
some of our chief mercies. We have erred,
both on the side of our hopes and fears ; we are
unfit to choose for ourselves ; we are convinced,
that the way of man is not in himself, it is not in
man that walketh to direct his steps. We know
not what to pray for as we ought. Let thy Spirit
help our infirmities ; and produce in us those
views and dispositions which will lead us to ask
according to thy will, and then we know Thou
hearest us.

With regard to temporal blessings, may we
never be importunate ; may we always refer
them to thy fatherly goodness ; for Thou knowest
that we have need of these things before we ask
Thee ; but may we seek first in time and attention,
thy kingdom and righteousness. May we value

6*

things by their relation to eternity. May we
never think we prosper, unless our souls prosper;
that we are rich, unless we are rich towards God;
that we are wise, unless we are made wise unto
salvation. May our spiritual and everlasting
welfare be our chief solicitude, and may we be
conscious to ourselves, that we would rather be
poor, and afflicted, and despised; if blessed with
much of the life of God in our souls, than to be
admired by our fellow men, and be successful in
our enterprises, and have more than heart can
wish—if these things should prove the means of
our forgetfulness of God.

Having found this world to be dreams and lies,
vanity and vexation of spirit, may we arise and
depart from it, and seek our happiness in thy
favour, and image, and presence, and service.
And though we are unworthy to be regarded by
Thee, especially after we have so often refused
Thee, receive us graciously; justify our persons,
and renovate our nature; and put thy laws into
our minds and write them in our hearts; and be
Thou to us a God, and may we be to Thee a
people. Endear to us that Saviour, whose unexampled love led Him to suffer the just for the
unjust, that He might bring us unto God. May
we never dare to think of coming to Thee in any
other way; but may we always have boldness and
access, with confidence, by the faith of Him:
yea, may we joy in God, through our Lord Jesus
Christ, by whom we have now received the atonement; and not only so, but may we glory in
tribulation also, knowing that tribulation worketh
patience, and patience experience, and experience
hope.

For blessed be thy name, we live not in a
fatherless world; nor are our minutest affairs forgotten before God. The hairs of our head are
all numbered; our losses and trials are not the
effects of chance, but events, in which thy wisdom
and mercy are, now concerned, and will be, here-

after, displayed. We know that all things work together for good, to them that love Thee ; may our character, therefore, and not our condition, be the object of our anxiety. May we ascertain that our heart is right with Thee, and be careful for nothing. Having given ourselves unto the Lord, may we remember that we have a right, from thy holy word, to depend upon Thee, to provide for us, and to manage all our concerns, even to the end.

Discharged from the toil and the torment of care, may we feel ourselves at liberty to enjoy the advantages and comforts of our condition in life, and above all to pursue our work as christians. May we be attentive to duty: may we inquire, how we can best serve our generation, and glorify Thee in our body and spirit. May holiness to the Lord be inscribed upon all our time, and talents, and substance ; and may the inquiry of our grateful hearts, every moment be, What shall I render unto the Lord for all his benefits towards me ?

Thou hast made the outgoings of another morning and evening to rejoice. Thou has crowned the day with thy goodness. Let the night witness thy care and kindness : and may we enter on another portion of our time, not only under fresh obligations, but with new desires and resolutions to be for ever thine.

Our Father, &c.

WEDNESDAY MORNING.

O THOU Most High! enable us to feel and to express, becoming regards towards Thee, as the Creator of the ends of the earth, the Preserver of men, the Governor of the universe, the Judge of all, the Saviour of sinners. Thy greatness is unsearchable, but thy goodness is infinite. It is because thy compassions fail not, that we are not consumed. Thou hast not only prolonged our

unworthy lives under numberless provocations,
but Thou hast afforded us every needful supply
and indulgence.   Thy mercies have been new
every morning, and every moment.   Through thy
good hand upon us, we have been rescued from the
perils of another night ; our repose has been unter-
rified and undisturbed ; sleep has refreshed our
bodies and renewed our strength ; and we find ourselves surrounded at the commencement of another
day, with all our accustomed privileges.

But O God, we can never be sufficiently thankful, that we have our existence in a christian country, and where we can hear words, by which we
may be saved.   O, how important, how suitable,
how encouraging are the discoveries, the doctrines,
the promises, the invitations of the gospel of peace.
We are lost ; but here is presented to us a free,
full, and everlasting salvation.   We are left without strength ; but here we learn, that help is laid
on one that is mighty.   We are poor and needy ;
but here we behold the unsearchable riches of
Christ.   We are blind and ignorant ; but in Him
are hid all the treasures of wisdom and knowledge.
We thank Thee O God for thine unspeakable gift,
and we cordially accept of thy mercy extended to
us, through the mediation of thy dear Son.   We
rejoice that he has been delivered for our offences,
and raised again for our justification ; and that He
is now exalted at thy right hand to be a Prince
and a Saviour.   We abandon every other refuge
to hide in, and every other foundation to build
upon, and make him our only hope, and our only
confidence.   And while we depend on his death,
and make mention of his righteousness only, we
admire his example, and desire to be conformed to
his image.   May we put on the Lord Jesus Christ,
and increasingly resemble Him, whose life was
beneficence ; whose soul was meekness and humility ; who pleased not himself ; and who, of obedience the most trying and difficult, could say, I de-

light to do thy will, O my God, yea thy law is within my heart. May his glory fill our minds; may his love reign in our affections; and at his cross, and at his tomb, may we burn with ardour to live, not to ourselves, but to Him that died for us and rose again.

Let the number of his followers daily increase, and may none of our friends be found among his enemies. Pour thy Spirit upon our seed, and thy blessing upon our offspring. Let our sons be as plants grown up in their youth, and our daughters as corner stones, polished after the similitude of a palace. May our domestics be the servants of God; may they do his will from the heart; and be prepared for that world, where those who serve, will be as those who are served, and all the distinctions now necessary, will be done away, and none remain, but those which arise from character. And whatever be our conditions in life, may we fill them as christians; may we escape the snares to which they expose us; discharge the duties that grow out of their circumstances; enjoy with moderation and gratitude their advantages; and improve with decision and diligence, their opportunities and resources of usefulness. May every place and every company, in which we are found, be benefited by us.

And whatever may be the opinion of our fellow creatures concerning us, may we be satisfied and happy, in having the testimony that we please God.

We are now going forth into the concerns of another day. Take us under thy protection and influence. Guide us in all our steps. Enable us to realize thy presence and thy providence. Succeed us, in all our lawful endeavours, or prepare us for disappointment; and assure us that we are in the number of those to whom all things are working together for good; and who will for ever acknowledge—marvellous are thy works. Lord God Almighty, just and true are all thy ways, **O thou King** of saints.   Amen.

WEDNESDAY EVENING.

GOD over all, blessed for evermore. We desire to acknowledge thy Being and agency; to adore thy perfections, and to admire the works of thy hands. Thou hast made summer and winter. Thou hast appointed the moon for seasons, and the sun knoweth his going down. The day is thine ; the night also is thine : and thou makest the outgoings of the morning and the evening to rejoice. To that throne, from which none were ever repulsed or sent away empty, we again approach for mercy and grace to help in time of need. Let our prayer come before Thee as incense, and the lifting up of our hands as the evening sacrifice. Preserve us from formality, in those exercises in which we so daily engage ; and alarm our fears, lest we should provoke Thee to say, in vain do they worship me.

For this purpose, enable us to realize thine all seeing eye, to remember with *whom* we have to do, and *what* we have to do with Him : may we deeply feel the guilt of the sins we confess, and hunger and thirst after the blessings we implore. And while we review the numberless blessings we have received from thy hands, may we be more than ever sensible of our unworthiness, that our hearts may be unfeignedly thankful, and that we may be disposed to show forth thy praise, not only with our lips, but in our lives, by giving up ourselves to thy service, and walking before Thee in holiness and righteousness all our days.

He that is our God is the God of salvation, and unto God the Lord belong the issues from death. We bless Thee this evening, as the Preserver of men. Another day has been added, by thy good providence, to the season of thy long suffering, and the time of our preparation for eternity. We lament that the design of our being placed and continued here, has been so imperfectly subserved; that in so many things we have offended, and in all, come short of the glory of God. If, where much is given, much will be required, and the servant who knew his Lord's will, and did it not, shall be beaten with many stripes—if Thou, Lord should mark *our* iniquities, O Lord, who shall stand? We cannot answer Thee for one of a thousand of our transgressions: the review of a single day is enough to plunge us into despair—our only relief is, that there is forgiveness with Thee; and that with Thee there is plenteous redemption.

But while we hope in thy mercy, we would not abuse it. We would not sin that grace may abound; or be evil, because Thou art good. But since Thou art good, and ready to forgive, we would the more sincerely grieve, that ever we have offended a Being, so worthy of our devotedness; and be the more concerned in future, to walk so as to please Thee.

Create in us a clean heart, and renew a right spirit within us. Set a watch, O God, upon our mouth; keep the door of our lips. And in simplicity and godly sincerity, not with fleshly wisdom, but by thy grace, may we have our conversation in the world, and in the church, and in the family.

We again commend ourselves to thy care. As Thou hast been through the day, our sun and our shield, be Thou through the night, our shade and our defence. Undisturbed by anxieties, unalarmed by fears, undistressed by pain, or indisposition, may we retire and enjoy repose. Remind us, by putting off our garments, and lying down to sleep, of putting off the body, and sleeping in the grave, the house appointed for all living. Prepare us for the night of death, the morning of the resurrection, and the day of judgment.

And all we implore, is through the Mediation of Him, who bore the sins of many, and made intercession for the transgressors, to whom, with the Father, and the Holy Spirit, be endless praises. Amen.

THURSDAY MORNING.

WE would address Thee, O God, in the language of the publican, which so well becomes us, and say, from our hearts, God be merciful to me a sinner. Sinners we are by nature and practice; sinners thy word proclaims us to be; sinners, we hope we feel ourselves to be; and acknowledge that Thou art justified when Thou speakest, and clear when Thou judgest.

Yet Thou hast not left us to despair; nor have we a mere peradventure to encourage us—who can tell if God will return and repent, and leave a blessing behind him that we perish not? We have all the assurance we could desire, that with the Lord there is mercy, and with Him, plenteous redemption. Conscious of the number and heinousness of our offences, we could not have approached thee with confidence, without a previous token for good. But thou hast stretched forth the golden sceptre, and said—"touch and live; I will be merciful to thy unrighteousness, and thy sins and iniquities will I remember no more." May we encourage ourselves, by a sense of thy all-sufficiency, by faith in thy promises, and by views of the experience of others, and ask and receive, that our joy may be full. To that dear refuge, in which so many have been sheltered from every storm, may we repair; and in that fountain for sin, always open, and free for all, may we be cleansed from all our defilements.

Lord, we believe—help thou our unbelief; that sin is exceeding sinful; it is the abominable thing which thy soul hateth ; and this, and this alone, separates between thee and us. Thou canst not contradict the essential perfections of thy nature ; and thou canst not make us happy *with* thyself, till thou hast made us holy, *like* thyself. O thou holy God, deliver us from all our iniquities, and make us such creatures as thou canst take pleasure in, and such creatures as can take pleasure in thee. While many are asking, Who will show us any good ? may the cry of our heart be, Lord, lift thou up the light of thy countenance upon us. May we consent to the law of God, that it is good ; may we delight in thy law, after the inner man. May we never complain of the strictness of thy demands, but mourn over our want of conformity to them. May we esteem all thy commandments, concerning all things to be right, and hate every false way. Put thy Spirit within us, that our practice may spring from principle, and our dispositions be congenial with duty, so that we may resemble him who could say, " my meat is to do the will of Him that sent me, and to finish his work.

We live in a world of changes : but with thee there is no variableness, nor shadow of turning. May we know that Thou, the eternal God, art our refuge, and that underneath us are thine everlasting arms. Creatures die ; friends and relations die ; the fathers, where are they ? And the prophets, do they live for ever ? But the Lord liveth, and blessed be our rock, and let the God of our salvation be exalted.

May we never forget that we are mortal ourselves. May we never put the evil day far off. May we frequently and seriously think of a dying hour ; may we faithfully inquire, What will be its issue with regard to us, and what preparation we have for it. And may we never rest satisfied, till we are enabled to view it, as the period of our release, and the end of our conflict ; till we can say with Paul, Thanks be unto God who has **given** us the victory, through our Lord Jesus Christ.

Take us, this day, under thy protection ; **and** make use of us for thy glory. Let thy presence go with us ; and do thou give us rest. Let thy love sweeten our comforts, and thy grace sanctify all our trials. We consecrate ourselves to Thee, body, soul, and spirit. Accept of our persons and services, and enable us to ascribe, blessing, and honour, and glory, and power, unto Him that sitteth upon the throne, and unto the lamb, for ever and ever. Amen.

THURSDAY EVENING

O God, all thy works praise Thee, and thy saints bless Thee. By thy mercies, we again surround this family altar, and engage in the exercises of devotion. May we be concerned to worship Thee, a holy God, in the beauty of holiness ; and to worship Thee, who art a Spirit, in spirit and in truth. Such worship alone thy word requires ; but such worship, thy grace alone can enable us to render. For we know from thy word, and from our own experience we know, that without Thee, we can do nothing. All our sufficiency is of Thee: do Thou work in us to will, and to do, of thy good pleasure.

We would call to remembrance our true character and condition before Thee. We would not go about to establish our own righteousness, or seek to deny or extenuate our guilt. We are not only unprofitable servants, but condemned criminals. We confess the number and offensiveness of our transgressions, and acknowledge that we deserve to perish. But we bless Thee for the everlasting consolation and good hope, through grace, which the gospel affords ; for the news of a

Mediator between Thee and us ; of a High Priest who has put away sin by the sacrifice of himself ; of an Advocate with the Father, who ever lives to make intercession for us, and of a Saviour, in whom it has pleased Thee, that all fulness should dwell.

Produce in us, all the feelings of those who are blessed with repentance unto life. Give us that faith by which we can be justified from all things, and have peace with God, through our Lord Jesus Christ. To the shadow of the Redeemer's cross may we retreat, and there find security and relief, refreshment and delight. Assure us of an interest in thy favour, which is life; and clothe us with thine image, which is the beauty and dignity of the soul.

We bless Thee for thy word, which we have been reading. May it dwell in us richly in all wisdom. May we yield a suitable attention to its various parts. May we make it, not only our song in the house of our pilgrimage, but the man of our counsel, a light unto our feet, and a lamp unto our paths. May we take it along with us, into all the concerns of life ; and whether we are rich or poor, whether we are parents or children, whether we are appointed to govern or serve, may we walk by this rule, that mercy and peace may be upon us.

May we ever be willing that the Lord should choose our inheritance for us, and readily and piously accommodate ourselves, to the dispensations of thy providence. May we never lean to our own understanding : may we never take a step, without asking counsel of the Lord, nor be unwilling to take one, at the intimation of thy pleasure. May we never think that Thou art less wise, and righteous, and good, in a cloudy and dark day, than in a shining one; when we cannot trace Thee, may we trust ; and walking by faith, and not by sight, be fully persuaded, that just and right are all thy ways, O Thou King of saints.

Regard those, who, under the pressure of affliction, are saying, Brethren pray for us. Be with
them in trouble. Thou knowest the anxieties of
thy people, lest by any of their temper or carriage
in the evil day, they should injure the religion they
profess: let thy grace be sufficient for them: let
faith and patience have their perfect work: let them
glorify Thee in all their trials.

Bless all in authority over us, and so rule their
hearts and strengthen their hands, that they may
punish wickedness and vice, and maintain true religion and virtue.

May all those who are placed above others in
condition, go before them in the profession of truth,
and the practice of holiness, and be examples to
all inferior ranks in society.

And may the grace of, &c.   Amen.

FRIDAY MORNING,

O Thou eternal God! with Thee is the fountain of life. Thou art the Father of men and angels. Thou art the Governor of the universe, and
the Judge of all. Thou dost from thy throne behold all the dwellers upon earth: and there is not
a word on our tongue, or a thought in our heart, but
lo! O Lord, Thou knowest it altogether. And
Thou art not a God that hast pleasure in wickedness, neither can evil dwell with Thee.

How then can we presume to enter thy presence,
who have rendered ourselves guilty before Thee,
and have provoked thy righteous displeasure. O
wretched creatures that we are! We have weari-
ed thy patience, we have abused thy goodness, we
have trampled on thy authority, and we have said
unto God, Depart from us, we desire not the knowledge of thy ways. We lie at thy mercy. If Thou
pity us not, we are undone. But Thou art long

suffering, not willing that any should perish. Hast Thou not sworn by thyself, that Thou hast no pleasure in the death of him that dieth? Hast Thou not delivered up thine own Son for us all? And wilt Thou not, with Him, also freely give us all things?

Through Him as the way, the truth, and the life, may we return to Thee; and find Thee, waiting to be gracious, and exalted to have mercy upon us. Awaken our consciences. Enlighten us in the knowledge of sin and of ourselves. May we feel our personal depravity, misery, and helplessness; and from self-despair, may we be led to value the discoveries of the gospel, and to flee for refuge to lay hold upon the hope set before us. May we rejoice in the suitableness, the all-sufficiency, and the perfect willingness of the Saviour; and find in Him, for ourselves, individually, wisdom, and righteousness, and sanctification, and redemption. As our Prophet, may we receive his instructions. As our High Priest, may we rely on his sacrifice and intercession. As our Prince, may we obey Him. As our example, may we follow Him: and whatsoever we do, in word, or deed, may we do all in the name of the Lord Jesus.

May integrity and uprightness preserve us. May we be Israelites indeed, in whom is no guile; and herein exercise ourselves, to have always a conscience void of offence, towards God, and towards man. May the same mind govern us, and the same spirit actuate us, in prosperity and adversity; alone, and in public; in thy house, and in our own; may we fulfil our course with diligence and perseverance; and at last, finish it with joy: When we have passed the wilderness, and our eyes behold the swellings of Jordan, bid our anxious fears subside; and give us an abundant entrance into the everlasting kingdom of our Lord and Saviour.

But, O Lord, we would not reach that felicity alone. May we awaken the attention of others, and

induce them to join us in the path of life ; ever re
membering, that if we convert a sinner from the
error of his way, we shall save a soul from death,
and shall hide a multitude of sins.   May we therefore seek every opportunity of usefulness ; may we
walk in wisdom towards them that are without ;
holding forth the word of life, and adorning the
doctrine of God our Saviour in all things—To whom,
be glory and majesty, dominion and power, both
now and for ever.   Amen.

FRIDAY EVENING.

O God, Thou art greatly to be feared in the assembly of the saints, and to be had in reverence of
all them that are about Thee.   Thou art King of
kings, and Lord of lords : Thou art the blessed and
only Potentate ; Thou only hast immortality—thy
greatness is unsearchable.   But thy name is love.
Thy compassions never fail.   Thy mercies are over
all thy works ; and Thou hast displayed the exceeding riches of thy grace, in thy kindness towards us, by Christ Jesus.

We are not only allowed, but even enjoined to
seek thy face ; and assured, that they who seek the
Lord, shall not want any good thing.   We acknowledge that we have forfeited all claim to thy regard, and are not only unworthy, but guilty.   We
are convinced, that if ever we are saved, it must
be according to thy mercy, for there is nothing in
us, from which our recovery can arise, or on which
our hope can fix.   But Thou hast commended thy
love towards us, in that while we were yet sinners,
Christ died for us—died for the ungodly.   And
Thou hast sent the gospel to announce the intelligence, and to certify, that whosoever believeth on
Him shall not perish, but have everlasting life.

O Thou God of all grace, as Thou hast given us
a Saviour, produce in us that faith by which we

shall be enabled to receive Him, and make Him all our desire, all our hope, and all our glory. May we enter Him as our refuge ; build on Him as our foundation ; walk in Him as our way ; follow Him as our guide ; and conform to Him as our example

May we never be ashamed of Jesus or of his words; but go forth to Him without the camp, bearing his reproach. May we never draw upon ourselves reflections by unholy or imprudent conduct, but count it a glory, when buffeted for a fault, to take it patiently ; but if we suffer for truth and righteousness' sake, may we rejoice that we are partakers of Christ's sufferings ; knowing, that when his glory shall be revealed, we also shall rejoice with exceeding joy.

May we never make the multitude our model . nor wait for the company and countenance· of others, when conviction, derived from thy word, excites us to advance. Like Caleb, may we have another spirit, and follow the Lord fully : and with Joshua, say to all around us, " Choose you, whom you will serve—but as for me and my house, we will serve the Lord."

Preserve us from the present evil world. May its smiles never allure, nor its frowns terrify us from the path of duty : may its vices never defile, nor its errors delude us. May we not live looking at the things which are seen and temporal ; but as heirs of immortality, may we feel that we are strangers and pilgrims on earth, and declare plainly that we seek a country. And may our title to it daily become more clear ; and our meetness for it more perfect ; and our foretastes of it more abundant.

May our house be the tabernacle of the righteous; and let it be ever filled with the voice of rejoicing and of salvation. May those who are stationed at the head of the family, know their duty towards those who are placed under their care ; and may they know their duty to us : and in our several relations may we walk by the rule of thy word, that mercy and peace may be upon us ; and that observers may exclaim, Behold, how good and how pleasant a thing it is for brethren to dwell together in unity.

Bless the religious denomination to which we belong; and let every christian church flourish. Wherever we see the grace of God, may we be glad ; and willingly leave, to the Author of all good, the choice of his own instruments. Bless the Government of our country. Regard in mercy, all its lawful interests, domestic and foreign. Sanctify, and perpetuate, and extend, our religious advantages. Let thy word have free course, and be glorified. Let thy way be known on earth, and thy saving health among all nations.

And now, unto Him that is able to do exceeding abundantly, above all that we ask or think, according to the power that worketh in us, unto him be glory in the church, by Christ Jesus, throughout all ages, world without end. Amen.

SATURDAY MORNING.

O God, Thou art glorious in holiness, fearful in praises, doing wonders. And it is not one of the least of thy wonderful doings towards the children of men, that we are on this side an awful eternity, and not reaping the due reward of our deeds. Our whole life has been a series of provocations against thy divine majesty. Our offences have not only been countless, but aggravated. Conscience has rebuked us; friends have admonished us ; the examples of the wise and good have reproached and encouraged us. Thou hast often called us to reflection and repentance, by the smart of the rod ; and invited and allured us, by a profusion of kindnesses. Our iniquities are increased over our head, and our trespass is gone up into the very heaven. And Thou hast seen all our sins; and Thou hast abhorred all; and Thou couldst have easily and justly punished us; yet Thou hast spared us; and instead of finding ourselves, this morning, in the place where even God has forgotten to be gracious, and lifting up our eyes in hopeless torment, we can lift up our eyes unto the hills, from whence cometh our help.

In ourselves we are poor, and wretched, and miserable; but Thou, whom we have offended, even Thou, hast provided every supply for our souls; and with the announcement, we have the invitation, Come, for all things are now ready. O Lord, we thankfully obey thy call; we accept of thy goodness: we acquiesce in all the appointments of the gospel. We believe the record Thou hast given of thy dear Son—that there is salvation in none other, but that in Him there is plenteous redemption; and apply to Him for all the benefits resulting from every office he sustains in the church. We give up our minds implicitly to his instruction; in the sacrifice he once offered, we trust and glory; we revere, we love his authority; and pray that his grace may reign in us, through righteousness unto eternal life. We would not—we will not— love a world that crucified *Him*. We will not cherish, or endure, the sin that put Him to grief; or suffer Him to be wounded in the house of his friends. At the same cross, which relieves our consciences from a burden too heavy for us to bear, we would learn lessons of self-denial, forgiveness, and submission: we would feel motives to obedience; and find resources for all the exigencies of the divine life.

For we rejoice to think, that by his being made a curse for us, the blessing of Abraham comes upon the Gentiles, and that we can receive the promise of the Spirit, by faith. For his sake, give thy Holy Spirit to them that now ask Thee as a

Spirit of grace and of supplication, of truth and of holiness, of peace and of consolation : and may we not only possess—but be filled with the Spirit.

May we never consider ourselves, as detached individuals. May we look, not every man on his own things only, but also on the things of others. Never may we ask with Cain, when reproved for unkindness, or urged to beneficence, Am I my brother's keeper? But may we love our neighbour as ourselves. May we do good even to the unthankful and the unworthy ; may we teach transgressors thy ways, and be the means of converting sinners unto Thee : and may none of our efforts be rendered fruitless, by inconsistency of character, and reproachfulness of conduct. May we *be* what we *profess;* and *do,* as well as *teach.* May all our connexions *see,* as well as *hear* our religion ; and be constrained to acknowledge, that we are the seed which the Lord hath blessed.

We bless Thee, that again we have laid us down in peace, and slept, because Thou, Lord, only makest us dwell in safety. Into thy hands we commit our bodies and spirits, for our going out and coming in, this day. We are more exposed by day than by night ; more surrounded with evil ; and more liable to the seductions of sin. May we ever regard sin as our greatest foe, and holiness as our noblest attainment. And whether we are in solitude or society, lead us not into temptation, but deliver us from evil ; for thine is the kingdom, and the power, and the glory, for ever and ever. **Amen.**

SATURDAY EVENING.

O GOD, Thou hast made, and Thou upholdest all things by the word of thy power. Darkness is thy pavilion. Thou walkest upon the wings of the wind. All nations before Thee are as nothing. One generation passeth away, and another cometh; and we are hastening back to the dust from whence we were taken. The heavens we behold will vanish away like the cloud that covers them; and the earth we tread will dissolve like a morning dream; but Thou, incapable of change, independent of the vicissitudes of time, and the perishing of worlds, art, from everlasting to everlasting, God over all, blessed for evermore.

Infinitely great and glorious as Thou art, we are thy offspring and thy care. Thy hands have made us and fashioned us. Thou hast watched over us with more than parental, more than maternal tenderness. Thou hast holden our soul in life, and not suffered our feet to be moved. Thy divine power has given us all things, not only necessary for life, but godliness. Bless the Lord, O our soul, and forget not all his benefits; who forgiveth all our iniquities; who healeth all our diseases; who redeemeth our lives from destruction; who crowneth us with loving-kindness and tender mercies; who satisfieth our mouth with good things, so that our youth is renewed like the eagles.

We raise this evening a fresh memorial, and inscribe it to the God of our salvation. Hitherto hath the Lord helped us. We have passed, not only through another day, but through another week. The sun has not smitten us by day, nor the moon by night. We have been preserved in our going out, and coming in. But thine has been the vigilance, that turned aside the evils which threatened us. Thine have been the supplies that have nourished us. Thine the comforts that have indulged us. Thine the relations and friends that have delighted us. Thine have been the means of grace which have edified us; and thine the book, which, amidst all our enjoyments, has told us, that this is not our rest; and in all our successes, that one thing is yet needful.

Nothing can equal the number of thy mercies, but our imperfections and sins. These O God, we would not conceal, or palliate ; but confess them, with a broken heart and a contrite spirit.

In what a condition would our closet-reviews leave us, this evening, were it not for the assurance that there is forgiveness with thee, that thou mayest be feared, and with thee plenteous redemption. Yet, while we hope for pardon through the blood of the cross, we pray to be clothed with humility ; to be quickened in thy way ; and to be more de-voted to the things that belong to our everlasting peace.

How soon has the week rolled away ! Its days have fled like a dream, a vapour, a shadow. So will all our days flee ; so will they all appear when the end arrives. O, help us to keep that end in remembrance ; and endeavour to view things now, as they will appear, from the borders of the grave. May we know how frail we are, that we may be cured of the folly of delay and indecision ; and so number our days, that we may apply our hearts unto wisdom.

May we call the approaching sabbath a delight, the holy of the Lord, honourable ; and may we honour thee, in not doing our own ways, nor find-ing our own pleasures, nor speaking our own words. May the private moments of the day, be sacred ; and the social—innocent and edifying. And may we keep our foot, when we go to the house of God, and offer not the sacrifice of fools. Let us not go as they go, and sit as they sit, and hear thy words, but do them not.

Preserve us from trifling with the things of the soul and eternity, or trusting in those privileges, which, unimproved, will only augment our guilt and our misery.

Thy people, the Jews, were distinguished by thy favours, above all the families of the earth ; but wrath came upon them to the uttermost. The churches of Asia, provoked thee to remove the candlestick out of its place ; and they were left in darkness. We have awful examples still nearer. How many, who once heard and professed the gospel, have been turned by the abuse of it, into apostates and infidels, blasphemers and persecutors ; ten fold more the children of hell than before ; while numbers who yet maintain the form of godliness, are too hardened to feel the power of it.

While, therefore, we go to thy house, in the multitude of thy mercies, may we in thy *fear* worship towards thy holy temple ; for thou art greatly to be feared in the assembly of the saints. O, let us not perish under means designed to save us. O, let not the savour of life unto life, prove to us only the savour of death unto death.

Make the place of thy feet glorious. Bring us to thy holy mountain, and if we are not made joyful in thy house of prayer, convince us, alarm us, humble us, banish the spirit of the world from our hearts, and fill us with all the fulness of God.

So we thy people and the sheep of thy pasture, will give thee thanks for ever, we will show forth thy praise throughout all generations. Amen.

SUNDAY MORNING.

O God, we desire with all reverence and humility to approach thee, as a Being infinitely great and glorious. Thou art the perfection of all excellency, the fountain of all life, and the source of all blessedness. How immense is the family of creatures, produced by thy word, and depending on thy care. Millions are visible ; and myriads of myriads, in the air, the earth, and the sea, are invisible ; and all these have their wants and their appetites, and are capable of receiving relief and pleasure. And the eyes of *all* wait upon thee, and thou givest them their meat in due season· thou openest thine hand and satisfiest the desire of every living thing.

But they never forfeited the care of their Creator, nor swerved from the end of 'their being ; while *we* have revolted from thee ; *we* have joined in alliance with thy foes ; and deserve, as children of disobedience, that the wrath of God should come upon us. And yet, such is the excellency of thy loving kindness, O Lord, that the *children of men*, unworthy and guilty as they are, are allowed to come and put their trust under the shadow of thy wings.

We bless thee for the Scriptures of truth, which make known thy designs concerning us, and assure us, that they are thoughts of peace,

and not of evil. We rejoice in thy word, as one
that findeth great spoil. We love to peruse its
doctrines, promises, and invitations ; to contemplate the great mystery of godliness, God ma-
nifest in the flesh ; and to dwell on the history and
experience of those who have obtained mercy.
For all who have ever been saved, have been
saved by thy grace, and have been thy workmanship. And thou art the same, yesterday, to-
day, and for ever ; thy hand is not shortened that
it cannot save, nor thine ear heavy, that it cannot
hear.

Bow down thy ear, and hearken to the voice of
our supplication : employ thy hand for our deliverance and relief. We are already the creatures of
thy power—O, make us the subjects of thy grace.
We are already the beneficiaries of thy providence—O, bless us with all spiritual blessings—
blessings for our souls, and for eternity. Though by
nature far off, may we be made nigh by the blood
of Christ : no longer strangers and foreigners, but
fellow-citizens with the saints, and of the household of God. Bless us, we pray Thee, with a present salvation——that being justified by faith, we
may have peace with God ; that the love and power of sin may be subdued in our hearts ; that we
may be dead to the world ; alive to the glory of
God ; and concerned to serve our generation according to thy will.

May we never be blots, or mere blanks, in life.
May we never cause the ways of truth to be evil
spoken of : may our liberty never prove an occasion to the flesh, but by love may we serve one
another. May every one of us please his neighbour, for his good to edification. May we attend,
not only to what is essential in our religious character, but what is ornamental. May we pursue
whatsoever things are lovely and of good report,
and render our professions of the gospel, not only

impressive, but amiable and inviting. May we hold forth the word of life, with our tempers as well as our tongues; with our lives as well as our lips; and thus be continually saying to those we meet——We are journeying towards a place, of which the Lord said, I will give it you; come with us, and we will do you good, for the Lord hath spoken good concerning Israel.

Send out thy light and thy truth; let them lead us, let them guide us to the holy hill, and to thy tabernacles. Bless, this day, the dispensation of thy gospel by means of preaching. While Paul plants and Apollos waters—it is all that they can do; give Thou the increase. May thy ministers be wise to win souls, and help those much who have believed through grace.

Especially bless thy dear servant, on whose labours we are this day to attend. Let him come forth from his sacred retirement in the fulness of the blessing of the gospel of peace : and may he enter the sanctuary, as Aaron entered the tabernacle of the congregation, when the holy oil was poured upon his head, and the fragrance filled the place—and O, let him not prove the savour of death unto death to any that shall hear him. Open our ear to discipline ; may we hear for ourselves ; hear for our souls ; so hear, as that our souls may live. And may great grace rest upon all the assemblies of thy people.

Despise not the prisoners of Thy providence. Follow those who are unable to follow Thee ; and while forbidden to hear the preaching of the word, may they hear the voice of the rod, and have reason to say, It is good for us that we have been afflicted. Make them thankful, that to will is present with them ; and that in their hearts, are the ways of them who repair to Zion. Prove thyself, a very present help in trouble, and render the bed of languishing, the chamber of sickness, the house of mourning—the house of God, and the gate of heaven.

And by all the discipline of thy Providence, and the ordinances of religion, may we be increasingly prepared for the remaining duties of life, the solemnities of a dying hour, and the services and joys that are beyond the grave.

We implore it through the intercession of Him who has encouraged us to address Thee—as Our Father, &c.

SUNDAY EVENING.

It is a good thing to give thanks unto the Lord, and to sing praises unto thy name, O, Most High : to show forth thy loving-kindness in the morning, and thy faithfulness every night.

We have this evening to acknowledge the blessings, not only of another day, but of another sabbath. We bless Thee that the sabbath was made for man, and that Thou hast hallowed such a portion of our time, for purposes more important, but which, alas, we are prone to neglect. Thus Thou art affording us opportunities to retire and compare the objects which court our attention : to learn, among all the cares of life, that one thing is needful ; and to hear the inquiry, what is a man profited, if he should gain the whole world and lose his own soul. Thus we have moments of abstraction and leisure, in which we can more fully investigate our character ; examine our condition ; and ask, for what purpose we entered this mortal stage, and what will become of us when the scenes close.

We thank Thee that the lines are fallen to us in pleasant places, and that we have a goodly heritage : so that we can add to private meditation and devotion, the public ordinances of religion ; and can sit under our own vine and fig-tree, none daring to make us afraid. We bless Thee, that we have not only the Scriptures, but the ministry of the gospel ; and have this day not only read, but heard the words of eternal life. We hope we have seen thy power and thy glory in the sanctuary, and have found the house of God to be the gate of heaven.

But, O God, the effects we experience while waiting upon Thee, though delightful, are as often transitory, and prove like the morning cloud, and early dew. Before the lapse of a single day, we are compelled to complain, My soul cleaveth unto the dust ; and to pray, quicken Thou me according to thy word. Render therefore the impressions made upon us, deep and durable : keep these things for ever in the imagination of the hearts of thy people ; and let thy word *dwell* in us richly, in all *wisdom.*

May the instructions we receive, attend us in every part of our ordinary life, and regulate, and excite us in the discharge of all our relative duties, so that whether we are husbands or wives, parents or children, masters or servants, we may adorn the doctrine of God our Saviour in all things. May we be satisfied with no knowledge, no belief, no professions, no feelings in religion—while our hearts are void of thy love, and we are strangers to that grace which bringeth salvation, and teacheth us to deny ungodliness and worldly lusts, and to live soberly, righteously and godly in the present world.

We take shame to ourselves, not only for our open violations of thy law ; but for our secret faults, our omissions of duty, our unprofitable attendance on the means of grace, our carnality in worshipping Thee ; and all the sins of our holy things. Our iniquities are increased over our head, and our trespass is gone up into the very heavens—and there, *He* is gone also, who is our Advocate with the Father, and the Propitiation for our sins. Behold his hands and his feet : and hear, O, hear the voice of the blood of sprinkling, that speaketh better things than that of Abel.

Pity those who have this day been deprived of the public means of grace by sickness or infirmity. Let them know that Thou art not confined to temples made with hands : be with them in trouble ; and give them their vineyards from thence, and the valley of Achor for a door of hope.

And remember the millions who were never favoured with the advantages we enjoy, and would be grateful for the crumbs that fall from our table. But they never smiled when a sabbath appeared. They never heard of the name of Jesus. They feel guilt, but know nothing of the blood that cleanseth from all sin ; they feel depravity, but know nothing of the renewing of the Holy Ghost. They are bleeding to death of their spiritual wounds, but no one proclaims among them the balm of Gilead, and the physician there. O, send out thy light and thy truth. Let thy way be known on earth ; thy saving health among all nations.

We now commit ourselves, with all our connexions, into thy hands. Guard us through the defenceless hours of sleep, from every evil to which we are exposed. If, as life is always uncertain, it should please Thee to call us hence this night—may we awake in glory, and be for ever with the Lord : or if Thou shouldst continue us in being—may we rise in health and comfort, to pay Thee the homage of a grateful heart, in a course of cheerful obedience.

In thy favour is life—Do *Thou* bless us, and we shall be blessed—safe from every evil, and sure of every good.

And prepare us at length for the rest that remains for thy people ; in which we shall join the general assembly and church of the first born, in ascribing—blessing and honour, and glory, and power, to Him that sitteth upon the throne, and to the Lamb, for ever and ever. Amen

O THOU, who hast characterised thyself as the hearer of prayer, unto Thee shall all flesh come: and that we may come with acceptance and success, we come in the name of the great Intercessor, Jesus Christ, the righteous—and Thou, Eternal Spirit of grace and supplication, do Thou make intercession for us, by making intercession in us, according to the will of God.

All they that are far from Thee shall perish; but it is good for us to draw near to Thee. We have found the duty our delight. Devotion has opened a resource, when all other comforts have failed: and in every perplexity, every alarm, every distress, a glorious high throne, from the beginning, has been the place of our sanctuary. We praise thy name, that ordinances have not been unprofitable observances to our souls; but channels, through which the God of all grace has replenished us; and means, by which we have enjoyed fellowship with the Father, and his Son Jesus Christ.

Bless the services in which we were engaged on the past day. Let a savour of divine things be left on our spirits; and be diffused in our conversation. And as the face of Moses, when he descended from communion with Thee, shone, so that the Israelites could not steadfastly behold him for the glory of his countenance; so may it be with us. Let those around us take knowledge of us, that we have been with Jesus; and may our profiting appear unto all men. May our light shine before men. May we be *manifestly* the disciples of Christ. Instead of confounding our neighbours and friends to determine, whether we are settlers, or strangers, and pilgrims on the earth; may we declare *plainly* that we seek a country. May we put on, as the elect of God. holy and beloved, bowels of mercies, kindness, humbleness of mind, meekness, long suffering, forgiving one another. May we be followers of God, as dear children: may we be perfect, as our Father, who is in heaven, is perfect.

At present, it is a day of small things with us. We have only light enough—to see our darkness; sensibility enough—to feel the hardness of our heart; spirituality enough—to mourn our want of heavenly mindedness. But we might have had more; we ought to have had more. We have never been straightened in Thee: Thou hast always placed before us an infinite fulness, accompanied with the command and the promise, Open thy mouth wide; I will fill it.

We confess and bewail, not only our deficiencies, but our backslidings also. It is not with us as in months past: O, recall us to thyself; enable us to feel our first love, and to do our first works. Yea, may we forget the things that are behind, and reach forth unto those that are before. May we not only have life, but may we have it more abundantly; and not only be fruitful, but bear much fruit.

May our improvements correspond with our privileges: and our practice with our knowledge. May our wills always bow to the decisions of our judgments; may we choose what we approve; and never condemn ourselves in the things that we allow.

May we never want the threatenings of thy law, and the terrors of hell, to keep us from every evil way. May thy goodness lead us to repentance; and thy love constrain us to holy obedience.

May all our churches continue steadfastly in the apostles' doctrine, and in fellowship, and in breaking of bread, and in prayer; and may the Lord add daily to their number, such as shall be saved.

May the dead hear the voice of the Son of God, and live. May those who are asking the way to

Zion, with their faces thitherward, find a teacher that will say to them, This is the way, walk ye in it, when they turn to the right hand, and when they turn to the left. Let the rich be poor in spirit ; and the poor be made rich in faith, and heirs of the kingdom which Thou hast promised to them that love Thee. Let the ignorant be enlightened ; and let those that are wise, become fools, that they may be wise.

We bless Thee, for all thy former loving-kindnesses to this family, and pray that they may be continued to us and sanctified to us. May the outgoings of the morning and evening of another day be made to rejoice. May we continually live under the shadow of thy wing, and the influence of thy grace ; and let the words of our mouth, and the meditations of our hearts, be acceptable in thy sight, O Lord, our strength and our Redeemer.

And unto Him that is able to do for us exceeding abundantly above all that we ask or think, according to the power that worketh in us, unto Him be glory in the church, by Christ Jesus, throughout all ages, world without end. Amen.

MONDAY EVENING.

Who in the heavens can be compared unto the Lord? Who among the sons of the mighty can be likened unto the Lord ? Thy wisdom, no difficulty can perplex ; thy power, no exertion can weaken ; thy bounty, no communication can exhaust or diminish. Thy goodness waits to be gracious, and is exalted to have mercy.

Thou hearest prayer ; and to assure our hearts before Thee, Thou hast not only commanded us to seek Thee, but Thou hast furnished us with the petitions we are to offer. Thou, even Thou hast told us, to take with you words and turn to the

Lord; and say unto Him—Take away all iniquity, receive us graciously, so will we offer the sacrifice of praise to God continually, that is the fruit of our lips, giving thanks to his name.

We feel the truth of our character, as drawn in the Scriptures; and we acknowledge our desert— and our helplessness too. Thy mercy is our only refuge and resource. O, be merciful unto us, and bless us, and cause thy face to shine upon us, that we may be saved. O, visit us with that salvation, which is present as well as future ; which changes, not only our state, but our nature ; and which, not only admits us into thy family, but makes us new creatures.

As Thou didst in the original creation, command light to shine out of darkness, so do Thou shine in our hearts. Give us the light of the knowledge of thy glory, in the face of Jesus Christ ; and may we so know Thy glory, in the face of Jesus Christ; and may we so know Thee, as to love Thee supremely ; serve Thee, as our only Lord ; and cleave to Thee, as our portion for ever. Subdue the rebellion of our wills, that we may submit to thy commands, and acquiesce in thy dispensations, without murmurings and disputings. Unite our hearts to fear thy name ; and may we be in the fear of the Lord all the day long. Make us Israelites indeed, in whom there is no guile. Enable us to maintain a conscience, void of offence, towards God, and towards man : may we be the same, when no eye sees us, as we are in the public walks of life : may we enter the closet as well as the temple ; and attend to our principles and motives, as well as our actions and pursuits.

We mourn over our numberless failures and backslidings ; our incorrigibleness under rebukes ; our want of profiting under ordinances ; the misimprovement of our talents ; and our neglect of opportunities of usefulness. Whatever view we take of ourselves, compels us to exclaim, Behold I am vile. Yet while we are humble, may we be grateful : and never be backward to acknowledge what Thou hast done for our souls.   If we are not like some of thy people, we bless Thee, that we are not like the rest of the world ; if we are not what we ought to be, we are not what we once were: and *Thou* hast made us to differ, and we have nothing which we did not receive from thee.

And if our religion be imperfect, may it appear to be real, and vital, by its activity, and its tending to growth.   May it awaken in us an unconquerable desire, to go from strength to strength, and to be renewed day by day.

May our religion always attend us, and dignify us in the ordinary scenes of life.   May we remember, that greatness consists, not in doing great things, but in doing little things with a great mind.

As the events of providence occur, may they always find in us, those dispositions which will keep them from injuring us, and which will convert them all into advantages.

In a vale of tears, may we look for a succession of trials : and may we also look for the accomplishment of the promise—I will be with thee in trouble.

May the joy of the Lord be our strength ; may it keep us from lusting after the vanities of the world ; bear up the heart and mind in the loss of every creature-comfort, and enliven us in the valley of the shadow of death.   And before we reach heaven, may we bear the image of the heavenly ; possess the earnests of our inheritance ; and enjoy the first fruits of the glorious harvest.

And to God, the Father, the Son, and the Holy Ghost, be all honour and glory, for ever and ever. Amen.

TUESDAY MORNING.

O God, Thou art the Creator, the Upholder, and the Proprietor of all things. Thy dominion is everlasting and universal. Thou dost according to thine own will in the armies of heaven, and among the inhabitants of the earth ; none can stay thy hand, or say unto Thee, What dost Thou?

We cannot escape from thy presence, or control ; nor do we desire it. It is our privilege, that we are under the agency, not only of Omnipotence, but righteousness, wisdom, patience, mercy, and grace. Thou art love. Thou hast loved us with more than parental affection ; thou hast commended thy love towards us, in that while we were sinners, Christ died for us. He that spared not his own Son, but delivered Him up for us all—how shall he not with him also, freely give us all things? Here may all our fears drop off from our minds ; here may we be filled with everlasting consolation, and good hope through grace.

Thou hast not only allowed, but commanded us to believe on the name of thy dear Son. O, let us not refuse to be comforted ; let us not reject the counsel of God against ourselves ; but, remembering, that we are as welcome as we are guilty, may we drink of the fountain of the water of life freely.

But while we know that we *may* come to the Redeemer, and *ought* to come—may we never think ourselves interested in the blessings of his salvation, unless we *have* come. May there be a real and living union between our souls and Him ; that being quickened together with Christ, we may be raised up, and made to sit with him in heavenly places. May we live a life of faith in thy promises, mingled with no doubt of thy truth, or suspicion of thy power. May we live a life of hope ; expecting that Thou wilt be our sun and our shield : that Thou wilt give grace and glory ; and

withhold no good thing from us, while we walk up
rightly.   And may we live a life of love; for he
that dwelleth in love, dwelleth in God, and God in
him.   O, shed abroad thy love in our hearts, the
animating and delightful principle, of all obedience.   May we love our neighbour as ourselves ;
and consider every one *as* our neighbour, who
falls within the reach of our knowledge and assistance.

We feel, that the work to which we are called,
is far above our strength.   We have tried our purposes and resolutions, and have found them vain.
The least temptation, has been too powerful for
us, when we have gone forth in our own strength.
O, teach us how to be strong in the Lord, and in
the power of his might.   And at every movement
in our journey, and our warfare, say to our heart,
Fear not, for I am with thee ; be not dismayed,
for I am thy God ; I will strengthen thee; yea, I
will help thee ; yea, I will uphold thee with the
right hand of my righteousness.

And may we never depart from Thee, by making
flesh our arm, or the creature our portion.   With
regard to the world, may our soul be even as a
weaned child ; but may we draw near to Thee as
our exceeding joy ; and contemplate, with appro-
priation, the period when we shall behold thy face
in righteousness, awake up after thy likeness, and
be satisfied with thy favour.

All which we implore through the mediation of
Him, who ever liveth to make intercession for us :
and to whom, with the Father, and the Holy
Spirit, be endless praises.   Amen.

MAY we approach Thee, with all the encouragement derivable from a conviction that Thou art the blessed God—Happy in thyself, and the source of happiness to thy creatures. The eyes of all wait upon Thee, and Thou givest them their meat in due season: Thou openest thine hand, and satisfiest the desire of every living thing. Thou art our maker and benefactor. Thou hast not only produced us, but sustained us : not only supported us, but indulged us: yea, Thou hast given us all things richly to enjoy. Thou hast provided for the welfare of our souls, as well as our bodies : Thou hast answered the awful question, How shall I come before the Lord, and bow before the High God ? Thou hast told us what we must do to be saved. May we follow the light of life which Thou hast given us, till it brings us to Him who appears in every attribute, and in every attitude of power and pity, to meet all our wants and miseries. And as we draw near, may we hear his gracious voice saying, him that cometh unto me, I will in no wise cast out. May we commit our eternal all into His hands ; and being reconciled by his death, may we be saved by His life. May we live by Him ; live to Him ; live like Him. While we behold Him as rich, for our sakes becoming poor, and dying that we may live, may his unexampled love constrain us into all holy obedience and zeal : and render our duty, our delight.

May we never wait for the company of others, or feel their approbation necessary to induce us to follow *Him*, who is all our salvation, and ought to be all our desire. May we go forth to Him without the camp, bearing his reproach. And if our faith is deemed folly, our hope delusion, our meekness meanness, our zeal madness ; may we rejoice that we are counted worthy to suffer shame

for his name ; and binding it as a garland around
our brow, say, If this be to be vile, I will yet be
more vile.   Thus, blessed Redeemer, wast Thou
treated in the days of thy flesh ; thus, was thy
name cast out as evil, thy actions misrepresented,
and thy Spirit blasphemed.   O, let the servants
be willing to be as the Master, and the disciples
as the Lord.

We hope in thy word ; but it is because it assures us, that Thou waitest to be gracious : and
dost not break the bruised reed, or quench the
smoking flax.   How poor and pitiable, how maim-
ed and dying a thing, has our religion been, under
every advantage to promote it.   Lord, hide pride
from us ; enable us to walk humbly with our God ;
and ask and receive that our joy may be full.
Hast Thou not promised to supply all our need,
from thy riches, in glory, by Christ Jesus ? Thou
knowest all our warfare, all our work, all our
trials ; and Thou knowest the degree and extent
of our weakness ; and yet Thou hast said, My
grace is sufficient for thee—Lord we believe—help
Thou our unbelief.

While we rejoice in our privileges, we would
remember the way in which they become ours.
We have nothing to glory in before Thee.   We
ourselves also, were once foolish and disobedient ;
and we would ever look to the rock whence we
were hewn, and to the hole of the pit whence we
were digged.   Thou hast made us to differ   and
we have nothing but what we have received.

And this encourages us with regard to others.
What Thou hast done for us, Thou art able to do
for them.   And Thou art willing.   Thou hast
therefore commanded us to pray, for all men.   O,
let none of those perish, whom we love as our own
souls.   Keep them as the apple of the eye ; hide
them under the shadow of thy wing.

Let grace and peace be multiplied to all them,
who have obtained like precious faith with us ;
and if Thou art pleased to try that faith, may the·

trial be found unto praise, and glory, and honour, at the appearing of Jesus Christ.

But we would not forget even the ignorant and profligate. Teach transgressors thy ways, and let sinners be converted unto Thee.

Dethrone the god of this world. Destroy the works of the devil. And may our globe which has so long groaned beneath the curse, be as the smell of a field which the Lord hath blessed. Send out thy light and thy truth; thy servants and thy labourers; and for them may the wilderness and the solitary place be made glad, and the desert rejoice and blossom as the rose. Amen.

Blessing and glory, and power, and might, be unto our God for ever and ever. Amen.

WEDNESDAY MORNING.

O Thou, with whom we have to do—suffer us not to live without Thee in the world. Thou art our Creator; our Preserver; our Governor; and we believe that Thou wilt be our Judge. It is well for us, that we can view Thee in another character—the Saviour of sinners; and that before we are called to appear before thy awful tribunal, we are invited, and commanded to come boldly to the throne of grace, there to obtain mercy, and find grace to help in time of need.

May we readily and thankfully avail ourselves of every opportunity to draw nigh to God, in the temple, in the retirement of the closet, and at the domestic altar; and let not our devotion be bodily exercise only. Quicken our souls to call upon thy name. Detach us from the influence of flesh and sense. Impress us with the power of faith; and produce in us that spirituality of mind which will render our services acceptable to Thee, and delightful and profitable to ourselves.

9*

Though Thou art Most High for evermore, Thou regardest the man that is poor and of a contrite spirit, and that trembleth at thy word. Thou fillest the hungry with good things, while the rich are sent empty away. O, bring us, however humbling and painful the process may be ; O, bring us, into that state which attracts thine eye, and prepares for the proofs of thy love. Show us our danger, that we may flee for refuge to the hope set before us. Make us sensible of our disease, and of the eternal death to which it is so rapidly tending. That we may value the physician, and cry—heal me and I shall be healed, save me and I shall be saved, for Thou art my praise.

Our deliverance must come entirely from thyself. And Thou hast not forgotten to be gracious. We bless Thee for the purpose of salvation ; for the engagements of the everlasting covenant ; and for the gift of thy dear Son, the proof and the pledge, that Thou wilt also freely give us all things. We thank Thee for the word of truth, which proclaims peace by the blood of the cross ; and beseeches us in Christ's stead to be reconciled unto God. O, let the message prevail. Let it slay the enmity of our hearts, and lead us to throw down every weapon of rebellion, and mourn over them. With weeping and supplication, may we return to Thee, from whom we have so deeply revolted. And while with shame and self-abhorrence, we confess that other lords beside Thee have had dominion over us, henceforth may we resolve, that by Thee only will we make mention of thy name. With zeal, may we engage in that service which is perfect freedom ; and with entireness, devote ourselves to that work which is honourable and glorious. May we employ every faculty, and use every blessing, as those who know, that they are not their own, but bought with a price, and bound to glorify God, in their body and in their spirit, which are God's.

Work in us to will and to do of thy good pleasure. Uphold us by thy free Spirit; and let the joy of the Lord be our strength.

May we be watchful over our ways, may we be jealous over our tempers; and may we keep our hearts with all diligence, knowing, that out of them are the issues of life. Divest us of pride, and clothe us with humbleness of mind. Eradicate every root of bitterness, and let the peace of God rule in our hearts.

When we droop, revive us; when we loiter, quicken us; restore us, when we go astray; and lead us in the paths of righteousness for thy name's sake.

Yea, though we walk through the valley of the shadow of death, may we fear no evil, knowing that Thou art with us, and that thy rod and staff will comfort us.

The Lord bless us and keep us. The Lord make his face to shine upon us, and be gracious unto us. The Lord lift up his countenance upon us and give us peace. Amen.

WEDNESDAY EVENING.

O God, Thou art greatly to be feared in the assembly of the saints, and to be had in reverence of all that are about Thee. Those glorious beings that never fell, veil their faces and sink into nothing before the Eternal all; and exclaim, Holy, holy, holy, is the Lord of hosts, the whole earth is full of his glory. With what emotion should we enter thy presence, whose foundation is in the dust; and who have contemned thy goodness, defied thy power, trampled upon thy laws, and rendered ourselves worthy of eternal death. Our iniquities are increased over our head: and our trespass has gone up to the very heavens. Enter not into judg-

ment with thy servants : our consciences assure
us, that if Thou, Lord, shouldst mark iniquity, we
could not stand.

But there is mercy with Thee, and with Thee
there is plenteous redemption; and therefore,
while a sense of our vileness depresses us, we encourage ourselves in thy word. We know that
our recovery can never spring from any cause in
us. We have destroyed ourselves, but we cannot
save. Yet our condition is not helpless. Help is
laid on One that is mighty ; and infinitely qualified
for His work ; and who has shown us, in His resurrection from the dead, and ascension into heaven,
the all sufficiency and acceptance of His sacrifice
on the cross, and proved, that by the one offering
of Himself, He hath perfected for ever them that
are sanctified.

Informed of this compassionate scheme, may we
gratefully fall in with the design ; may we unfeignedly believe the record that Thou hast given
us of thy Son ; embrace Him as our only hope ;
rejoice in Him as our highest glory ; and henceforth, may the life that we live in the flesh, be by
the faith of Him who loved us, and gave Himself
for us.

And while we live by Him, may we live to
Him, and may we live like Him. May we never
consider ourselves christians, but as we resemble
Christ. May our conformity to His principles,
temper, and conduct, be hourly growing, and become more apparent, not only to ourselves but
to others. And may we continue in his word,
that we may be his disciples indeed ; rooted and
built up in Him, and established in the truth as
we have been taught, and abounding therein with
thanksgiving.

May no length of watching or length of waiting
cool our love and zeal ; whatever discouragements
we meet with, may we never grow weary in well
doing—yea, may we not only persevere, while

many draw back—but fear God above many who go forward; and hear the Saviour-Judge saying, I know thy works, and the last to be more than the first.

May we not only *be* blessed; but *prove* blessings. May we often look closely at our talents, relations, and circumstances in life, to see how we can be serviceable to the bodies and souls of our fellow-creatures, and especially how we may do good to them that are of the household of faith.

We are continually meeting with wants and miseries which we are utterly unable to remove or release; but we rejoice that in our contracted agency, prayer opens a resource to our benevolence; we can pray; and prayer has power with God, and can prevail.

Let the leisure and affluence of the rich, afford them means and opportunities of beneficence; and may they be ready to communicate; and be rich in good works.

Let the afflictions of the afflicted render sin hateful, wean them from a vain world, endear to them the word of grace, the throne of grace, and the spirit of grace; and work out for them, a far more exceeding and eternal weight of glory.

Let our ignorance of futurity, keep us in a state of constant dependence upon thy providential care; and lead us earnestly to seek large supplies of the Spirit of Jesus Christ, to fit us for all events.

Thou hast redeemed us, O Lord God of Truth; and therefore, into thine hands we commit ourselves, and our interests, beseeching Thee to do for us, exceeding abundantly, above all we are able to ask or think, through our only Lord and Saviour. Amen.

O God, help us to approach Thee, under a very lively conviction of thy abundant mercy, and the exceeding riches of thy grace. We ought to admire thy wisdom, to stand in awe of thy power, and to abase ourselves before thy spotless purity. But it is the discovery of thy goodness alone, that can banish our fear, and allure us with humble confidence into thy presence, there to divulge our sorrows, and confess our sins.

And, O, how encouraging is it, under a review of our past guilt, and a consciousness of present unworthiness, to know, that we have to do with a Being who waits to be gracious, and is exalted to have mercy. We therefore bless Thee, that an attribute so essential to our happiness and hope, is not founded on conjecture, or obscurely revealed. Thou hast not left Thyself without witness in the seasons of the year, and the bounties of nature, and Providence. But Thou hast given us thy word, which Thou hast magnified above all thy name. There we see Thee, not sparing thine own Son, but delivering Him up for us all; there we behold the provisions of thy house; there we hear the proclamations of thy servants—Come, for all things are now ready.

Lord, make us willing to be saved, and to be saved in thine own way. Condemned by the law which we have so often transgressed, may we turn for all our relief to the gospel; and perceiving nothing in ourselves, may we find in the hope of Israel, wisdom, righteousness, sanctification, and redemption. May the message which concerns a dying, rising, interceding Saviour, be received into our very hearts, and become there a well of water, springing up into everlasting life. And may we not only receive Christ Jesus the Lord, but also walk in Him; in a state of dependence upon

Him, communion with Him, and conformity to
Him. May we be followers of Him as dear children; imperfect, but still pressing forward; not
complaining of labour, but valuing rest; not murmuring under our trials, but thankful for a state.
O, that we were sure of reaching it! where our
sun shall no more go down, nor our moon withdraw herself, but God shall be our everlasting
light, and the days of our mourning shall be
ended.

We live in the midst of observation. Many
watch for our halting, and wish our good to be
evil spoken of. May we walk the more circumspectly; and by well doing, may we put to silence the ignorance of foolish men; yea, by our
good works which they behold, may we constrain
them to glorify God in the day of visitation.

We appear not alone in Thy presence; but are
variously connected in life. Regard those who
are dear to us by the claims of nature or friendship. We ask not that Thou shouldst set them
upon the high places of the earth; but O, number
them with Thy saints in glory everlasting; O, let
none of them die without an interest in Christ, and
be separated from us in the day when Thou wilt
make up thy jewels.

Bless those who are related to us in religious
bonds. And such, we are delighted to 'consider
all the followers of the Lamb, under whatever
name, distinctive or reproachful, they may pass
among men; may the Lord add to his people,
how many soever they be, a hundred-fold; and
may grace and peace be multiplied unto them.

And forget not, we beseech Thee, those to whom
we are politically allied. May all who are in
places of public trust, be faithful to the public interest. Teach our senators wisdom. May all
our magistrates be men fearing God and hating
covetousness, terrors to evil doers, and a praise to
them that do well; and may all ranks in the com-

munity, pursue that righteousness which exalteth a nation ; that, being a holy, we may be a happy people, whose God is the Lord.

So we thy people, and the sheep of thy pasture, will give Thee thanks for ever ; we will show forth thy praise throughout all generations. Amen.

THURSDAY EVENING

WHEN we enter Thy presence, O God, we see Thee in all the glory of thy perfections, seated on a throne of universal and everlasting empire, thousands ministering unto Thee, and ten thousand times ten thousand standing before Thee. Impress our minds with a consciousness of thy greatness; not to drive us back from Thee, but to inspire us with reverence and godly fear, in approaching Thee ; not to diminish our confidence in Thee, but to lead us to admire the vastness of thy condescension, in deigning to open communications with creatures so mean and vile as we are. Lord, what is man, that Thou art mindful of him ; or the son of man, that Thou visitest him.

And, yet Thou *hast* been mindful of *us ;* Thou hast visited us. We have been thy charge from the womb ; and Thou hast, in all conditions, cared for us. We have been constantly fed at thy table ; and clothed from thy wardrobe. How often hast Thou drawn the curtain of night around us, and ordered creation to be quiet, while thy children have slumbered and slept. Thy mercies have been new every morning. Thy goodness has inspired our relations and friends with all the sentiments of tenderness and respect, they have ever expressed towards us. And we would not overlook the blessings of the life that now is—

But, O Lord, suffer us not to forget that we want better blessings than these. We want a hope beyond the grave. We are guilty, depraved, dying creatures. We need pardon and holiness, and wisdom, and strength, and peace and joy ; we want the earnests and foretastes of immortality. And blessed be thy name, what we so much need, and hope we can say, so much desire, Thou hast provided. We thank Thee for thy unspeakable gift. We rejoice, that we have our existence in a land of gospel privileges ; and where one of the first sounds that entered our infant ears, from the lips of maternal piety, was the name of Jesus. We rejoice that we have been led to view Him, not only as a teacher, and an example, but as the Lamb of God, that taketh away the sins of the world ; and that now in Christ Jesus, we, who sometimes were far off, are made nigh by the blood of Christ ; and have boldness and access with confidence, by the faith of Him.

May we look after actual and personal benefit from Him, and never be satisfied, till we can say, I know whom I have believed, and am persuaded, that He is able to keep that which I have committed to Him against that day. Possess us with more of that faith, which is the principle and medium of all vital godliness ; may we be rich in faith ; may we be strong in faith. By faith may we live ; and by faith may we walk. May we feel the joy of faith ; and do the work of faith. May we abound in hope ; may the charity of every one of us, towards each other, increase ; and may we be filled with all the fruits of righteousness, which are, by Jesus Christ, to the glory and praise of God.

We ought to feel a broken heart, and a contrite spirit. We grieve to think, how insensible we have been, to the claims of thy authority, and the endearments of thy love ; how little we have credited thy truth, trusted thy promises, feared thy threatenings, obeyed thy commands, or improved any of our advantages. We have had line upon

line, and precept upon precept. How numberless
have been our admonitions, and warnings; and
Thou hast said—He that being often reproved,
hardeneth his neck, shall suddenly be destroyed,
and that without remedy.

We thank Thee, that notwithstanding our desert, this is not, at present, our doom. As yet, we
are in the number of those, for whom Thou art
waiting to be gracious. We are yet in the land
of the living. Through another day Thou hast
spared us, and blessed us. May thy goodness lead
us to repentance, and thy long-suffering prove our
salvation. Let no evil befall us, and no plague
come nigh our dwelling, this night; and in the
morning may we rise to walk, before the Lord, in
the land of the living, and to show forth all his
praise.

We implore it in the name of Him who died
for our sins, rose again for our justification, and
ever liveth to make intercession for us; and to
whom, with the Father, and Holy Spirit, be ascribed everlasting praises. Amen.

FRIDAY MORNING.

Our voice shalt Thou hear in the morning, O
Lord; in the morning, alone, and in our family,
will we direct our prayer unto Thee, and will look
up. How well does it become us to be thankful!
Many, during the past night, have had no place
where to lay their head. Many, the victims of
disease, have been full of tossing to and fro, until
the dawning of the day; so that their bed has not
comforted them, nor their couch eased their complaint. Many have been deprived of rest while
watching over their connexions in pain and sorrow. How many have slept the sleep of death,
and will not awake till the heavens are no more!

Others, whose lives are prolonged, have risen to be surrounded with want and wo : and thousands, who have all things richly to enjoy, have risen only to live another day, without God in the world.

And why is not this the case with us ? Thou, O God, hast remembered, and distinguished, and indulged us. Bless the Lord, O *my* soul, and all that is within me, bless his holy name. O magnify the Lord with me, and let us exalt his name *together*.

And thy mercies have been new every morning, yea, every moment. All our desires have not been gratified ; but it was love that denied us, when the accomplishment of our wishes would have proved our ruin or our injury *:* we have had our trials, but they have been few compared with our sins ; they have been attended with numberless alleviations ; and when we have kissed the rod, it has fallen out of thy hand.

Thou hast often wiped away our tears, and restored peace to thy mourners ; Thou hast never chastened us but for our profit ; we already see the design of many of our griefs, and can say, It is good for me that I have been afflicted, and in all other cases where darkness yet clouds the dispensation, we desire to walk by faith. We believe that Thou hast done all things well, and that thy work is perfect.

But, O, what do we owe Thee for the word of thy truth—the throne of thy grace—the Son of thy love—thy unspeakable gift ; what do we owe Thee, if we have any reason to hope that we are in Christ, and free from all condemnation ; and that when He, who is our life, shall appear, we shall also appear with Him in glory, and be for ever with the Lord !

Surely, a gratitude becomes us that will not evaporate in a morning acknowledgment with the lip, but such as will keep us in the fear of the Lord all the day long, and lead us to ask, What shall I render unto the Lord for all his benefits towards me ? We, therefore, by the mercies of God, present our bodies a living sacrifice, holy and acceptable unto Thee, which is our reasonable service.

And now, O Thou Author of all good, we come to Thee for the grace another day will require— the grace its duties will require—the grace its events will require ; for we know not when we leave our apartments in the morning, what a day will bring forth. But we know that we are step- ping into a wicked world, and that we carry about us an evil heart : we know that without Thee we can do nothing : and we know that there is nothing with which we shall have any concern in the day, however harmless in itself, but may prove an oc- casion of sinning and falling, unless we are kept by the power of God. We, therefore, desire to pray ourselves out of our own keeping into thy keeping. Hold *Thou* us up, and we shall be safe. Preserve our understandings from the subtlety of error ; our affections from the love of idols ; our senses from the ungovernable impressions of out- ward objects ; our character from every stain of vice, and our profession from every appearance of evil : and may the God of peace sanctify us wholly, and may our whole spirit, soul, and body, be preserved blameless unto the coming of our Lord Jesus Christ.

May we engage in nothing on which we cannot implore thy blessing, and to which we cannot wel- come thy inspection. Prosper us in our lawful undertakings, or prepare us for disappointment. Give us neither poverty nor riches. Feed us with food convenient for us, lest we be full and deny Thee, and say, Who is the Lord ? or, lest we be poor, and steal, and take the name of our God in vain.

May every creature be good to us, being sanc- tified by the word of God and prayer. Teach us how to use the world as not abusing it. Enable us to improve our talents, and to redeem our time. May we walk in wisdom towards them that are without, and in kindness towards them that are within; and do good, as we have opportunity unto all men, especially unto them that are of the household of faith.

And unto Him that is able to keep us from falling, and to present us faultless before the presence of His glory with exceeding joy : to the only wise God, our Saviour, be glory, and majesty, dominion, and power, both now and ever. Amen.

FRIDAY EVENING

O Thou incomprehensibly great and glorious Jehovah! the King of kings, and Lord of lords, who only hast immortality. We adore Thee and abase ourselves. Though we are allowed to approach Thee, we would not be mindless of the views and feelings which so well become those, who, as creatures, are less than nothing, and, as sinners, are worse than nothing before Thee.

For, if we say, we have no sin, we deceive ourselves, and the truth is not in us; the heavens would reveal our iniquity, and the earth would rise up against us. And why should we endeavour to deny our guilt, since even our thoughts have not been screened from thy sight, and Thou hast set our most secret sins in the light of thy countenance? and why should we desire it, since we know, that if we confess our sins, Thou art faithful and just to forgive us our sins, and to cleanse us from all unrighteousness? From a view, therefore, of their exceeding sinfulness, we would confess them with a broken heart, and a contrite spirit, earnestly longing to be delivered from them, and be led in the way everlasting.

10*

Enable us to remember that blood which cleanseth from all sin ; to believe in that grace which can subdue all our iniquities ; and to resign ourselves to that agency which can deliver us from the bondage of corruption, into the glorious liberty of the sons of God. While many envy the men of the world, who have their portion in this life, may we, with Moses, choose rather to suffer affliction with the people of God, than enjoy the pleasures of sin for a season. While many seek great things for themselves on earth ; things which perish in the using, and afford no satisfaction in the possessing—may the prayer of David become ours. Remember me, O Lord, with the favour Thou bearest unto thy people. O visit me with thy salvation, that I may see the good of thy chosen, that I may rejoice in the gladness of thy nation, and glory with thine inheritance.

We sometimes hope that Thou hast already begun a good work in us ; and to whom should we go for the continuance, the progress, and the completion, but to Thee, the God of all grace, and who art not only the Author, but Finisher, of our faith ? we rejoice in what Thou hast done for others ; in their deliverance and elevation we see what Thou art able and willing to do for us. We bless Thee for the promises upon which Thou hast caused us to hope, and in which Thou hast engaged to perfect that which concerneth us : we thank Thee for the means of grace, in the humble and diligent use of which, Thou art pleased to draw near to those who draw near to Thee.

May we love the closet as well as the temple and sanctify to us, not only the preaching of the gospel, but also the reading of thy word. Believing, with a faith unfeigned, that it is given by inspiration of God, may we find it profitable for doctrine, for reproof, for correction, and for instruction in righteousness. In every perplexity, may it be the man of our counsel : may we repair to it in every distress, and in the multitude of our thoughts within us, may thy comforts delight our souls.

May we have an increasing conviction of our liableness to err, and our exposure to sin, that we may place ourselves under thy guiding and guardian care. As we see the vanity of the world, and meet with trials and disappointments, may we take a firmer hold of that covenant which is ordered in all things, and sure ; and may *this* be all our salvation, and all our desire, when our house is not so with God, and Thou makest it not to grow. May we rejoice in hope ; be patient in tribulation ; and continue constant in prayer.

May we feel more of the purifying, more of the dignifying, more of the softening influence of the religion we profess. May we have compassion one of another ; love as brethren—be pitiful—be courteous. May we never render railing for railing, but contrawise, blessing : may we not be overcome of evil, but overcome evil with good.

May we never incur the curse of the angel of the covenant, for not coming to the help of the Lord., May we deem it an honour to be employed by Thee, and long to be instruments in thy hands. Ready to seize every opportunity of usefulness ; and willing to use all our talents in thy blessed service, may we daily ask, Lord, what wilt Thou have me to do ?

Bless our country. May we be for a name and a praise unto Thee in the whole earth. Largely have we been the recipients of thy goodness ; and freely may we give. Sanction the institutions and efforts by which we are endeavouring to spread the benefits of the gospel. God be merciful unto *us,* and bless *us,* that His way may be known on earth, His saving health among all nations.

O remember the number called, in various ways, to suffer. Bless their daily rod, as well as their daily bread. May they feel impressions which shall never wear off; may they learn such lessons as shall never be forgotten ; may they enjoy such consolations, as shall enable them to say, It is good for me that I have been afflicted.

And to God, only wise, be glory and dominion, for ever and ever.   Amen.

SATURDAY MORNING.

O Thou everlasting God, the Creator of all the ends of the earth, and the Father of the spirits of all flesh. We have destroyed ourselves, but in Thee is our help. Our nature is defiled ; all the powers of our souls are degraded ; we are vile, we are miserable ; we are without strength. We condemn ourselves, and confess that we deserve to perish. If ever we are saved, it must be by goodness the most undeserved and astonishing ; not only by mercy, but abundant mercy ; not only by grace, but the exceeding riches of thy grace.

And such mercy and grace Thou hast been pleased to reveal, and to promise, and to exemplify. Thou hast told us thy designs, and unlike the forebodings of our guilty minds, they are thoughts of peace, and not of evil.

We bless Thee for devising means to rescue us from the perdition of sin, and restore us to a state of happiness, and honour, and safety, superior to our original condition. We bless Thee for the provisions of the everlasting covenant, and for the constitution of a Mediator between Thee and us. We rejoice that He failed not, nor was discouraged, but accomplished the work that was given Him to do, and said on the cross, It is finished. We rejoice that now thy justice is satisfied, thy truth established, thy law magnified, and a foundation laid, even in thy own glory, for our hope.

May we look after present and personal interest
in Christ, and never rest, till we can say, Surely,
He hath borne our grief, and carried our sorrow;
the chastisement of our peace was upon Him, and
by His stripes we are healed. May we know,
that in Him we have righteousness, and strength,
and are blessed with all spiritual blessings. While
we are justified by His blood, may we be saved
by His life. While we glory in His cross, may
we bow to His sceptre, and long to have the same
mind in us which was also in Him; knowing, that
if we have not the Spirit of Christ, we are none
of His.

.We are convinced, that it is our happiness, as
well as duty, to walk in thy ways, to keep thy
statutes, and to submit to thy appointments; but
we are equally convinced, that thy grace alone is
sufficient for us, and that without Thee we can do
nothing. We cannot even stand, but as we are
upheld by thy free Spirit. But with Thee is the
residue of the Spirit; and Thou hast engaged to
give thy Holy Spirit to them that ask Thee. Yea,
Thou hast said, Open thy mouth wide, and I will
fill it. Bless us, therefore, with constant and increasing supplies of grace and strength; work in
us to will and to do of thy good pleasure, and fulfil all the good pleasure of thy goodness, and the
work of faith with power.

May our religion, instead of being an occasional
and partial thing, be universal and invariable in
its influence and effects. May we be in the fear of
the Lord every day, and all the day long. May
we hold communion with Thee in thy works, as
well as thy word, and in the dispensations of thy
providence, as well as in the ordinances of thy
house.

May we always distinguish between the form of
godliness, and the power thereof; and between
life, and a name to live. What is the hope of the
hypocrite, though he hath gained, when Thou

takest away his soul ? O, make us Israelites in deed, in whom is no guile. Often may we examine ourselves, and inquire whether our religion will bear the eye of God. If we are not right, set us right, and keep us right. Search us, O God, and know our heart ; try us, and know our thoughts, and see if there be any wicked way in us, and lead us in the way everlasting.

Impress us with a conviction of the vanity of the world, and the brevity and uncertainty of the time of our continuance here, that we may keep the end of life in view, and apply our hearts unto wisdom.

We are ignorant, and liable to a thousand delusions, but Thou knowest what is good for us ; to Thee, therefore, we commit our works, and our way ; and to Thee we refer the choice of our inheritance.

Only be with us, and keep us in the way that we go, and give us bread to eat, and raiment to put on, so that we come to our Father's house in peace ; and the Lord shall be our God.

And may the grace of our Lord Jesus Christ, and the love of God, and the communion of the Holy Ghost, be with us all, now and for ever. Amen.

SATURDAY EVENING.

O God, Thou hast been the refuge and the dwelling place of thy people in all generations. To Thee, the poor and the needy have always repaired for succour ; and they that know thy name, will put their trust in Thee. And to whom should we go, but unto Thee ? Thou hast the words of eternal life. There is no blessing we can implore, but Thou art *able* to give, and hast *promised* to give, and hast already *given* to a

countless multitude, all unworthy and guilty like
ourselves. Yea, Thou hast not spared thine own
Son, but delivered Him up for us all; and wilt
Thou not with Him, also, freely give us all
things?

O make us more willing to receive, the supply
of all our need, from thy riches, in glory, by
Christ Jesus. And for this purpose, convince us
of sin. Show us our true character and condition
in thy sight. Take away the stone out of our
hearts, and give us hearts of flesh. May we feel
and bewail our folly and ingratitude; our pride
and unbelief; the rebellion of our lives, and the
corruption of our nature. May we sorrow after a
godly sort, and abhor ourselves, repenting in dust
and ashes. Through the law, may we die unto the
law, and despair of obtaining life, but from thy
own sovereign mercy. May we look with wonder, and submission, and gratitude, and delight,
to the provision which Thou hast made for the
glory of thine own name, in the salvation of sinners. May we believe in Him, whom Thou hast
set forth as a propitiation for sin, and as the end
of the law for righteousness—may we know Him
in the power of his resurrection and the fellowship
of his sufferings, and be made conformable unto
his death.

Give us that hope which maketh not ashamed.
Inspire us with that love which excites to all holy
obedience. Pour into our hearts that joy of the
Lord which is the strength of thy people; and
enable us to say with Paul, The life that I now
live in the flesh, I live by the faith of the Son of
God, who loved *me*, and gave himself for *me*.

And when we cannot pronounce on our own interest in divine things, may we still persevere in
duty; may we wait on the Lord, and keep his
way; and be humble and earnest suppliants at thy
footstool, assured, that they who hunger and thirst

after righteousness, are blessed—and shall be filled.

Preserve us from that levity and indifference which are so unbecoming creatures, who live continually under the eye of God, and are always on the brink of an eternal world.

May we discover nothing like selfishness and unkindness, while professing to be the followers of Him, who pleased not himself; who, when rich, for our sakes became poor; and went about doing good.

May we hold ourselves at thy disposal, not only with regard to the duties, but events of life. Whatever preferences we feel, may we submit them all to thy infinite wisdom, and say, Nevertheless, not my will, but thine be done. If we are called to resign any of our enjoyments, may we remember that it is the absolute proprietor, and our best friend who requires them; and yield, in the spirit of Him, who, when stripped of all, could say, The Lord gave, and the Lord hath taken away; blessed be the name of the Lord.

But make us thankful for the continuance of our comforts; and that in a world of such changes and misery, our indulgences have been so many, and our trials so few.

Especially, would we be grateful for the means of grace, and the ordinances of religion, which still await us, notwithstanding all our unworthiness and provocations. O Lord, teach us to profit by them more than we have done; and as to-morrow is the rest of the holy sabbath unto the Lord our God, may we be in the spirit on thy own day; and enter it in a state of mind suited to its solemnities, duties, and privileges. May we leave every thing worldly at the foot of the mount, while we go to worship God above. May we experience the blessedness of the man, whose strength is in Thee, and in whose heart are the ways of them. May we go from strength to strength ; and at last may every one of us in Zion appear before God.

O Lord God of hosts, hear our prayer, give ear O God of Jacob. Behold, O God, our shield, and look upon the face of thine Anointed. Amen.

Fourth Week.

SUNDAY MORNING.

O Thou most high. Thine eyes are in every place, beholding the evil and the good; thine eyes behold, and thine eye-lids try the children of men. We hope we can appeal to thy Omniscience, and say, In the way of thy appointments, we are now waiting for Thee, while our desire is to thy name, and to the remembrance of Thee.

We are sinners, but not insensible of our state. Our iniquities are great and numberless; but with a broken heart and a contrite spirit, we pray to be delivered from them, and led in the way everlasting. Our case is desperate in itself, but there is hope in Israel concerning this thing. The combined help of men and angels could not reach our misery; but Thou art adequate to our relief.

Thou art rich in mercy. The blood of Jesus Christ, thy Son, cleanseth from all sin. The agency of thy Holy Spirit can subdue the most powerful corruptions. Heal us, and we shall be healed; save us, and we shall be saved; for Thou art our praise. Hide thy face from our sin, and blot out all our iniquity. Create in us also, O God, a clean heart, and renew a right spirit within us. Illuminate our understandings with the light of life. May we know the truth, and may the truth make us free. Give us tender and wakeful consciences; and may they always smite and torment us when we sin against God. May we be consistent and uniform in the whole of our conversation and conduct; the same alone and in company: in prosperity and adversity; esteeming

all thy commandments concerning all things to be
right, and hating every false way—Israelites indeed, in whom there is no guile.

May we never be satisfied with any present progression in the divine life; but this one thing may
we do, forgetting the things that are behind, and
reaching forth unto those that are before, press
towards the mark, for the prize of our high calling
of God in Christ Jesus. May we add to our faith
virtue; and to virtue knowledge; and to knowledge temperance; and to temperance godliness;
and to godliness brotherly kindness; and to brotherly kindness charity; and may all these things,
not only be in us, but abound.

And while we never forget what is necessary to
constitute the Christian character, may we never
neglect what is needful to complete it. May we
be concerned to adorn the doctrine of God our
Saviour; to recommend the religion of Jesus to
all around us; and to induce observers to say,
We will go with you, for we have heard that
God is with you.

Enable us to accommodate ourselves to the dispensations of thy providence, with the views and
feelings of Christians. May we know how to be
abased, and how to abound; may we learn in
whatsoever state we are, therewith to be content;
yea, in every thing, may we give thanks; knowing
that all the ways of the Lord, are mercy and truth,
to those that trust in Him.

May we feel the ties that unite us to our fellow-
creatures, especially to our fellow-christians. By
sympathy, and praise and prayer, may we make
their mercies and miseries our own; rejoicing with
them that rejoice, and weeping with them that
weep.

Regard the sons and daughters of distress; and
as afflictions are not immutable dispensations, and
we are allowed to pray for temporal blessings con-
ditionally, if it be thy pleasure, command de

liverance for them ; or should thy wisdom con
tinue the trial, keep them from sinking or sinning
in the evil day ; let thy strength be made perfect
in their weakness ; and in the multitude of their
thoughts within them, may thy comforts delight
their souls.

Be with those who will pass the day in absence
from thy dear abode. Though Thou art with thy
people in trouble, yet Thou hast taught them, by
experience, to value thy ordinances, and to esteem a day in thy courts, better than a thousand.
O, let them not pass an unprofitable, though a silent sabbath ; let their meditation of Thee be
sweet ; and though not in thy house, may they be
in thy Spirit, on thy own day.

And make those thankful, who are exempted
from spiritual privations ; and have liberty, and
health, and strength, to go into thy house, in the
multitude of thy mercies.

We bless Thee that this is our privilege. May
we know the day of our visitation, and embrace
the things that belong to our peace. May we
hear with solemnity of mind, knowing that for
all these things, God will bring us unto judgment.
May we hear with prayer, remembering that whoever may plant or water, Thou alone canst give
the increase. May we be doers of the word, and
not hearers only ; and may we keep in memory
what is preached unto us, that we may not believe in vain.

May we carry into ordinary life the various portions of divine truth, which successively engage
our attention, and use them as seasons and circumstances render them suitable ; may its doctrines
inform, its warnings caution, its rules guide, and
its promises comfort us, till we have received the
end of our faith, the salvation of our souls.

Bless the congregation in whose devotions we
are to mingle. Let thy minister be clothed with
salvation, and let thy saints shout aloud for joy.

O, Thou holy and beautiful house, where our fathers praised Thee, peace be within thy walls— For our brethren and companions' sakes we will now say, peace be within Thee.

And bless, we beseech Thee, all thy churches, and all thy servants of every name. Plead thy own cause. Build up Zion. Establish and make Jerusalem a praise in the whole earth. May many run to and fro, and knowledge be increased; and may all know Thee from the least even to the greatest. Our Father, &c.

SUNDAY EVENING.

QUICKEN our souls to call upon thy name; pour upon us the spirit of grace and supplication; and in our enlivened and enlarged experience, may we know that Thou art not only the gracious reward-er, but the Almighty helper of them that diligently seek Thee.

For such O God, is the ignorance of our minds, the vagrancy of our thoughts, the earthiness of our affections, and the unbelief of our hearts, that without Thee we can do nothing. But the preparation of the heart, and the answer of the tongue are from Thee; thy Spirit helps our infirmities; thy grace is sufficient for us. Unite our hearts to fear thy name; enable us to come even to thy seat; and may our fellowship be with the God of love.

May we approach Thee, not as the Eternal Jehovah, but as our Father and our Friend, our exceeding joy, the strength of our heart, and our portion for ever. May we not only exercise that faith, by which we understand the worlds were made by the word of God. May we not only believe in Thee as the God of nature and providence, but in Jesus Christ, whom Thou hast sent, and sent to put away sin by the sacrifice of Him-

11*

self. We feel discouragements resulting from our guilty fears, and find it hard to believe, that on our return thou wilt meet us in peace. We therefore bless Thee, for the displaying of the exceeding riches of thy grace, in thy kindness towards us by Christ Jesus : and we rejoice in the blessed intelligence, that God was in Christ reconciling the world unto Himself, not imputing their iniquities unto them.

These glad tidings we have this day been hearing ; and O Lord, Thou knowest how often we have heard the joyful sound ; and Thou knowest the manner in which we have received it. We have reason to fear, that many have received it in vain; that their hearing has only added to their guilt ; and that their sabbaths have been only employed in treasuring up wrath against the day of wrath. O, what would the spirits in prison, give for one of our opportunities, one of our offers of mercy. How many now sitting in darkness, and in the regions of the shadow of death, would exult at the entrance of that light, against which we shut our eyes, or which we behold with indifference.

Awaken, O Lord, in our consciences, the inquiry, how shall we escape, if we neglect so great salvation ?

May we believe the report we have this day heard· keep in memory what has been preached unto us, lest we believe in vain. May we hide thy word in our hearts, that we may not sin against Thee ; and may the truth, as it is in Jesus, illuminate in us all that is dark, sanctify in us all that is unholy, establish all that is wavering, comfort all that is wretched, and accomplish in us all the good pleasure of thy goodness, and the work of faith with power, that the name of our Lord Jesus Christ may be glorified in us, and that we may be glorified in Him.

We sometimes hope, Thou hast commenced a good work in us ; we hope that we have begun to see the evil of sin, to hunger and thirst after right eousness; that we are asking the way to Zion, with our faces thitherward; and are praying, remember me, O, Lord, with the favour Thou bearest unto thy people.

Command and enable us to go forward. Take us by the hand, and lead us on from strength to strength. Let the dawn break into the perfect day; and the blade become the full corn in the ear.

We live in a world of changes but Thou art the same: may we know that Thou hast made with us an everlasting covenant, ordered in all things and sure. We are pressing through a vale of tears; but we bless Thee for the opening glory at the end. Enable us to realize, as our own, a better, even a heavenly country. Prepare us for every part of our pilgrimage; uphold our goings in thy word; and let no iniquity have dominion over us.

May we rejoice as though we rejoiced not; and weep as though we wept not; and buy as though we possessed not; and use this world as not abusing it.

We would sympathize with those that are in distress. Give to them that mourn in Zion, beauty for ashes, the oil of joy for mourning, and the garment of praise for the spirit of heaviness.

Bless all the institutions which are established to diffuse the Scriptures, and to send forth missionaries. Remember those who have gone forth to preach among the Gentiles, the unsearchable riches of Christ. Preserve their health, their morals, their spirituality, their zeal; let them be examples of all they teach; and be Thou a little sanctuary to them among the heathen. May all the events that take place, in the nations of the earth subserve the spread of the Redeemer's empire; and may we exult in the period, when the earth shall be filled with the knowledge of the Lord, as the waters cover the sea.

And to God the Father, the Son, and Holy Ghost, be praises for ever and ever. Amen.

MONDAY MORNING

THE heavens declare thy glory, O, God, and the firmament showeth thy handy work. Day unto day uttereth speech, and night unto night showeth knowledge ; and there is no speech nor language, where their voice is not heard. We behold displays of thy wisdom, power and goodness, in all thy works, from the largest, to the least.

But Thou hast magnified thy word, above all thy name ; and we can never be sufficiently thankful, for the revelation of thy will in the Scriptures of truth. We bless Thee that this sacred volume has been preserved, and translated, and published, and multiplied, so that we all have it in our possesion, and can read, in our own tongue, the wonderful works of God. Here we see, not only thy greatness, but thy grace ; and not only thy pity, but thy rectitude ; we see mercy and truth meeting together, righteousness and peace kissing each other. Here Thou hast shined in our hearts, to give us the light of the knowledge of thy glory, in the face of Jesus Christ.

For in Him Thou hast reconciled the world unto thyself, not imputing their trespasses unto them. Thou hast made him to be sin for us, who knew no sin, that we might be made the righteousness of God in Him. And Thou hast raised Him up from the dead, and given Him glory, that our faith and hope may be in God. May the hearts thus tenderly wooed, be effectually won. At the view of this infinite kindness, may we resign all our unworthy and suspicious thoughts ; and placing our confidence in Thee, return and say—Lord, I am thine, save me. Look Thou upon me, and be merciful unto me, as Thou usest to do unto those that love thy name.

We ask not to be enrolled among the rich and the great of this world, but to be numbered with

those who are blesed with all spiritual blesssings,
in heavenly places in Christ. The graves are
ready for us; and we shall soon be in a state, that
will render it a matter of indifference to us, whether
we have filled a cottage or a palace—but it will
be eternally important to us, that we have been
justified by thy grace, and sanctified by thy spirit,
and adopted into thy family. May we, therefore,
be wise unto salvation: and make it our present,
our supreme, our persevering concern, to obtain
those blessings which are spiritual in their nature;
eternal in their continuance; satisfying in their
possession; and which unerringly indicate, that
we are the friends of God.

Preserve us from a false estimate of the whole
of our character, or of any part of it. May we
regard our principles, as well as our conduct; our
motives, as well as our actions. May we never
mistake the excitement of our passions, for the
renewing of the Holy Ghost. May we never judge
of our religion, by occasional impressions and im-
pulses; but by our constant and prevailing disposition. May our heart be right with God, and our
life such as becometh the gospel.

May we maintain a supreme regard to another
and a better world, and feel, and confess ourselves
to be only strangers and pilgrims in this. How
often by bodily infirmities and pains, by relative
afflictions, and by dissatisfactions growing out of
every enjoyment—how often have we been told—
O, when shall we be taught, that this is not our
rest? O God, not only command, but enable us, to
arise and depart hence. Afford us all the direction, all the defence, all the support, all the consolation, our journey will require. Give us, in
large abundance, the supply of the spirit of Jesus
Christ, that we may be prepared for every duty:
that we may love Thee in all our mercies; that
we may submit to Thee in every trial. May we
trust Thee when we walk in darkness, and have

no light; and amidst all the changes of the present, and the uncertainties of the future, may our minds be kept in perfect peace, being stayed upon God

Hast Thou not made with us an everlasting covenant, ordered in all things and sure? The very hairs of our head—are they not all numbered? Are not all thy ways mercy and truth? Lord, we believe, help Thou our unbelief. And now unto Him that is able to keep us from falling, and to present us faultless, before the presence of His glory, with exceeding joy. To the only wise God our Saviour, be glory and majesty, dominion and power, both now and for ever. Amen

MONDAY EVENING

O Lord, Thou art over all by thy providential agency, and rich unto all that call upon Thee, in the exercise of thy mercy and grace. With Thee is the fountain of life, and in thy light shall we see light.

Help us to consider the way, the new and living way, in which a fallen creature can approach Thee with acceptance. May we behold the Lamb of God, that taketh away the sin of the world. May we contemplate the dignity of His person, the perfection of His sacrifice, and the prevalency of His intercession, who is the great High Priest over the house of God. And may we feel the distance between Thee and us done away, and rejoice that now, in Christ Jesus, we, who sometimes were afar off, are made nigh by the blood of Christ.

A glorious high throne, from the beginning, has been the place of thy people's sanctuary; and we have found it good to be there. O, what a source is devotion! When under all the toils that weary us, the cares that corrode us, the infirmities that press us down, the fears that disturb us—in every thing, by prayer and supplication, with thanksgiving, we can make known our supplication unto God, and feel a peace which passeth all understanding, keeping our hearts and minds through Christ Jesus.

We were as sheep going astray, but are now returned unto the Shepherd and Bishop of our souls. Yet, we feel the same grace that restored us, to be necessary to preserve us, and to supply. And hast not Thou promised to lead us, to guard us, to suffer us to want no good thing, to make all grace to abound towards us ? And art not Thou a faithful God, and able also to perform ? Lord, we take Thee at thy word. Do as Thou hast said.

We have tasted that Thou art gracious, and the relish has provoked our desires after more, and they who hunger and thirst after righteousness *are* blessed, and *shall* be filled. Make us to lie down in green pastures, and feed us beside the still waters, where we shall often exclaim, O, how great is His goodness, and how great is His beauty!

We often meet with those who have far more grace than we ourselves have : but this encourages our hope, since they were once poor, and He who supplied them is as rich as ever—and as accessible—and as free. We are continually meeting with duties and trials, which call for more grace than we have in ourselves, but not more than we have in our divine treasury, in whom it hath pleased Thee that all fullness should dwell. To Him, therefore, may we continually repair, and from His fulness receive, and grace for grace, till every void made by sin, be replenished, and we ourselves filled with all the fulness of God. We bless Thee that Thou dost not despise the day of small things ; but we aspire after a day of great ones. We are not straightened in Thee : may we never be contracted in ourselves ; may our desires be enlarged, and our hopes emboldened ; may we honour Thee by the entireness of our dependence, and the greatness of our expectation; and living and walking in the Spirit, may we go from strength to strength, and be changed from glory into glory, till we appear perfect before Thee in Zion

We know not what a day may bring forth; nor would we, if it were in our power, draw back the veil that hides the future, and learn the times and the seasons which the Father hath put into His own power. But, O be Thou with us in all, and prepare us for all. Prepare us for the smiles of prosperity : prepare us for the frowns of adversity ; prepare us for those losses in substance, and those bereavements in friends—so possible, so probable in a world like this : prepare us for the days of darkness, for they may be many : prepare us for the change, and when heart and flesh fail us, and we have no more a portion in all that is done under the sun, be Thou the strength of our heart, and our portion for ever.

May our very memory be blessed. May those who follow us, praise God that we have ever lived ; and may we leave behind us those instructions, examples, and effects, which shall glorify our God on earth, while our spirits have joined the spirits of just men, made perfect in heaven.

And may the grace of our Lord Jesus Christ, and the love of God, and the fellowship of the Holy Ghost, be with us all evermore. Amen.

TUESDAY MORNING.

O Thou, whose name alone is Jehovah, the Most High over all the earth, we desire to adore the perfections of thy nature, and to admire the works of thy hands. May the united displays of thy greatness, and thy goodness, impress our minds, and influence our thoughts and affections, while we approach Thee.

Heaven is thy throne, and the earth is thy footstool. The universe, with all its myriads of creatures, was made by thy word, and is upholden by thy power; and Thou dost according to thine own will in the army of heaven, and among the inhabitants of the earth; none can stay thy hand, or say unto Thee, what doest Thou?

But Thou art the Father of mercies, the God of all grace, and the God of all comfort. Even we, poor, mean, dying creatures, are not beneath thy care. Thou hast been mindful of us; Thou hast visited us; and thy visitation hath preserved our spirits. The lines are fallen to us in pleasant places; yea, we have a goodly heritage; we live in a land of vision; we have the Scriptures in our hands, and our ears hear the joyful sound of the gospel. We know that Thou hast not spared thine own Son, but delivered Him up for us all. We know that He has borne our grief, and carried our sorrow; that his blood cleanseth from all sin, and that whosoever believeth on Him, shall not perish, but have everlasting life.

We come in *His* name, and make mention of His righteousness only. We plead the obedience and sufferings of *Him* who magnified the law, both in its precept and penalty, and made it honourable. May we be justified by His blood; and may we be saved by His life. May we be joined to the Lord, and of one spirit with Him. May we deny ourselves, and take up our cross, and follow Him. May the agency of thy grace prepare us for all the dispensations of thy providence. May we be willing that the Lord should choose our inheritance for us, and determine what we shall retain or lose; what we shall suffer or enjoy.

If indulged with prosperity, may we be secured from its snares, and use its advantages as not abusing them. And may we patiently and cheerfully submit to those afflictions, which are necessary to hedge up our way when we are tempted to wan-

der, to excite an abhorrence of sin, to wean us from
the present evil world, and to make us partakers
of thy holiness. Only assure us, and we shall
learn in whatsoever state we are, therewith to be
content—only assure us, that Thou wilt be with
us in trouble, and, that at the end of the vale of
tears, we shall enter Emmanuel's land, where the
inhabitants no more say, I am sick ; where our sun
shall no more go down, nor our moon withdraw itself, but God shall be our everlasting light, and the
days of our mourning shall be ended.

May our friends and relations be fellow-heirs
with us of the grace of life. Let our house be the
tabernacle of the righteous : let our children and
servants be a seed to serve Thee : and among none
of those who surround this family altar, may there
be weeping and wailing, and gnashing of teeth,
when they shall see Abraham, and Isaac, and Jacob, in the kingdom of God, and they themselves
shut out.

Lord, help us all to view our religious opportunities as talents, for which we are accountable :
to remember, that our greatest danger results from
our highest privileges ; and to fear, lest a promise
being left us of entering into thy rest, any of us
should seem to come short of it.

Thou hast determined the bounds of our habitation ; and by the events of thy providence, many
of those in whose society we delight, are separated
from us. When we are absent in body, may we
be often present in spirit. We commend our absent friends and kindred to thy covenant care.
May no evil tidings concerning them, wound our
hearts : spare them in mercy : may we often embrace each other in circumstances of health and
comfort : or if we have had our last interview on
earth, may we all meet in our heavenly Father's
house, and be for ever with each other, and for
ever with the Lord.

' In hope of which, with every other blessing, we devoutly ascribe to the only wise God, our Saviour, praise and glory everlasting. Amen.

TUESDAY EVENING.

O Thou King of Glory, we desire to approach thy divine Majesty with reverence and godly fear, and to worship Thee in the beauty of holiness. Every perfection adorns thy nature, and sustains thy throne. The heavens are thine ; the earth also is thine ; the world is thine ; and the fulness thereof. Thy power drew the universe from nothing. Thy wisdom has managed all its multiplied concerns, presiding over nations, families, and individuals, and numbering the very hairs of our head. Thy goodness is boundless : the eyes of all wait upon Thee, and Thou givest them their meat in due season. Thou openest thine hand, and satisfiest the desire of every living thing. How precious are the thoughts of thy mercy and grace— and so excellent is thy loving kindness, that even the children of men, put their trust under the shadow of thy wing.

Thou art the blessed and happy God. O, teach us to place our happiness in thyself. May we never seek the living among the dead, nor ask with the deluded many, Who will show us any good ? But, may we prize the light of thy countenance ; implore the joy of thy salvation ; and passing by the attractions of creatures, be able to say, Whom have I in heaven but Thee, and there is none upon earth that I desire beside Thee.

Thou hast been infinitely more attentive to our happiness than we ever have been, or ever can be. Thou madest man upright, and when, by voluntary transgression, we fell away from Thee, Thou didst not treat us with the severity, or the neglect, we deserved. In thy love and pity Thou wast pleased to provide for us a Saviour, who bore our grief and carried our sorrows, and put away sin by the sacrifice of Himself.

Apply this redemption to our hearts, by the justification of our persons, and the sanctification of our natures. We confess our transgressions—Have mercy upon us. We are heavy laden—Give us rest. We are ignorant—Make us wise unto salvation. We are helpless—Let thy strength be made perfect in our weakness. We are poor and needy. Bless us with all the unsearchable riches of Christ. Having begun a religious course, may we run and not be weary, and walk and not faint. And though perplexities, and trials, and dangers await us, yet may we travel on, unchecked and undismayed, knowing, Thou hast said, I will never leave thee, nor forsake thee.

Thus far, blessed be thy name, Thou hast led us on, and we have found Thee faithful to thy promises. We have had our sorrows ; but Thou hast been a very present help in every time of trouble. We have had our fears ; but Thou hast not suffered the enemy to triumph over us. We have sometimes been on the verge of despair, and have said, I am cast out of thy sight : but we have been enabled to look again towards thy holy temple : and the shadow of death has been turned into the morning. Hitherto hath the Lord helped us. Thy vows are upon us, O God : we will render praises unto Thee. For Thou hast delivered our souls from death : wilt not Thou deliver our feet from falling, that we may walk before God in the light of the living ?

We would feel the connexions which unite us to others, and by sympathy, and prayer, and praise, make their miseries and mercies our own. We would rejoice with those that rejoice, and weep with those that weep. Provide support and employment for the poor, and may their hands be sufficient for them. Make the widow's neart to sing for joy; and in Thee, may the fatherless find mercy. Visit those who are on beds of sickness, and prepare them for thy pleasure : that if they live, it may be to serve Thee ; and if they die, it may be to enjoy Thee. Bless our nation. May every department of our government be under the control of infinite wisdom and goodness ; and let righteousness and peace be the stability of our times. Do good, in thy good-pleasure, unto Zion ; build Thou the walls of Jerusalem : and may all our churches, like the original disciples, continue steadfastly in the apostle's doctrine, and in fellowship, and in breaking of bread, and in prayers.

Protect and refresh us through the night season : and then cause us to hear thy loving-kindness in the morning ; for in Thee do we trust ; cause us to know the way wherein we should go, for we lift up our souls unto Thee. We implore it through the intercession of thy dear Son, and our Saviour.

And blessing, and honour, and glory, and power, be unto Him that sitteth upon the throne, and unto the Lamb, for ever and ever. Amen.

WEDNESDAY MORNING.

O God, Thou art incomprehensible, and in none of thy works and ways, can any of thy creatures find Thee out, unto perfection. Yet Thou hast not left thyself without witness, nor called us to worship an unknown God. Thou hast been pleased to reveal thyself to us, as far as our wants and welfare require ; and, among other endearing characters, we can discern Thee, as a God, hearing prayer.

Thou never saidst to the seed of Jacob, Seek ye me in vain. A glorious high throne, from the beginning, has been the place of thy people's sanctuary. And thither would we repair, in all our difficulties, necessities, and distresses, and find it good to draw near to God. Possess us with the spirit of grace, which is always a spirit of supplication. May we live in a prayerful frame of mind, that will always allow of our immediate and pleasing intercourse with Thee: in the ordinary concerns of life, may our thoughts and desires often ascend the skies; and in habitual devotion, may we find a resource, that will sooth our sorrows, sanctify our successes, and qualify us for all our dealings with our fellow creatures.

We bless Thee that Thou hast made us capable of knowing Thee, the Author of all being; of resembling Thee, the perfection of all excellency; and of enjoying Thee, the source of all happiness. Though we are unworthy to share in thy loving kindness, it is thy pleasure that we seek after it; and Thou hast said, their hearts shall live that seek God. Therefore, look Thou upon us, and be merciful unto us, as Thou usest to do unto those that love thy name. May we be accepted in the beloved, and know that in Him, we have redemption through his blood, even the forgiveness of our sins. May we view him as the end of the law for righteousness to every one that believeth; and as the source of all that grace, by which we are renewed in the spirit of our minds. May we always contemplate our duties in connexion with those promises, which insure ability for the performance of them; and while weak in ourselves, may we be strong in the Lord, and in the power of his might.

Attend us, O, God, in every part of our arduous and trying pilgrimage. We need the same counsel, the same defence, the same comfort, we implored as at the moment of our setting out—Cast us not away from thy presence, and take not thy Holy Spirit from us. May we live in the Spirit, and may we walk in the Spirit. And may our path be as the shining light, that shineth more and more unto the perfect day.

Let our religion be more and more obvious to our consciences ; and more perceptible to the eye of those around us. May all that see and hear us, take knowledge of us, that we have been with Jesus. While He is representing us in heaven, may we represent Him on earth ; while He pleads our cause, may we plead His ; and be concerned in all things to show forth *His* praise, who is making all things work together for our good.

Arise, O God, and plead thine own cause. Give the word and let the company of those that publish the glad tidings of thy kingdom, be great. May thy house be filled with inhabitants, and thy table furnished with guests ; and let all that love thy salvation say continually, the Lord be magnified.

Be gracious to our absent connexions—our hearts' desire and prayer to God for them is, that they may be saved.

Continue the gentleness of thy goodness to this household.

To the care which has watched over as through another night, we give up ourselves in prospect of the duties and events of the day. Let thy presence go with us ; and thy blessing attend us ; and whether we wake or sleep, may we live together with Christ.

In whose words we address Thee, as Our Father, &c. Amen.

WEDNESDAY EVENING.

O, Thou ever blessed God, we desire to approach Thee, adoring thy perfections, and admiring thy works, which are sought out of all them that have pleasure therein. May we feel becom ing regards towards Thee as our Creator, the Preserver of men, and the Saviour of sinners.

Thy name is most excellent in all the earth, and Thou hast set thy glory above the heavens. Thy compassions fail not, and therefore are not consumed. We are filled with wonder, at thy condescension in noticing creatures so poor and worthless; and at thy mercy and grace, in providing for the deliverance and happiness of creatures so miserable and guilty. We can never sufficiently bless Thee, that we were born in a christian country, where the true light shineth, and we can hear words whereby we may be saved. How suitable and encouraging are the discoveries, the invitations, and the promises of the gospel of peace. Here are announced, pardon for rebels, liberty for captives, health for the sick, and a free, full, and everlasting salvation for them that are lost. Here we are informed, that Thou hast not spared thine own Son, but delivered Him up for us all; that He has fulfilled and magnified the law; that His blood cleanseth from all sin; that in Him all fulness dwells; and that whosoever believeth on Him shall not be confounded.

In His beloved name we come, and avail ourselves of the plea, which Thou thyself hast afforded us. For His sake be merciful unto us, and bless us, and cause thy face to shine upon us, that we may be saved. May we be justified by his blood, and have access into that grace, wherein we shall stand, and rejoice in the hope of the glory of God. May thy image be reimpressed upon our souls, in knowledge, righteousness, and true holiness. May thy Holy Spirit take full possession of our hearts, and lead us into all truth, and enable as to walk in all thy commandments and ordinances blameles; may we be fruitful in every good word and work to do thy will.

Raise us above the world; where duty is concerned, may we feel neither its frowns nor its smiles. May it ever be a light thing with us, to be judged of man's judgment. May thy approbabation be our only aim; and thy word our only rule; and with Enoch may we all enjoy the testimony that we please God. Keep us from, or preserve us in, the hour of temptation. May we abhor and avoid whatever would grieve thy Holy Spirit, and cause Thee to hide thy face from us. May we walk in the fear of the Lord, that we may walk in the comforts of the Holy Ghost; and may we always suspect the confidence and consolation, which can be enjoyed along with a worldly temper, and a careless conversation.

May we have no fellowship with the unfruitful works of darkness; but rather reprove them; yet may we in meekness instruct those who oppose themselves, and be gentle and patient towards all men. And may we—do, as well as teach. May we be not only professors of the gospel—but examples, displaying in every relation, and office, and condition of life, its excellency, loveliness, and advantages, that we may put to silence the ignorance of foolish men, and even constrain them to glorify God in the day of visitation.

How well does it become us to be humble. How little have we illustrated our principles, or improved our advantages. How often have we injured, instead of recommending the cause of our Redeemer! How little have we served our generation; and how few are those to whom we have been a blessing! In many things we have offended; and in all, come short of thy glory. Pardon our inquity, for it is great.

Forgive the imperfections, omissions and sins, of another day; and make us thankful for the continuance of its numberless blessings.

Shelter us through the night; and in the morning, with renewed strength and grateful hearts, may we rise to love Thee more, and serve Thee better, than we have done this day—through our Lord and Saviour. Amen.

THURSDAY MORNING.

O LORD our God, blessed is the man whom Thou choosest, and causest to approach unto Thee. In thy presence there is fulness of joy, and at thy right hand there are pleasures for evermore. With Thee is the fountain of life, and in thy light alone can we see light.

We therefore entreat thy favour, with our whole heart. We acknowledge that we have forfeited all claims to it; and if we had no better ground of hope, than our deservings, we must sink into despair. For against Thee, Thee only have we sinned, and done evil in thy sight, that Thou mightest be justified when Thou speakest, and clear when Thou judgest.

But with Thee there is mercy, and with Thee there is plenteous redemption. We bless Thee for the assurance, that Thou hast sent thy own Son into the world, not to condemn the world, but that the world, through Him, might be saved. We rejoice, that neither the number nor heinousness of our trangressions, is a bar to that forgiveness, which is founded on the sufferings and sacrifice of the cross. The blood of Jesus Christ, thy Son, cleanseth from all sin. By the blood of that covenant which He has ratified, sent forth thy prisoners out of the pit wherein there is no water. Graciously absolve us from our guilt; and pronounce our discharge from all condemnation, not only in the court of heaven, but in the court of conscience, that being justified by faith, we may have peace with God, and enjoy the glorious liberty of his children.

But, O, save us from the hope of the hypocrite, which shall perish. Never suffer us to impose upon ourselves, in any thing that relates to our eternal state. May we never suppose that we are in Christ, unless we are new creatures; or that we are born of the Spirit, unless we mind the things of the Spirit. May we never rest satisfied with any professions of belief, or any outward forms or services, while the heart is not right with God. May we judge of our sincerity in religion, by our fear to offend Thee ; by our concern to know what Thou wilt have us to do ; and by our willingness to deny ourselves, and take up our cross and follow the Lamb, whithersoever he goeth.

May nothing render us forgetful of thy glory ; may nothing turn us aside from thy commands ; may nothing shake our confidence in thy promises. Take from us the evil heart of unbelief ; the cause of all our waverings and wanderings ; may we believe, that we may be established in our goings ; and be always abounding in the work of the Lord.

Prepare us for whatever we have to meet with, between this morning, and the grave. We know not what lies before us ; but Thou knowest, and thy grace can make us sufficient for every service and every suffering.

Let not our temporal occupations ever injure our spiritual concerns ; or the cares of this life make us forget, or neglect, the one thing needful ; may we learn the holy art of abiding with God in our callings ; of being in the world without being of it ; and of making every thing not only consistent with religion, but conducive to it.

May we do, and may we say nothing, by which we shall offend against the generation of thy children. If strong, may we bear the infirmities of the weak, and not please ourselves. If preserved, may we restore a brother that has been overtaken in a fault, in the spirit of meekness, considering ourselves, lest we also be tempted.

Bless those who have done us good, and render seven fold into their own bosom, and forgive those who have done us evil, and enable us to forgive them.

Bless those who are near and dear to us; may
they be near and dear to Thee. Bless them in
their outward comforts; but above all, may their
souls prosper.

Be gracious to our native land. Be mindful of
our rulers. Teach our senators wisdom; and so
control the minds and hearts of those, who are entrusted with the public welfare, as that they may
glorify Thee, and secure the best good of the
people. Bless the gates of Zion, and all the
dwellings of Jacob. Let thy secret reside in the
families of them that fear Thee; and may those
that have neglected to call upon thy name, immediately adopt the resolution of Joshua, As for me
and my house, we will serve the Lord.

This morning sacrifice, we offer in the all prevailing name of our adorable Redeemer—And
unto Him that loved us, and washed us from our
sins in his own blood, and hath made us kings and
priests unto God, and to his Father, to Him be
glory and dominion, for ever and ever. Amen.

THURSDAY EVENING.

O God, by the return of this hour of devotion,
Thou hast again said, Seek ye my face; and our
hearts have answered, Thy face Lord will we
seek.

We value every opportunity of approaching
Thee, not only as our duty, but as our unspeakable privilege. We rejoice, that there is opened a
new and living way into the holiest of all; and
that as we enter, we can see Jesus the Mediator
of the new covenant, and hear the voice of the
blood of sprinkling, that speaketh better things
than that of Abel. We are unprofitable servants.
Our obedience, instead of meriting recompense,
deserves condemnation for its numerous defects.

We are ashamed even of our devotions; and often question, whether any part of our religion will bear the eye of God.

But it is our encouragement, that if we cannot come to Thee as saints, we may come as sinners, with the assurance, that Thou wilt in no wise cast us out. We therefore come as sinners; yet sinners who hate themselves for their abominations, and long for deliverance. Hear the groaning of the prisoners, and loose those who are appointed unto death. Heal us, and we shall be healed; save us, and we shall be saved, for Thou art our praise. Save us from the curse of the law which we have violated; save us from the power and love of every sin; save us from an evil heart of unbelief in departing from the living God; save us from the present evil world; save us from our adversary the devil, who goeth about as a roaring lion, seeking whom he may devour; that being delivered out of the hand of our enemies, we may serve Thee without fear, in holiness and righteousness before Thee, all the days of our lives.

We sometimes hope Thou hast begun a good work in us, and we take comfort from the assurance, that Thou wilt perform it until the day of Jesus Christ. We ought to be humble, but we would not be ungrateful, nor refuse to acknowledge what Thou hast done for our souls; for by thy grace alone, we are what we are: Thou hast shown us the evil of sin, and the beauty there is in holiness: Thou hast led us to hunger and thirst after righteousness; we glory in the cross of our Lord Jesus Christ; we long to be conformed to his example; and we have taken hold of the skirt of him that is a Jew, and have said, We will go with you, for we have heard that God is with you.

O Thou, who despisest not the day of small things, perfect that which concerneth us. May we not only have hope, but abound in hope; may we not only have faith, but be rich in faith; may we not only be fruitful, but be filled with all the fruits of righteousness, which are by Jesus Christ, unto the glory and praise of God.

Let us not be of the number of those who are always learning, and never able to come to the knowledge of the truth. May we have clear and consistent views of divine truth ; and may every doctrine we admit into our judgments, have a powerful influence over our hearts. May it bring, as well as reveal, salvation—and teach us to deny ungodliness and worldly lusts, and to live soberly, righteously, and godly, in the present world. May the love of God subdue the lust of the flesh, the lust of the eye, and the pride of life, and whatever is not of the Father, but is of the world.

May we love our neighbour as ourselves, and never hide ourselves from our own flesh. May we look, not every man on his own things, but every man also on the things of others, and especially the things that are Jesus Christ's.

May we never crucify Him afresh, and put Him to an open shame. May we rather die than cause His worthy name to be blasphemed. May our devoted hearts be hourly asking, What shall I do for Him, who, when rich, for our sakes became poor, and died that we might live.

May He obtain the purchase of his blood in our revolted world; and see of the travail of his soul, and be satisfied. Let all kings fall down before Him, and all nations serve Him. And blessed be His glorious name for ever, and let the whole earth be filled with His glory. Amen and Amen.

FRIDAY MORNING.

O Thou ever blessed God! It is good for us to draw near to Thee ; and if we had no other privilege to be thankful for, we ought continually to praise Thee, for permission and encouragement to approach the throne of thy grace, there to spread before Thee all our wants and all our desires.

We are not worthy of the blessing ; we are not worthy of the least of all thy mercies. We are far gone from the original righteousness in which we were created ; and the depravity of our nature has appeared in the disobedience and rebellion of our lives. How early did we discover tendencies to discontent, and pride, and envy, and revenge. O, remember not against us the sins of our youth ; nor the multiplied transgressions of riper years—our misimproved time and talents, our abused mercies and means, our wasted and perverted Sabbaths and seasons of grace, our neglect of thy great salvation, and our disregard of the Friend of sinners, who loved us so as to die for us.

Our iniquity is increased over our head, and our trespass is gone up into the very heaven. While we confess our guilt, may we individually and deeply feel it, and be filled with self-abhorrence and self-despair.

But help us to remember, that there is hope in Israel concerning this thing. Enable us to hear the voice that proclaims, Behold the Lamb of God, that taketh away the sin of the world. Through Him may we return to Thee, and find Thee a God, ready to pardon sin, and able to subdue it. Through Him may we give up ourselves to Thee, as our portion to enjoy, and our master to serve, for ever. At thy footstool, in the spirit of submission, may we ever say, Speak, Lord, for thy servant heareth. May we not only obey, but delight to do thy will, yea, may thy law be within our heart.

Conscious of our danger, may we watch ; and sensible of our inability to keep ourselves, may we pray, lest we enter into temptation. Hold Thou us up, and we shall be safe. Preserve our understandings from error, our affections from the love

of idols, our lips from speaking guile, our life from
every stain of vice, and our character from the
very appearance of evil.

And may we not only be harmless and blameless, the sons of God without rebuke, but may we
be exemplary and useful, holding forth the word of
life, and adorning the doctrine of God our Saviour
in all things.

If the Saviour has manifested himself to us, as
he does not unto the world, may we declare that
which we have seen and heard unto others, that
they also may have fellowship with us ; and
having tasted that the Lord is gracious ourselves,
may we ever be saying to those around us, O, taste
and see that the Lord is good, blessed is the man
that trusteth in Him. And may we walk in wisdom towards them that are without. May our efforts be guided by prudence, as well as animated
by zeal. May we distinguish things that differ ;
and—not by a sacrifice of principle, but by a ju-
dicious use of circumstances and opportunities,
may we become all things to all men, if by any
means we may gain some. And, O, let our endeavours be successful ; for he that converteth a sinner from the error of his way, shall save a soul
from death, and shall hide a multitude of sins.

Especially, may our solicitude and exertion be
available with regard to our connexions and relations. Let those, who are dear to us in the bonds
of nature or friendship, become fellow-heirs with
us of the grace of life, and fellow-labourers with
us in the Lord's vineyard.   .

Let the rising generation be a seed to serve
Thee. Excite them by the command—Remem
ber now thy Creator, in the days of thy youth ·
and encourage them by the promise—I love them
that love me, and they that seek me early shall
find me.

Regard the aged. Alarm the old in sin : convince them that it is high time, and that it will

shortly be too late, to seek the things that belong to their everlasting peace. Support those who have long known Thee, and whose gray hairs, as a crown of glory, are found in the way of righteousness. Cast them not off in the time of old age, and forsake them not when their strength faileth.

Now, the God of peace, who brought again from the dead, our Lord Jesus, that great Shepherd of the sheep, through the blood of the everlasting covenant, make us perfect in every good work, to do his will, working in us that which is well pleasing in his sight, through Jesus Christ; to whom be glory for ever and ever. Amen.

FRIDAY EVENING.

O God, thy command and thy promise, our duty and our privilege, induce us to avail ourselves of every opportunity of approaching the throne of thy grace. We are all indigence and inability. It is not in the power of men and angels to reach our case ; and afford us the blessings we so much need, and so much desire. Our only hope is in the name of the Lord God, who made heaven and eartn.

But Thou art over all ; and rich unto all that call upon Thee ; and Thou Lord hast not forsaken them that seek Thee. We love to reflect upon the displays of thy perfections ; and to contemplate, what Thou hast done for others as poor and destitute, as sinful and guilty, as we are : and to remember that thy hand is not shortened that it cannot save, nor thy ear heavy that it cannot hear.

Behold a company of suppliants at thy footstool, in all the effects of the fall, and let our ruined condition be under thy agency. O, Thou God of all grace, work Thou in us to will and to do of thy

13*

good pleasure; and vile as we are in ourselves, make us an eternal excellency, the joy of many generations. Our understandings are darkened. Our hearts are hearts of stone. Our very conscience also is defiled. Our affections are earthly and sensual. Open Thou the eyes of our understanding. Give us hearts of flesh. Purify our consciences from dead works to serve the living God. Set our affections on things that are above: and as He who has called us is holy, so may we also be holy in all manner of conversation and godliness.

Deliver us from the bondage of corruption, and bring us into the glorious liberty of thy children: that being made free from sin, and become servants unto God, we may have our fruit unto holiness, and our end everlasting life.

Preserve us from all self-delusion, especially where our souls are concerned. May we never be flattered by the good opinion of our fellow creatures, against the convictions of our own consciences; but remember, that if our hearts condemn us, God is greater than our hearts, and knoweth all things. May we never substitute mere opinions, and outward forms and ceremonies, in the room of that grace, which renews the soul and sanctifies the life. Ever keep alive in our minds the belief, that in Christ Jesus, neither circumcision availeth any thing, nor uncircumcision, but a new creature: and in the examinations of our religious state and character, may we look after that kingdom, which is not meat and drink, but righteousness, and peace and joy in the Holy Ghost.

Inspire us with a well grounded hope of being, one day, presented before the presence of thy glory; when we shall see Thee without obscurity, approach Thee without sin, serve Thee without imperfection, and enjoy Thee without sorrow. How remote now do we often feel from this exalted state? And how improbable does it frequently seem, that we should ever attain it? We have never yet been better than a bruised reed, and a smoking flax : and thy patience alone could have borne with our imperfections and perverseness. Yet we trust the root of the matter is found in us ; and we bless Thee, if thy grace—by which alone we are what we are, has caused us to loathe sin, and abhor ourselves, and to hunger and thirst after righteousness, and to place our happiness in serving and enjoying Thee.

And we pray, that our path may be as a shining light, that shineth more and more unto the perfect day. Complete that which is lacking in our faith. Lead us into all truth : and establish our hearts with grace. Fill our minds with the sublime and elevating objects of revelation, that worldly things may find no room in our minds : and keep near us, all the affecting and awful motives of the gospel, that we may not be able to sin, but in the view of thine all-seeing eye, a burning world, a judgment to come, and the cross of our Lord Jesus Christ.

And the Lord make us, also, to increase and abound in love, one towards another, and towards all men. Let all bitterness, and wrath, and anger, and clamour, and evil speaking, be put away from us, with all malice ; and may we be kind, one towards another, tender hearted; forgiving, also, one another, even as God, for Christ's sake, hath forgiven us.

Prepare us for all the duties and trials that lie before us. We bless Thee for thy promises, which provide against every want we feel ; and for every condition in which we can be found. In God will we praise his word. In God have we put our trust. We will not fear what flesh can do unto us. Thou tellest our wanderings. Put Thou our tears into thy bottle. Are they not in thy book ?

We commend ourselves with all our relations and friends, this evening, to thy forgiving mercy, and providential care. O Thou, that givest thy beloved sleep, indulge us with refreshing repose ; or if Thou holdest our eyes waking, in the night may thy song be with us, and our prayer unto the God of our life. Guide us by thy counsel through life, and afterward receive us to glory.

And to the only wise God, our Saviour, be glory and majesty, dominion and power, for ever and ever. Amen.

SATURDAY MORNING.

O Thou who hast said, I will be sanctified in them that come nigh me, and before all the people will I be glorified ; may we have grace, whereby we shall serve Thee acceptably, with reverence and godly fear. Thou inhabitest eternity ; but our age is as nothing before Thee. Thy understanding is infinite, but we know nothing. Thou art Almighty, but we are crushed before the moth. Thou art of purer eyes than to behold iniquity, but we are vile ; what shall we answer Thee ? We cannot answer Thee for one of a thousand of our transgressions : and had we followed the forebodings of our consciences, we could not have approached Thee.

But Thou hast proclaimed thy name, the Lord God, merciful and gracious ; Thou hast caused all thy goodness to pass before us ; Thou hast opened a new and living way into the holiest of all, by the blood of Jesus ; and we have boldness, and access with confidence, by the faith of Him.

We bless Thee that in Him all fulness dwells, and that ignorant, and guilty, and depraved, and miserable, as we are in ourselves, from Him we can derive wisdom, righteousness, sanctification and redemption. And we rejoice, that these blessings are attainable, without money and without price ; and that we may know they are our's, by

every title God himself can give; and shall be
our's for ever.

O, let such undeserved, such infinite goodness
melt our hearts, and lead us to throw down the
weapons of rebellion, and weep over them. May
we sorrow after a godly sort, that ever we offended
a Being so worthy of all our love and our obedience; and while compelled to acknowledge,
with a broken heart and a contrite spirit, O Lord,
other lords, beside Thee, have had dominion over
us: enable us to say, But henceforth, by Thee
only will we make mention of thy name. As our
reasonable service, to Thee may we dedicate ourselves immediately without delay, and fully without reserve. To Thee may we yield our understanding and our intellectual powers; our wills
and our active powers; our senses and our bodily
powers; our time, our substance, and all our relative powers—may our words, and our actions,
and our callings in life, be all holiness unto the
Lord.

May we come out from the world, and touch
not the unclean thing, and be received and acknowledged as the sons and daughters of the
Lord Almighty. And though they are few in
number, and the world knoweth them not, may we
choose thy people as our companions, and delight
in them as the excellent of the earth. With them,
at thy gates, may we daily watch, and wait at the
posts of thy doors; with them, may we coura-
geously fight the good fight of faith; with them,
may we patiently labour in thy vineyard.

May we love them all; and as we have opportunity, may we unite with them all in holy communion, and co-operate with them all in schemes
of civil and sacred beneficence. We bless Thee
for the country and the age in which we live. We
bless Thee for the spirit which has been awakened,
and the efforts that are now making, to promote
the temporal, and above all, the spiritual welfare

of mankind, by individuals and communities, and combinations of communities. O let them not labour in vain; let the pleasures of the Lord prosper in their hand; let thy work appear unto thy servants, and thy glory unto their children; and let the beauty of the Lord our God be upon us, and establish Thou the work of our hands upon us; yea, the work of our hand, establish Thou it.

And prepare us for suffering thy will, as well as doing it. May we never look for unmingled felicity here, but expect to find life, as all who have gone before us have found it light and darkness, pain and pleasure, good and evil. When we meet with trials, may we never think them strange things; nor murmur and repine under them. Rather may we be thankful, that they are so few and alleviated; rather may we rejoice, that they are all founded in love to our souls, and designed to make us partakers of thy holiness. Sustain us under them; improve us by them; and assure us in due time of our deliverance from them; and of our entering the rest that remains for the people of God, where all sorrow and sighing shall cease, and all tears shall be wiped from our eyes.

And may the grace of our Lord Jesus Christ, and the love of God, and the communion of the Holy Ghost, be with us all, now and for ever. Amen.

SATURDAY EVENING

O God—Thou art the God of all the families of the earth; for they are formed by thy will, and supported by thy providence. But Thou art, in a peculiar manner, the God of those families, in which thy name is known, and loved, and honoured. Thy curse is in the house of the wicked, but Thou blessest the habitation of the just.

Whatever be the dispositions of others, we desire to say, with increasing resolution and zeal, As for us, and our house, we will serve the Lord. Thy yoke is easy, thy burden is light; thy work is honourable and glorious ; and in keeping thy commandments, there is great reward. Thou art the best of all masters; Thou hast promised to bear with our infirmities, and to suffer us to want no good thing.

Already Thou hast laid us under infinite obligations, as the God of providence and of grace : Thou hast dealt well with thy servants, O Lord. Bless the Lord, O our souls, and all that is within us, bless his holy name. Bless the Lord, O our souls, and forget not all his benefits.

By thy good hand upon us, we have been conducted through the perils, not only of another day but another week ; a period, during which, many have been carried down to their graves, and we have been brought so much nearer to our own. Impress us with the lapse of our time, and so teach us to number our days, that we may apply our hearts unto wisdom. Many have been involved in perplexities, and exposed to want; many nave been confined to the house of mourning, or the bed of sickness ; but we have been indulged with liberty, and ease, and health, and strength ; we have seen thy loving-kindness every morning, and thy faithfulness every night ; and have had all things richly to enjoy.

But, O, how little have we been affected by the instances of thy undeserved goodness; how imperfectly have we improved our religious privileges ; how negligent have we been in seizing opportunities of doing good to the bodies and souls of our fellow-creatures—and how well does it become each of us to exclaim, Behold, l am vile ; what shall I answer Thee ? wherefore I abhor myself, repenting in dust and ashes.

We stand before Thee this evening in our trespass ; enter not into judgment with thy servants,
O Lord.　Our only hope is, that to the Lord·our
God belong mercies and forgiveness, though we
have rebelled against Him.　Have mercy upon
us, O God, according to thy loving kindness, according to the multitude of thy tender mercies,
blot out our transgressions.

And may a confidence in thy goodness, instead
of encouraging us to sin, that grace may abound,
inspire us with that godly sorrow which worketh
repentance unto life.　May we hate and forsake
every false way.　May we be attentive to our
condition, and study our character ; may we bri
dle our tongue, and keep our heart with all diligence.

May we often look back and see, how at any
time, we have been ensnared or overcome : and
watch and pray in future, lest we enter into temptation.　And do Thou keep us by thy power;
uphold us by thy free Spirit ; and not only restrain us from sin, but mortify us to it.　　—

May sleep refresh our bodies, and fit them for
thy service on the ensuing day ; and may thy
grace prepare our minds.　May we leave all the
cares of the world for a while, behind ; that we
may attend on the Lord without distraction.　May
we repair to the hallowed exercises of devotion,
as the heart panteth after the water brooks.　May
we call the sabbath a delight, and be glad when
they say to us, Let us go into the house of the
Lord.

And, O Thou God of all grace; do as Thou hast
said ; fulfil thy word unto thy servants, upon which
Thou hast caused them to hope.　Bless abundantly the provisions of thy house, and satisfy thy
poor with bread.　Clothe thy priests with salvation and let thy saints shout aloud for joy.

And to the God of all grace, the Father, the
Word, and the Holy Ghost, be all honour and
glory, now and for ever.　Amen.

SUNDAY MORNING.

O God, Thou art very great; Thou art clothed with honour and majesty ; and it becomes us to approach Thee, with reverence and godly fear. We can also come before Thee, with humble confidence ; for thy condescension equals thy grandeur, and thy goodness is thy glory.

If we are unworthy, we rejoice that we are not unwelcome. If we are guilty, Thou art gracious; if we are miserable, Thou art merciful ; if we are all indigence, thy riches are unsearchable. By not sparing thine own Son, but delivering Him up for us all, Thou hast shown thy boundless compassion towards a perishing world ; and proved, that with Him, Thou wilt also freely give us all things. Thus a foundation is laid for our hope ; a refuge is opened for our safety ; and a new and living way is consecrated into the holiest of all, for our approach to Thee.

O, bless us with that conviction of sin, that brokenness of heart, that self-despair, which will endear to us the gospel message, as a faithful saying, and worthy of all acceptation ; and induce us to say with the apostle, that I may win Christ, and be found in Him ; that I may know Him and the power of His resurrection, and the fellowship of His sufferings, being made conformable unto His death. How happy are they that are found interested in Him ! They are delivered from the wrath to come ; they are justified from all things ; they

14

have peace with God ; they are heirs of the glory that is to be revealed.

May we feel a holy and increasing concern, to know whether these exalted privileges are claimable by us. For this purpose, may we frequently and faithfully examine ourselves. May we search after—that deadness to the world, that love to the Saviour, that attachment to his house, that devotedness to His service, which characterise the subjects of His salvation.

And may these things not only be in us, but abound. It is an unspeakale blessing if we have life : but it is our duty and privilege to have it more abundantly. It becomes us to be thankful, if Thou hast begun a good work in us ; but we are allowed to pray, that Thou wilt perfect that which concerneth us. According to the riches of thy glory, therefore, strengthen us with might by thy Spirit in the inner man ; that Christ may dwell in our hearts by faith ; that we being rooted and grounded in love, may be able to comprehend with all saints, what is the height, and depth, and breadth, and length, and to know the love of Christ, that passeth knowledge, that we may be filled with all the fulness of God.

May every part of our character and conduct, be adapted to make, not only a serious, but an amiable impression, on the minds of those around us ; that they may say, I will go with you, for I have heard that God is with you.

May all that we meet within our passage through life, whether pleasing or painful, instead of injuring the prosperity of our souls, turn to our salvation, through prayer, and the continual supply of the Spirit of Jesus Christ.

Send us help this day from the sanctuary, and strenghen us out of Zion. We know that thine own appointments, were never intended to make us independent of thy agency ; without thy superadded blessing, the best means will prove in vain.

But Thou hast promised to bless the provisions of thy house, and to fill thy poor with bread. Thou hast said, in all places where I record my name, I will come unto thee, and I will bless thee. And all have found Thee to be faithful to thy word. We have known Thee in thy palaces for a refuge: we have seen thy power and thy glory in the sanctuary; and have often praised Thee with joyful lips.

We therefore bless Thee for the return of these precious advantages: we pity those who are denied them; sanctify their privations; and compensate the want of ordinances, by thine own presence and communications. Enter, as an instructer and comforter, all the abodes of sorrow. Be the father of the fatherless, and the husband of the widow. Guide those who are perplexed; guard those that are tempted; and let all that love Thee, be as the sun when he goeth forth in his might. We ask it through the intercession of Him, who has taught us when we pray, to say, Our Father, &c.

SUNDAY EVENING.

O God, the heavens declare thy glory; the earth is full of thy riches; the universe is thy temple; thy presence fills immensity. It is thy pleasure to produce life, and to communicate happiness. From Thee we have derived all we are, and all we own; and in Thee we live, and move, and have our being continued. Thy good providence has determined the bounds of our habitation, and wisely administered all our affairs.

But above all we bless Thee for the exceeding riches of thy grace, in thy kindness towards us, by Christ Jesus. Thanks be unto God for his unspeakable gift: and for the unclouded revelation

of Him, in the word of truth. There we behold
His person and character; His grace and glory.
There we see Him, when rich, for our sakes, becoming poor; and dying that we may live: delivered for our offences, and raised again for our
justification. May we deeply feel our need of this
dispensation, in all its parts, and in all its influences; and with Peter exclaim, Lord, save—I
perish; and with the publican—God be merciful
to me a sinner.

Convince us of the pollution of sin, as well as
of its guilt, that we may not only have our fear
excited, but our aversion ; that with Job we may
see, that we are vile; and abhor ourselves, repenting in dust and ashes. May we feel the necessity of renovation, as well as forgiveness, in
order to our serving and enjoying Thee, in time
and eternity. O, Thou Holy God, who hast no
fellowship with iniquity, subdue in us the love of
sin; create in us a clean heart ; and renew in us
a right spirit

May we not be in the number of those who are
always learning, and never able to come to the
knowledge of the truth ; but may our hearts be
established with grace. May we never rest in a
mere system of doctrine, however scriptural, that
does not bring salvation, or teach us to deny ungodliness, and worldly lusts; and to live soberly, righteously, and godly, in the present world ; looking
for that blessed hope, and the glorious appearing
of the great God, and our Saviour Jesus Christ.
May we live in the spirit ; and may we walk in
the spirit : and instead of relying on our own convictions and resolutions, may we be strong in the
Lord, and in the power of His might.

In all our duties, conflicts, and trials, may his
grace be sufficient for us. To Him who gives rest
to the weary and heavy laden, may we repair in
all our spiritual distresses, in all our outward troubles, and in all the dissatisfactions experienced in

creature-enjoyments. From a world, where all is vanity and vexation of spirit, may we retreat to Him, who is full of grace and truth ; a friend that loveth at all times ; who is touched with the feeling of our infirmities ; and who is able to do for us exceeding abundantly, above all we can ask or think.

Prepare us for our final hour, and for all the scenes through which we have to pass in the remainder of our pilgrimage. May we know how to be abased, and how to abound. May we learn in whatsoever state we are, therewith to be content. May we stand complete in all the will of God.

Do us good by all thy dispensations ; and especially sanctify to us all the means of grace. We bless Thee that we have been favoured with another sabbath ; and have had opportunities of repairing to the sanctuary, to mingle our prayers and praises with the devotions of thy people, and to hear the words of eternal life. We grieve to think, that so much of the precious seed, sown by thy servants, should fall by the way side ; so much upon stony places ; and so much among thorns ; and that so little fruit is brought forth to perfection. May it appear that we have not received the grace of God in vain ; but that thy word in us, is like good seed sown in good ground, which springeth up and bringeth forth, in some an hundred fold, in some sixty, and in some thirty.

And suffer us not to confine our religion to extraordinary occasions ; but help us to acknowledge Thee in all our ways. May we never limit our devotion to particular seasons ; but be in the fear of the Lord all the day long. May we be godly, not only on the sabbath, but in the week ; not only in the house of God, but in our own. May our piety be, not a dress, but a habit ; not only a habit, but a nature, a life ; the life of God in the soul of man. And at last, by thy grace and gui-

14*

dance, may we enter that world, where there is no temple, but the glory of God and of the Lamb are the temple thereof.

But, O, how can we endure to see the destruction of our kindred? O Lord, let those that are united to us by so many tender ties, be precious in thy sight, and devoted to thy praise. Sanctify and succeed domestic devotion and instruction, discipline, and example ; and may our houses be nurseries for heaven, from which our churches, as the gardens of the Lord, shall be enriched with trees of righteousness, the planting of the Lord, that He may be glorified.

O, let none of those who are amiable, and moral, and possess so many attractions, like the hopeful youth in the gospel, fall short of heaven at last.

Where the conscience is tender, and the heart is soft, and the word alarms or delights, let not these promising appearances be blasted ; but bring forth judgment unto victory.

Bless all who are connected with us by religious ties. Save thy people and bless thine inheritance ; feed them also, and lift them up for ever.

Regard us as a nation. Inspire all ranks and degrees of men among us, with a love to that righteousness, which exalteth a nation ; and deliver us from that sin, which is a reproach to any people.

And as all mankind, of whatever country or condition, are our brethren, bless them with the same civil and religious privileges, which this highly favoured land enjoys. Let thy way be known on earth, thy saving health among all nations.

And may the grace of our Lord Jesus Christ, and the love of God, and the communion of the Holy Ghost, be with us all, now and for ever. Amen.

MONDAY MORNING.

O God, thy greatness is unsearchable ; but we rejoice to think, that thy love passeth knowledge. We have sinned against Thee, but Thou art ready to forgive. We have gone far astray from Thee ; but Thou art more than willing to admit our return. Thou hast even provided the way to accomplish it. Thou hast appointed and made known a Mediator, who has once suffered for sin, the just for the unjust, that He might bring us unto God. In Him we behold Thee reconciling the world unto thyself, not imputing their trespasses unto them. And in Him a multitude which no man can number, redeemed, justified, and renewed, are exulting, My soul shall be joyful in my God, for he hath clothed me with the garments of salvation, He hath covered me with the robe of righteousness, as a bridegroom decketh himself with ornaments, and as a bride adorneth herself with her jewels.

O, that it were thus with us ! O that we could ascertain our spiritual condition, and read our title clear to the inheritance of the saints in light. Praise waiteth for Thee, O God in Zion ; and we are longing to be able to adore Thee, as the strength of our souls, and our everlasting portion. Say to them that are of a fearful heart, Be strong, fear not. Him that cometh unto me, I will in no wise cast out ; whosoever will, let him come and take of the water of life, freely : O, say unto our souls, I am thy salvation.

And, O Lord, we hope that we are not concerned for our safety only ; we trust we not only wish to know that we have the grace of God in truth, but to feel a progression in the divine life ; to increase with all the increase of God. We wish to be qualified for our work ; to stand complete in the will of our heavenly Father ; and to adorn the doctrine of God our Saviour in all things.

Grant us, therefore, we pray Thee, more of the supply of the Spirit of Jesus Christ; to give more decision to our character; more vigour to our purposes; more elevation to our hopes; more fervour to our devotion; more constancy to our zeal, so that we may run and not be weary, and walk and not faint.

Thou dost not despise the day of small things, nor refuse to encourage a little strength; but Thou hast commanded us to grow in grace, and in the knowledge of our Lord and Saviour; and Thou hast said, To him that hath, shall be given; and hast promised, that the feeble among them shall be as David. Be it unto us according to thy word. Fulfil all the good pleasure of thy goodness, and the work of faith with power, that the name of our Lord Jesus Christ may be glorified in us, and we in Him. May we be examples of the religion we profess, the most impressive and attracting; may we have a testimony in the bosoms of those who observe us, that we are the seed which the Lord hath blessed; and may every thing around us say to them, Come with us, and we will do you good.

To Thee we desire to submit all our desires, and to Thee would we commit all our concerns, casting all our care upon Thee, conscious that Thou carest for us.   And

> Who so fit to choose our lot,
> Or regulate our ways—

as a Being who loved us, so as not to spare his own Son, who knows what is best for us in every circumstance, and is able to make all things work together for our good.

In every difficulty with which we are called to struggle, may we not only think of thy promises, but also call to remembrance, the years of the right hand of the Most High. We have often been brought low, and Thou hast helped us; and when we have been looking for nothing but darkness, at evening time it has been light. O, how does it betray our depravity, that after all thy kindness and care, after all the proofs of thy patience, power, and fidelity, we are yet so little capable of trusting in Thee. We would cry out with tears, Lord, we believe, help Thou our unbelief.

Do us good by all the dispensations of thy providence, especially those of an afflictive kind. And why should we consider them strange things, since Thou hast told us, that in the world we shall have tribulation, and that the same afflictions have been accomplished in all our brethren ? And why should we desire exemption from them ? Seeing they are founded in love, and intended for our profit. May we ever realize thy design by them, and see thine hand in them ; may we believe that Thou wilt be with us in trouble : and look forward with joy to that state, where it will be safe for us to be without sorrow, and God shall wipe away all tears from our eyes.

And if we have a portion in this world, keep us from making this world our portion. May we never look for that in the creature, which can only be found in the Creator ; nor for that on earth, which is only to be found in heaven. Among our caresses and indulgences, may we never lose the heart of a stranger, or forget that this is not our rest. May the streams of comfort lead us to the fountain of all good : and may we love and serve our Benefactor in all his benefits.

And thus may we know how to be abased, and how to abound ; and in every varying condition, display the principles and dispositions of those, who are born from above, and bound for glory.

And to the Father, the Word, and Holy Ghost, be ascribed all honour and praise, world without end. Amen.

O Thou, whose name alone is Jehovah. Thou art the Most High over all the earth ; and Thou hast set thy glory above the heavens. All thy works praise Thee, O Lord, and thy saints bless Thee. Thou art our father's God, and we will exalt Thee; Thou art our own God, and early will we seek Thee, for in thy favour is life.

Open Thou our lips, and our mouth shall show forth thy praise. Thou hast made us, and not we ourselves. Thine eye did see our substance, yet being imperfect, and in thy book all our members were written, which in continuance were fashioned, when as yet there were none of them. Thou hast taught us more than the beasts of the field, and made us wiser than the fowls of the air. There is a spirit in man, and the inspiration of the Almighty giveth him understanding. Thy providence has watched over us from the womb, supplied all our wants, arranged all our affairs, and determined the bounds of our habitation.

And, O, what reason have we to exclaim, the lines have fallen to us in pleasant places, yea, we have a goodly heritage. We live in a land of vision. How superior are our advantages to those of thine ancient people, the Jews. The sun of righteousness, which was below the horizon to them, has risen upon us, with healing in his wings ; and we are all the children of the day. Let us not, therefore, sleep, as do others ; but while we have the light, may we walk in the light, lest darkness come upon us.

May we ever be impressed with the conviction, that where much is given, much will be required : and that our greatest danger results from our distinguishing advantages—our sabbaths ; our sanctuaries ; the Scriptures of truth : the preaching of the gospel ; and all the events which have urged our attention to it.

What more could have been done for us, than Thou hast done? And yet how little fruit have we brought forth. How well do we deserve to be cut down as cumberers of the ground, and cast into the fire! Yet, O Lord spare us, at the intercession of thy Son, our Saviour; for His sake, renew our season of trial: and employ fresh means for our improvement; and accompany them with a divine power. Convince us of our sin and danger. Awaken in us the solemn inquiry, what must I do to be saved? And let not our concern, when awakened, lead us into any refuge of lies, or induce us to build on any false foundation; but may we believe on the Lord Jesus Christ, and find his rest to be glorious.

Produce in us that brokenness of heart, and that self-despair, which will render the faithful saying—worthy of all acceptation; and make the Saviour precious to us— as He is to all them that believe. May He be delightful to us in all His offices; may we love Him in His commands, as well as in His promises; may we wear His yoke, and carry His burden; and find His yoke easy, and His burden light. Make us in our views, principles, and dispositions, new creatures, may we shine in all the beauties of holiness; and reflect the praises of Him who hath called us out of darkness into His marvellous light. Explain to us thy secret which is with them that fear Thee; and show us thy covenant in its provisions and stability; and in every distress, may this be all our salvation, and all our desire.

With affections weaned from the world, and with evidences bright for heaven, all the days of our appointed time may we wait till our change comes: may we die, supported by the consolations of the gospel, and surrounded with the glory of God; and have an entrance ministered unto us abundantly, into the everlasting kingdom of our Lord and Saviour

Prepare us for our passage, as well as for our end. While we are here, may we fulfil the duties and bear with firmness, the trials of our respective stations; may we glorify our Father, who is in heaven; and serve our generation according to His will.

Continue thy goodness to us as a family. Remember our absent friends. Let thy ministers enjoy thy presence; and thy churches be filled with thy glory. Let this nation be under thy care, and ever prove the seat of learning and science; of civil and religious freedom; of social blessedness; and of gospel privileges; and be the source of usefulness to the ends of the earth.

May princes come out of Egypt. May Ethiopia stretch forth her hands unto God. And may all nations whom Thou hast made, come and worship before Thee.

For thine, O God, is the power; and thine shall be the glory, through our Lord and Saviour. Amen.

TUESDAY MORNING.

O LORD God of hosts, hear our prayer; give ear, O God of Jacob; behold, O God our shield, and look upon the face of thine Anointed.

It is in his dear and all-prevailing name we come. We have nothing of our own to plead; no works, no worthiness, no promises. We have all, like sheep, gone astray. We have been transgressors from the womb. We have knowingly opposed thine authority, and abused thy goodness. We have been ungrateful under thy indulgences; incorrigible under thy rebukes; and have improved none of our religious advantages. We stand before Thee condemned by our own consciences, as well as by thy word. Yet, in the way of thine appointment, Thou art waiting to be gracious: and hast said, that whatsoever we ask, believing in his name, we shall receive.

Through Him, display thyself, in our experience, as a God, pardoning iniquity, and subduing it. Justify us freely from all things; and sanctify us wholly, body, soul, and spirit. May we be thy workmanship, created in Christ Jesus, and prepared unto every good work. We groan within ourselves, longing, not only for deliverance from the wrath to come, but from the sin that dwelleth in us: and praying, not only for an interest in thy favour, but a participation of thy image.

If Thou hast begun the good work in us, carry it on unto the perfect day. Assure us of present assistance and final success, whatever difficulties or oppositions we meet with; that we may go on our way rejoicing, and be strong in the grace that is in Christ Jesus. If we feel little,—and, O, how little do we feel of the joys of thy salvation; uphold us by thy free Spirit; and enable us to persevere in the path of obedience, and in the use of the means which Thou hast appointed, assured that none of those shall be ever ashamed that wait for Thee. And should we walk in darkness and have no light, may we trust in the Lord, and stay upon our God—Yet suffer us to implore, that Thou wilt make thy face to shine upon us, and give us the full assurance of hope—which hope may we have, as an anchor of the soul, both sure and steadfast, in all the storms of life.

We bless Thee for all that is past. Unless the Lord had been our help, our souls had almost dwelt in silence: but when we said, My foot slippeth, thy mercy, O Lord, held us up. But we are still in the body, and in the wilderness; we need thine aid as much as ever; we have a growing sense of our ignorance, weakness, and danger—O, withdraw not thy presence, and take not thy Holy Spirit from us. Whether we are called to do thy will, or to bear it, may we feel that our

15

help is in the name of the Lord, who made heaven and earth. If our course conducts us through rough and trying scenes, say to us, Thy shoes shall be iron and brass, and as thy days, so shall thy strength be. In view of our encounter with our spiritual foes, clothe us with the whole armour of God; teach our hands to war, and our fingers to fight; and in the heat of action tell our hearts, that we shall be more than conquerors, through him that loved us.

And may we be concerned that the blessings we ask for ourselves, may be imparted to others. Teach us to love our neighbour as ourselves; and may we often examine our conditions in life, our offices, our talents, and our opportunities, to see how we may be serviceable in our day and generation.

Comfort those that mourn in Zion. Let all the afflicted find Thee a very present, and an all-sufficient help in the day of trouble. Provide for the poor and needy. Guide those that need instruction; and may integrity and uprightness preserve them while they wait upon Thee.

Sanctify and continue to us, and to our latest posterity after us, all our national blessings, civil and religious; and may our country, by its institutions, character, and usefulness, be a praise in the whole earth.

These are great blessings for such sinful creatures as we are, to ask—but Thou hast given us a name to plead, which is above every name. Behold—not our guilt, but that blood which cleanseth from all sin; not our unworthiness, but that righteousness with which Thou art well pleased. And accept us in the beloved. Our Father, &c. Amen.

O God, we are thine, and Thee we are bound to worship. We grieve to think how many there are who cast off fear, and restrain prayer before Thee. But, whatever be the determinatiun of others, our purpose, by thy grace, is taken; and as for us and our house, we will serve the Lord.

We would not live a day, or an hour, without Thee in the world, careless of thy favour, or regardless of thy glory. Impress us, individually and deeply, with a sense of thy omniscience ; that Thou art about our path, and our lying down, and acquainted with all our ways. Especially may we feel it, when we enter thy more immediate presence, and engage in the exercises of devotion. *Then* may we remember, that thine eyes are upon us ; that Thou requirest truth in the inward parts ; and that nothing can screen, even our motives and principles, from thy penetration.

Too little, we acknowledge, has this been our experience in former engagements : we have often been careless, where we should have been full of reverence ; we have been strangers to the power of godliness, while familiar with its forms. Thou hast been nigh in our mouths, but far from our reins. Much of our guilt has originated from our religious means and privileges ; from the low estimation in which we have holden them ; the little advantage they have contributed to our growth in grace, and in the knowledge of our Lord and Saviour.

Over all this may we sorrow after a godly sort, and may the sincerity of our repentance, be seen in our future alarm, and endeavours ; and especially in our self-renunciation, and dependence upon another—for when we are weak, then, and then alone, we are strong. May we every moment feel, how necessary it is to be more intimate with

Him who came, not only that we might nave life, but that we might have it more abundantly; whose grace is sufficient for us; whose spirit helps our infirmities, and can strengthen in us the things that remain, that are ready to die.

We bless Thee for an Advocate with the Father; for a propitiation of infinite value; for a fulness that filleth all in all. In Him, believing, may we rejoice with joy unspeakable, and full of glory. And may we know how to obtain relief for a burdened conscience, without feeling reconciled to our imperfections. May we abhor the thought of turning the grace of our God into lasciviousness, or sinning, that grace may abound. Because we are not under the law, but under grace, may we reckon ourselves to be dead indeed unto sin, but alive unto God, through Jesus Christ our Lord; by thy mercies, presenting our bodies a living sacrifice, and asking, What shall I render unto the Lord for all his benefits towards me? Through sanctification of the Spirit, and belief of the truth, may our affections be set on things that are above, and may this be the growing desire of our souls; O, that my feet were directed to keep thy precepts.

We would not seek great things for ourselves; but be content with such things as we have. Deliver us, O Lord, from the love of money, which is the root of all evil. May we value our substance, not as the medium of pride and luxury, but as affording us the means of support and usefulness; and may we guide our affairs with discretion, that we may owe no man any thing, and be able to give to him that needeth. Establish in us the royal law; may we love our neighbour as ourselves; and feel it, not only our duty, but our pleasure, as we have opportunity, to do good unto all men; especially unto them that are of the household of faith.

Bless all the churches of the faithful. Thou hast given them rest: may they walk in the fear of the Lord, and in the comforts of the Holy Ghost, and be edified and multiplied.

Display thy power and thy glory in the sanctuary. Be with thy servants, who show unto men the way of salvation. Make them wise to win souls; may they speak the things only that become sound doctrine; may they never expect success, as the result of their eloquence and reasonings, but from the excellency of the power that is of God.

May our highly favoured country be safe and flourishing, under the shadow of the Almighty.

Regard our friends and relations. Those that are absent from us, we commend to the care and direction of an ever-present God. Let those that know Thee not, be made wise unto salvation; let not those, who are endeared by so many ties, be separated from us for ever—How can we endure to see the destruction of our kindred?

Keep us in all places and circumstances. Hide us this night in the secret of thy pavilion, and in the morning encompass us with songs of deliverance.

And now, blessed be the Lord God of Israel, who only doeth wondrous things; and blessed be his glorious name for ever: and let the whole earth be filled with his glory. Amen and Amen.

WEDNESDAY MORNING.

O Thou, that hearest prayer, and inhabitest the praises of Israel; with Moses and Aaron among thy priests, and Samuel among them that call upon thy name, we would, this morning, exalt the Lord our God, and worship at his footstool, for He is holy.

We thank Thee, O Father, Lord of heaven and earth, for all thy inexpressible and inconceivable

15*

goodness to the children' of men, and of which, our own history and experience afford such numberless proofs. In thy works of creation, we read thy name, the Lord God Almighty ; in the dispensations of thy providence, we acknowledge Thee as the only wise God ; but in the gospel of thy grace, we behold Thee as the God of love ; and so loving the world, as to give thine only begotten Son, that whosoever believeth on Him should not perish, but have everlasting life. In Him Thou hast provided for our deliverance, from all the effects of sin ; for the justification of our persons, the sanctification of our natures, and our perseverance in the path of life. till we receive the end of our faith, the salvation of our souls.

We bless Thee, that, exposed as we are to the terrors of thy law, which we have so often transgressed, here we have a refuge from the storm ; and learn, that there is no condemnation to them that are in Christ Jesus. We bless Thee, that while we are compelled to exclaim, Unclean, unclean, here is an open fountain, the efficacy of which, cleanseth from all sin. We bless Thee, that while in us dwelleth no good thing. there is a fulness accessible to all, and incapable of reduction, from which we can receive, and grace for grace.

O Lord, we ask not for worldly riches or honours, but pray, that we may be blessed with all spiritual blessings, in heavenly places in Christ. We envy not those whom the multitude admire ; they will be cut down as the grass, and wither as the green herbs : but remember us, O Lord, with the favour Thou bearest unto thy people : look Thou upon us, and be merciful to us, as Thou usest to do unto those that fear thy name. They are happy—now : and are inviting and encouraging us, to taste and see, that the Lord is good. May a vital union be immediately established between Him and us—He the head, and we the members—He the vine, and we the branches—He the shepherd, and we the sheep of his pasture—He the chief corner stone, and we also as lively stones, built up a spiritual house, an habitation of God through the Spirit.

Let us not walk as other Gentiles, in the vanity of our minds, and having our understandings darkened; but may we estimate things according to the testimony of thy word, and feel a persuasion, that to obtain salvation by our Lord Jesus Christ, is a concern, in comparison with which, every other interest is a shadow, and a dream.

And, O Lord, save us from presumption. Keep us from suspending our attention to the things of eternity, and on a more convenient season, or any future period, which may never arrive; but reflecting upon the shortness and uncertainty of life, and knowing how frail we are, may we seek the Lord while He may be found, and call upon Him while He is near. May we immediately begin to live the life of the righteous, that we may die the death of the righteous, and that our last end may be like his.

And O, save us from the delusion of those who go far, but not far enough, in religion; who are convinced, but not converted; who have another heart, but not a new one; and who, with all their light, and zeal, and confidence, have not the spirit of Christ, and therefore are none of his. May we judge of our christianity, not only by our dependence upon Christ, but our love to Christ, and our conformity to Christ: and know that He dwelleth in us, and we in Him, because He hath given us of his spirit.

May our religion not only be real, but progressive; may we not only hold on our way, but wax stronger and stronger. May we live, and may we walk, in the spirit. May we profit by every correction, and be injured by no indulgence.

Accept of our personal and combined acknowledgments, that Thou hast been our salvation in the night watches ; and that we are not only living to praise Thee this morning, but have all things richly to enjoy.

Bless the word which we have been reading. Let not the cares of this life, or the deceitfulness of sin, render it unfruitful. May thy word abide in us, and operate. May it attend us in all the businesses of the day, that we may not sin against Thee ; and that whether we eat or drink, or whatever we do, we may do all to the glory of God—

To whom be glory in the church, by Christ Jesus, throughout all ages, world without end. Amen.

WEDNESDAY EVENING.

O Thou, that inhabitest eternity, and with whom a thousand years are as one day. If we were angels, we should veil our faces as we approach Thee, and exclaim, holy, holy, holy, is the Lord of Hosts, the whole earth is full of His glory. With what emotions then should we enter thy presence, who are but sinful dust and ashes. Give us grace, whereby we may serve Thee acceptably, with reverence and godly fear.

May we always combine thy majesty with thy mercy, that we may not trifle before Thee, or incur the reproach of the hypocrite, and the formalist, who draw nigh unto Thee with their mouth, and honour Thee with their lips, while their heart is far from Thee. And may we always connect thy goodness with thy greatness, that we may draw near in full assurance of faith. May our consciences, at this moment, believe that Thou art good, and ready to forgive, and plenteous in mercy to all that call upon Thee.

And do Thou have mercy upon us, O God, according to thy loving kindness, according to the multitude of thy tender mercies. Thou art under no obligation to save us; we lie, as guilty, at thy sovereign disposal. Thou hast a right to exercise thy mercy in thy own way; and Thou hast sent thy own Son into the world, not to condemn the world, but that the world through *Him*, might be saved. Thou hast made Him to be sin for us, who knew no sin, that we might be made the righteousness of God in Him. We bow O, God, to thine appointment; and gratefully comply with thy command, for this is thy commandment, that we believe on the name of thy Son Jesus Christ our Lord. We would flee to no other refuge; we would wash in no other fountain; we would build on no other foundation; we would receive from no other fulness.

May the life that we henceforth shall live in the flesh, be by the faith of Him, who loved us, and gave Himself for us. In His name may we rejoice all the day, and in His righteousness be exalted.

May we feel a growing conformity to the image of thy Son, and like Him learn obedience by the things we suffer. May the law of the spirit of life in Christ Jesus, make us free from the law of sin and death.

In all our dealings with all our fellow-creatures, may we do justly; in all cases requiring relief and compassion, may we show that we love mercy: and with regard to all the dispensations of thy providence and grace, may we walk humbly with our God.

May we be strong, and of good courage, to follow our convictions, regardless of the opinions of others; and to obey God, rather than man. Having obtained the knowledge of thy will, from thy word, may we go forth and be steadfast, unmoveable, always abounding in the work of the Lord. And let us not be slothful, but followers of them, who through faith and patience inherit the promises.

O, how great is the goodness, which in thy promises and in thy kingdom, Thou hast laid up for them that fear Thee! Number us with them; and enable us to say, Thou hast given me the heritage of them that fear thy name. This assurance O, God, we want, to animate us in duty; to support us in our trials—for they are many; and to raise us above the fear of death and the dread of eternity. For we know that we are not to live here always, nor to live here long. Dangers surround us; within us are sown the seeds of disease; our breath is in our nostrils; and there is but a step between us and the grave. How soon is another day gone! and how solemnly does it remind us, That all our days are as a shadow! Great God, so teach us to number our days, that we may apply our hearts unto wisdom. Amidst all the uncertainties of time, may we know in ourselves, that in heaven we have a better and an enduring substance: when the earthly house of this tabernacle is dissolving, may we see prepared to receive us, a building of God, an house not made with hands, eternal in the heavens.

We feel our weakness, and our wants. We depend on all the elements for our subsistence, and there is no creature, but can be our help or our hurt. We need day by day, our supplies of food. We labour for a few hours, and we feel ourselves exhausted. We would not say to Him, that made us, why hast Thou made me thus; but bless Thee for the promise we have, that when we lie down, Thou wilt make us dwell in safety; and for a state, where we shall feel no languor, need no rest; where there shall be no night; and they need no candle, neither light of the sun; for the Lord God giveth them light, and they shall reign for ever and ever. We ask it in the name, and for the sake of our adorable Redeemer. Amen.

THURSDAY MORNING.

O THOU, who wast, and art, and art to come, the Almighty. Thou art the Creator of all the ends of the earth. Thou art *our* Maker, and not only the framer of our bodies, but the former of our souls. May we remember that Thou madest us upright, but that we have sought out many inventions. Let us not forget what we *now* are—what we deserve—and what we want.

Nor let us be ignorant of the provisions, of thy mercy and grace; nor of Him, in whom it hath pleased Thee, that all fulness should dwell. In all our outward troubles, and in all our spiritual distress, He is the hope and the consolation of Israel. May we receive the record, that Thou hast given to us eternal life, and that this life is in thy Son. To Him may we always look for relief, and to Him *only;* persuaded that there is none other name given under heaven and among men, whereby we must be saved. May we be equally convinced of the guilt and the pollution of sin; may we alike feel our need of the Prince and the Saviour, and implore of Him repentance, as well as forgiveness. May we love holiness, and be pure in heart. O, that our feet were directed to keep thy statutes. O, that we had the same mind in us, which was also in Christ Jesus; and were enabled to tread in His steps, who has gone before us in every path of duty and trial.

As long as we are in the world, keep us from the evil; and may we be always alive and awake to discharge every obligation, resulting from our condition in life, and the particular events of thy providence.

We would not be at our own disposal; but rejoice to think, we are under the care of one, who is too wise to err, and too kind to injure. However ignorant of the future, we will trust and not be afraid; and begin even in this vale of tears, the song we hope for ever to sing ; Marvellous are thy works, Lord God Almighty, just and true are all thy ways, O Thou King of saints.

Thou hast been pleased again to renew our time, and our strength, and our comforts ; help us to renew our purposes and resolutions, to obey and serve Thee. In all our ways, may we this day acknowledge Thee, and do Thou direct our paths. Let thy presence go with us, and thy free spirit uphold us.

May we prove a stumbling block to none, by our temper or conduct ; but recommend and endear the religion we profess to all around us. May we decline no opportunity of usefulness, that our circumstances may present ; may we not withhold good, from him to whom it is due, when it is in the power of our hand to do it. May we dread the sentence, Whoso stoppeth his ears at the cry of the poor, he also shall cry himself, and not be heard. May we therefore be merciful ; ready to communicate ; feeling the grace of our Lord Jesus Christ, who, when rich, for our sakes became poor, that we through his poverty, might be rich.

Let those who are advanced in years, be anxious to bring forth fruit in old age. Let those who are in the midst of life, abide with God in their calling ; and while they are not slothful in business, may they be fervent in spirit, serving the Lord. And O, preserve the young from the snares and temptations of youth. May they be soberminded. If sinners entice them, let them not consent. With the infidel, and the vicious, and the despiser of the sabbath, may they not go, lest they learn of their ways, and get a snare to their souls. Let them say, I am a companion of all them that fear Thee ; and choose that good part, which shall not be taken away from them.

Bless us as a nation, in all the dependencies, and interests of the country : in all its civil and sacrd institutions : let glory dwell in our land, and upon all the glory, may there be a defence.

We rejoice that Thou wilt have all men to be saved, and come to the knowledge of the truth ; and that Jesus Christ gave himself a ransom for all, to be testified in due time.

Call in the Jews with the fulness of the Gentiles. Say to the north, give up, and to the south, keep not back ; bring my sons from far, and my daughters from the ends of the earth. Bless all those who by their exertions and sacrifices, are proving the sincerity of their prayers for the spread of the Redeemer's cause ; and let many run to and fro, and knowledge be increased, till all shall know Thee, from the least even to the greatest.

Our Father, &c. Amen.

THURSDAY EVENING.

Give ear to our words, O Lord ; consider our meditation ; and enable us to approach Thee, with becoming conceptions of thy nature, relations, and designs.

Thou inhabitest eternity ; but our age is nothing before Thee. Thou dwellest in the heaven of heavens, and this cannot contain Thee ; but we dwell in houses of clay, whose foundation is in the dust. Thy power is Almighty, but we are crushed before the moth. Thy understanding is infinite, but we know nothing, as we ought to know. Thou art of purer eyes than to behold evil, and canst not look upon iniquity : but we are vile—What shall we answer Thee ? We cannot answer Thee for one of a thousand of our iniquities. And had we listened to the language of our guilty consciences alone, we could not have entered thy sacred presence.

But Thou hast called us to thy footstool; Thou hast shown us a new and living way into the holiest, by the blood of Jesus; and we have boldness, and access with confidence, by the faith of Him. We, therefore, draw nigh, in full assurance of faith; believing that we are as welcome as we are unworthy; and that the blessings we are come to implore, are as free, as they are great and numberless. O, receive us graciously. Be merciful to our unrighteousness. Adopt us into the household of faith; and say to our souls, I am thy salvation.

We have often feared that we have no part nor lot in the matter; and that our heart is not right in the sight of God. We have often questioned whether we know any thing of the new creature; whether we have ever excercised repentance towards God, and faith towards our Lord Jesus Christ. And what, if after all our advantages, we should perish; and after all our profession, have a name only that we live, while we are dead. O Lord, decide the doubtful point; and bear witness with our spirits that we are the children of God.

We would not deceive ourselves in a business of everlasting moment: but if we are in a *state* of grace, enable us to know it, for our own comfort and the glory of thy great name.

And, O Lord, we pray that we may *grow* in grace. If we have the reality of religion, how far are our works from being found perfect before God. Strengthen in us the things that remain, that be ready to die; and help us to reach after the higher attainments and privileges of the divine life, and not always live at this poor dying rate. May we be followers of God as dear children, and feel it the joy of our lives, to be holy, as Thou art holy; and merciful, as Thou art merciful. May thine eye be more to us, than the inspection of all fellow-creatures; and thy approbation, be dearer, than the applause of a thousand worlds.

May no grace of the spirit be wanting in us; may no duty of our calling be neglected, or carelessly performed. May our faith, be a strong faith; our hope, a lively hope; our charity, a fervent charity; our conversation, a conversation becoming the gospel of Christ. May we stand complete in all the will of God; and may our light so shine before men, that they may see our good works, and glorify our Father, who is in heaven.

May we long to serve our generation according to thy will: may wisdom select and regulate our means; and a blameless and lovely consistency of character, give weight to our endeavours. And may all our works begin, continue, and end in Thee. On Thee may we depend for light to know, and disposition to choose, and strength to perform, and submission to suffer, and patience to wait.

And when we have done all, may we acknowledge that we are unprofitable servants, and confess that we deserve condemnation for the defects of our obedience, rather than a reward for its excellency. And looking off from our duties, as well as our sins, to find a foundation for our hope, may we rejoice in Christ Jesus, and have no confidence in the flesh. And may our persons and services, be accepted in the Beloved—To whom be glory and dominion, for ever and ever. Amen.

FRIDAY MORNING.

WE would lift up our hearts, with our hands, unto God in the heavens. Behold, before Thee, a company of highly indulged, but sinful beings: for if we say, we have no sin, we deceive ourselves, and the truth is not in us. None of our fellow-creatures know half so much of our depravity, as we ourselves know: and our knowledge is ignorance, compared with thy wisdom.

Thou readest the heart. Thou viewest actions in their principles and motives. Thou seest more defilement in our duties, than we ever saw in any of our sins, in thy sight the heavens are not clean; and Thou chargest thine angels with folly. And if we hate ourselves, and are ready to flee from ourselves, because of our abominations, how wonderful is it that Thou dost not abhor us, and swear in thy wrath, that we shall not enter into thy rest.

But be astonished, O heavens, and wonder, O earth! instead of such a deserved exclusion, Thou hast even devised means, that they who are banished be not finally expelled from Thee; means the most astonishing and glorious, and which the angels desire to look into. For Thou hast so loved the world, as to give thine only begotten Son, that whosoever believeth on Him, should not perish, but have everlasting life. In Him mercy and truth meet together; righteousness and peace kiss each other; and thy honour is not only secured, but prominently displayed, even in our escape from thine own threatenings. In Him the enslaved can find redemption; the guilty pardon; the unholy renovation. In Him is everlasting strength for the weak, and unsearchable riches for the needy; in Him we find all the treasures of wisdom and knowledge for the ignorant—in Him all fulness dwells.

We bless Thee for the provision, which thy infinite goodness has made for our everlasting welfare; and for the gospel of our salvation, which makes it known; and which not only reveals it to our view, but proposes it to our hope, and presses it upon our acceptance.

O Lord, at thy gracious call, we hear; we look; we come; we apply; we receive. We not only submit to the scheme of mercy, but we acquiesce in it: we glory in the cross of our Lord Jesus Christ; we joy in God through our Lord Jesus Christ, by whom we have now received the atonement. We bless Thee, that in this grace we *stand:* Thou hast rendered the blessings as secure as they are glorious; and we are persuaded, that neither death, nor life, nor angels, nor principalities, nor powers, nor things present, nor things to come, nor height, nor depth, nor any other creature, shall be able to separate us from the love of God, which is in Christ Jesus our Lord.

Yea, for ever blessed be thy name, Thou hast not only provided for our safety, but our prosperity. Thou hast not only promised that the righteous shall hold on their way, but wax stronger and stronger. Thou dost not despise the day of small things; but Thou givest more grace; and hast commanded us to ask and receive, that our joy may be full.

And now, O Lord, what shall we render for all thy benefits towards us? We can never discharge the obligations we are under—but we pray that we may be sensible of them; and though we can make no adequate returns, may we make suitable ones: and ever ask from the heart, as well as with the lip, Lord what wilt Thou have me to do?

And may we show forth thy praise. May we speak well of thy name. May we be concerned to bring others to love and serve Thee; and to share with us, in all the good which Thou hast spoken concerning Israel.

O, let our children be thy children; our friends thy friends; our servants thy servants.

May our neighbours, and our enemies too, be visited with thy salvation.

Dwell in our families. Let thy goings be seen in our sanctuaries. Let the people praise Thee, O God, yea let all the people praise Thee. Let the whole earth be filled with thy glory.

Bless the Lord, ye His angels, that excel in strength, that do His commandments, hearkening unto the voice of His word. Bless ye the Lord, all ye His hosts, ye ministers of His that do His plea
15*

sure.　Bless the Lord all His works, in all places of His dominion.　Bless the Lord, O my soul Amen and Amen.

FRIDAY EVENING.

AGAIN, O Lord of all, we desire to bow in thy presence.　May we approach Thee with all the encouragements that can be derived from thy character, as the God of love.　We are not left to feel after Thee in the darkness of nature ; or to worship Thee as the unknown God.　We cannot find Thee out unto perfection ; but we know that Thou art good and ready to forgive, and plenteous in mercy unto all them that call upon Thee.

For Thou hast given us thy word, which Thou hast magnified above all thy name : and Thou hast favoured us with the gospel, so that on us who were sitting in darkness, and the shadow of death, has risen a great light, the light of life.

But we acknowledge, how ungratefully we have received the benefit, and how little we have improved our privileges, to the purposes for which they have been given.　We have made light of these things, though angels desire to look into them ; we have neglected the great salvation : we have turned away from Him that speaketh from heaven.　And all that Thou hast kindly employed, to enforce the messages of thy word, we have disregarded : for we have contemned the examples of the good, the admonitions of friendship, the reproaches of conscience, the rebukes of thy providence, and the strivings of thy Holy Spirit ; and well do we deserve, that the kingdom of God should be taken away from us.　O, let us not confess our sins without feeling and lamenting them ; but with a broken heart and a contrite spirit, with self-abhorrence, self-condemnation, and self-despair.

And under a deep impression of 'our guilt, may
we seek, alone, from Him who is the hope and the
consolation of Israel. Viewing Him as dying for
the ungodly, may we believe in His name May
we know that He bore our sins in His body on
the tree, and that by His stripes we are healed.
And may we find in Him, not only righteousness
but strength. May He impart to us, not only forgiveness of sins, but repentance unto life. May
we never separate in our regards what He has
joined together in the Scriptures ; or suppose that
we are justified by His blood, unless we are sanctified by His Spirit.

We believe we can never be happy in sin, and
we do not desire it : Lord, deliver us from it, and
lead us in the way everlasting. Make us holy like
thyself, that we may be made happy in thyself.
We are naturally disqualified for all communion
with a holy God ; work in us to will and to do of
thy good pleasure ; produce in us those principles
and dispositions, which will attach us to thyself as
our exceeding joy ; and enable us to say, whom
have I in heaven but Thee, and there is none upon
earth that I desire beside Thee.

Under all our ignorance, weakness, fears, and
depressions, may thy Spirit help our infirmities,
with supplies of wisdom, strength, and comfort.

May we faithfully study our character, and be
always willing to come to the light, that if evil.
our deeds may be reproved. May we peculiarly
observe ourselves, under the operation of those
events which are designed to try us ; that we may
judge of the reality and degree of our grace. May
we often review life, and see how we have at any
time been ensnared, or overcome, that we may, in
future, become more wise and circumspect. And
while we watch, may we also pray, lest we enter
into temptation. May we never trust in our own
hearts, or depend upon any past experience, or
present resolution ; but be strong in the grace that
is in Christ Jesus.

Thus far Thou hast helped us. Hitherto our enemies have not triumphed over us. And though we have seen many decline from their profession we hope, if Thou wert to ask, Will ye also go away? We should be able to say, with more conviction and affection than ever, Lord, to whom should we go but unto Thee, Thou hast the words of eternal life. Thou hast been with us in trouble; and many a shadow of death hast Thou turned into the morning. We can now discern thy wisdom and kindness, in dispensations, which once perplexed and dismayed us: and what we know not now, we shall know hereafter.

Never leave us nor forsake us; but support and lead us through all these dark and sorrowful regions: and enable us with confidence to hail the hour, when our sun shall no more go down, nor our moon withdraw herself; for God shall be our everlasting light, and the days of our mourning shall be ended.

We implore it through the intercession of Him who gave himself for our sins, that he might deliver us from this present evil world, according to the will of God and our Father; to whom be glory for ever and ever. Amen.

SATURDAY MORNING

Let not the Lord be angry, while we, who are but dust and ashes, take upon us to speak unto the living God. Pardon our unworthiness; help our infirmities; and hearken unto the voice of our cry, our King and our God, for unto Thee will we pray.

Thou art good to all; and we have largely shared with thy creatures, the bounties of thy providence: but O, remember us with the favour Thou bearest unto thy people. We bless Thee for characterizing them; and we bless Thee that Thou hast placed the distinction in no high and discouraging attainments : for Thou takest pleasure in them that *fear* Thee ; in them that *hope* in thy mercy. May these dispositions be found in each of us. May we dread thine anger, revere thy perfections, stand in awe of thy majesty, and tremble at thy word. And hide not thy mercy from us : enable us to trust in it, and to plead it ; and, with a broken heart and a contrite spirit, may we earnestly cry, God be merciful to me a sinner. In how many ways do we need the exercise of it ; but Thou art rich in mercy ; and abundant in mercy ; and delightest in mercy.

We are all so many proofs of it : because thy compassions fail not—we are not consumed. Our forfeited lives have not only been continued, but crowned with thy goodness. Thou hast provided for our souls as well as for our bodies ; and we hear a thousand voices inviting us to the feast, and saying, Come, for all things are now ready. Thanks be unto God, for his unspeakable gift : we bless Thee for a Saviour, who died for our sins, and rose again for our justification, and is now ascended far above all heavens that He might fill all things.

May we be made the partakers of Christ, and not only of his righteousness—but of his spirit : that we may be—not only pardoned but renewed ; and not only have a title to heaven, but a meetness for it. No longer alienated from the life of God, may our meditations of Thee be sweet, and may we draw near to Thee as to our exceeding joy. May we confide in thy promises, and rely on thy constant protection and care. May we be devoted to thy service, and find it perfect freedom. May we love obedience ; may thy law be within our heart.

May thy cause be dear to our souls. We pray that thy word may have free course and be glorified. Let thy church not only be multiplied in number, but increased in knowledge, and sanctity, and peace, and concord, and joy ; so that it may be a praise in the whole earth. Let the light of the moon be as the light of the sun, and the light of the sun be seven-fold, as the light of seven days. For brass, bring gold; and for iron, silver; and wood, brass; and for stones, iron.

Thou dost not stand in need of us: but in thy condescension and wisdom, Thou art pleased to make use of means; and we desire the honour and happiness of being instruments in thy hand. Lord, what wilt Thou have us to do? We would value every day afforded us, as a new period of usefulness. May we be anxious to accomplish all we can, to alleviate human wo, and to advance the temporal and spiritual welfare of all around us.

And may we be not only zealous, but persevering. May we never be discouraged. May we never grow weary in well-doing.

While many go back after following the Saviour, may we cleave to Him with purpose of heart; and at last, hear Him say, Ye are they who have continued with me in my temptation, and I appoint unto you a kingdom, as my Father also hath appointed unto me.

We would not forget the afflicted. Hear the sighing of the needy; cause the widow's heart to sing for joy; and in Thee may the fatherless find mercy. Remove indisposition and disease from those who are exercised thereby; or assure them of that world where the inhabitant no more says, I am sick.

Be with us all through the changing scenes of life, and at the hour of dissolution; when heart and flesh fail—and fail they soon will—be Thou the strength of our heart, and our portion for ever. If death should be sudden, let it not find us unprepared; if it should be awful in the apprehension, let it be safe in the result; and if we cannot depart in triumph, may we expire in humble hope saying with numbers before us,

> A guilty weak and helpless worm,
>   On thy kind arm I fall;
> Be thou my strength and righteousness,
>   My Jesus and my all.

And through eternal ages, may it be our privi
lege to unite with those, who are singing, Unto Him
that loved us, and washed us from our sins in his
own blood, and hath made us kings and priests unto
God, and to his Father, be glory and dominion, for
ever and ever. Amen.

SATURDAY EVENING.

O LORD God of Hosts ; Thou hast established
thy throne in the heavens, and thy kingdom ruleth
over all. It is a source of joy to our minds, and of
encouragement to our hopes, that the Lord God
Omnipotent reigneth. In thy greatness, we see
thy all-sufficiency to accomplish all that Thou hast
promised ; to confer upon us all we need ; and to
do for us exceeding abundantly, above all we can
ask or think.

It is, therefore, good for us to draw near to Thee ;
and it is our mercy to know, that we can approach
Thee with confidence of acceptance and success,
founded not on any worthiness or works of our own,
but on thy own grace, in the appointment of a
Mediator, who has put away sin by the sacrifice of
Himself, and opened a new and living way, into
the holiest of all, by his own blood.

We have no other name to plead ; and we need
no other. Behold, O God, our shield, and look
upon the face of thine Anointed : and for his sake
who groaned in the garden and died upon the cross
and now appears in thy presence for us, pardon our
iniquity for it is great ; cleanse us from all unrighteousness ; deliver us from the power of darkness ; and translate us into the kingdom of thy
dear Son.

May we no longer be strangers and foreigners,
but fellow-citizens with the saints, and of the
household of God : and because we are sons, send

forth the spirit of thy Son into our hearts, crying Abba, Father. May our intercourse with Thee, be free and delightful, and constant ; and not on peculiar occasions only, but in every thing, by prayer and supplication, with thanksgiving, may we make known our requests unto Thee. May we live in thy presence.

May we walk with God—and walk humbly with God; sensible of our deficiencies and desert ; admiring thy condescension and patience ; and bowing to all thy dispensations, without murmuring or repining.

May we walk circumspectly, not as fools, but as wise, redeeming the time. May we be zealous in the discharge of all those duties, the performance of which, depends on a season so fleeting and precarious. May we consider one another, and provoke one another to love and to good works ; not forsaking the assembling of ourselves together, as the manner of some is ; but exhorting one another, and so much the more—as we see the day approaching.

Enable us to realize the universality and perfection of thy agency, in all our affairs ; and since all thy ways are mercy and truth, may we learn in whatsoever state we are, therewith to be content ; yea in every thing may we give thanks.

May we not only submit to our trials, but be grateful for them. They are designed for our profit, that we may be partakers of thy holiness. They evince a care of which we are unworthy, and which we have never properly repaid. Lord, what is man, that Thou shouldst magnify him ? that Thou shouldst set thy heart upon him ? that Thou shouldst visit him every morning, and chaster him every moment ? So impatient, and wayward, and foolish, have we been under thy hand, that we have forfeited all claim to the rod, and deserve to be stricken no more. It would be just in Thee to say, They are joined to idols, let them alone. But

O Lord, abandon us not to ourselves ; treat us not with neglect. Employ whatever means are necessary to save and sanctify our souls. Try us as Thou pleasest ; only, while we are chastened of the Lord, let us not be condemned with the wicked.

Humble us under a review of our depravity, through another day, and another week, which is now hastening to join the days and weeks before the flood. Who can understand his errors? In many things we all offend. Hide thy face from our sins. Heal our backslidings, and receive us graciously.

On the coming day, let thy good Spirit lead us to thy holy hill, and to thy tabernacle. May we go unto the altar of God as to our exceeding joy, and taste the blessedness of those that dwell in thy house, and are still praising Thee. Teach us to value properly, the means of grace, and be concerned to derive from them, the benefit they are designed to afford. May we remember our accountableness for them. May we remember, that they never leave us as they find us ; but always prove the savour of life unto life, or of death unto death.

Let not our attendance add to our sin and condemnation. Let us not sing without devotion, pray without desire, and hear in vain ; but be found in the number of those, who know the joyful sound, and walk in the fear of the Lord, and in the comforts of the Holy Ghost.

And may those who will not be able to hear the word, hear the rod, and hear it saying, As many as I love, I rebuke and chasten. Let meditation, and reading, and pious conversation, and above all, thy special presence, be substitutes for public ordinances. Thus send portions to those for whom nothing is prepared, and let them that tarry at home, divide the spoil. And have mercy upon all men, as we implore it through the mediation

16

of the ever blessed Redeemer, in whose words we address Thee—Our Father, who art in heaven, hallowed be thy name, thy kingdom come, thy will be done on earth, as it is in heaven, give us this day our daily bread, and forgive us our trespasses as we forgive those that trespass against us. and lead us not into temptation, but deliver us from evil, for thine is the kingdom, the power and the glory, for ever. Amen.

FORMS OF PRAYER, &c

CHRISTMAS DAY.

MORNING.

O GOD, Thou art worthy of universal and ever-lasting adoration. Thy nature is incomprehensible; thy perfections are infinite: and thy ways are past finding out. Thou art the Creator and upholder of all things. And all thy works praise Thee, O Lord, and thy saints bless Thee. All our lives have been full of thy undeserved goodness.

But we are called this morning, to behold the exceeding riches of thy grace, in thy kindness towards us, by Christ Jesus. Herein is love; not that we loved God, but that He loved us, and sent his Son to be the propitiation for our sins.

May we contemplate this matchless event, with all those views and affections which its importance demands. May those who observe the day, observe it unto the Lord. May our festivity, becoming the occasion, be harmless and holy. Let us not disgrace the season, by reviving those works of the devil, which the Son of God was manifested to destroy, nor rest satisfied with the mere remembrance of his advent, as founded in truth, and attended with wonders; but inquire, for what end He was born, and for what cause He came into the world. And since we are informed, that He came to seek and to save that which was lost, and suffered, the just for the unjust, that He might bring us unto God; may we deem the report no only a faithful saying, but worthy of all acceptation: and may it be in us as a well of water, springing up into everlasting life.

May none of us disregard Him, from ignorance, worldly-mindedness, presumption, self-righteousness, or despondency. As our Prophet, may we repair to his feet for instruction. May we look to his sacrifice, and find relief for our burdened consciences. May we acknowledge his authority, and obey his commands. In all our approaches to Thee, may we make mention of his righteousness only, and in his strength, go forth into all the duties and trials of life.

May we never feel miserable, even in a vale of tears, while we think of the consolation of Israel but rejoice in Him, with joy unspeakable and full of glory.

Reflecting upon his grace in becoming poor, that we through his poverty might be rich; may all selfishness, and uncharitableness, be extirpated from our hearts; may we love one another, as he has loved us; and may we delight to go about doing good.

May no coldness, no indifference, ever approach our spirits, whenever we are engaged in serving a master who has all the claims of a benefactor; yea, who died for us, and rose again.

To Him may we consecrate all our faculties and possessions; and, on our time and our substance, our souls and our bodies, may there be inscribed holiness unto the Lord. May we grieve to hear his name blasphemed, and weep to see his laws transgressed.

May his cause lie near our hearts; and may we long for the time, when He shall be known and adored, from the rising of the sun to the going down of the same; when to Him shall every knee bow, and every tongue confess; and the glad tidings of great joy shall be to all people—Unto *you* is born a Saviour. which is Christ the Lord.

Through his mediation we address Thee ; and in his words we conclude our imperfect supplications. Our Father, &c.

——————

CHRISTMAS DAY.

EVENING.

Though Thou art exalted above all blessing and praise ; yet, O God, we love to explore thy ways, to admire thy works, and to adore thy perfections. Thy understanding is infinite, thy power is Almighty, thy mercy endureth for ever. Thy goodness transcends all our conceptions, as far as the heavens are higher than the earth.

We call on our souls, and each other, this evening, to praise and magnify thy holy name. We bless Thee for our creation, and the degree we hold in the rank of being. We bless Thee for our preservation, and for all the supplies which have rendered life supportable ; and all the indulgences, which have rendered it comfortable. But above all, we thank Thee for thine unspeakable gift. For Thou hast surpassed all thy works, and crowned all thy benefits, by remembering us in our low estate, and laying help on one that is mighty.

And we have again heard the intelligence, that God so loved the world, that He gave his only begotten Son, that whosoever believeth on Him, should not perish, but have everlasting life. Convince us of our need of this dispensation of mercy and grace ; and may we acquiesce in it, not with coldness of assent, but with gladness of heart. May we exclaim with the angels—Glory to God in the highest, on earth peace, good will towards men ; and with the multitude of disciples, shout— Hosanna, blessed is He that cometh in the name of the Lord

16*

Though the world knew Him not, and his own received Him not, and He is still despised and rejected of men; may we receive Him as all our salvation, and all our desire.

May we rejoice to view Him, in a nature, which leads Him to call us brethren; in which, as our example, He can go before us, in the duties of obedience and submission; in which, He can sympathize with us, in all our wo—and in which, He has suffered for sins, the just for the unjust, that He might bring us unto God.

May we look to Him for all we want, and live a life of faith upon his fulness. In Him may we know that we have redemption through his blood; that we have righteousness and strength; that we have all the treasures of wisdom and knowledge.

May we connect with his work *for* us in the flesh, his work *in* us by the Spirit. While we are reconciled by his death, may we be saved by his life; and remember that his name is Jesus, because he saves his people from their sins.

And as He came not only that we might have life, but have it more abundantly, may our expectations be large, and our desires importunate; may He dwell in our hearts by faith, that we being rooted and grounded in love, may be able to comprehend with all saints, what is the height, and depth, and breadth, and length, and know the love of Christ, which passeth knowledge, and be filled with all the fulness of God.

Once in the end of the world hath He appeared, to put away sin by the sacrifice of Himself; and unto them that look for Him will He appear a second time, without sin unto salvation. O, prepare us for that solemn day. May we believe in Him as a Saviour, before we meet Him as a Judge: that when the tribes of the earth shall wail because of Him, we may lift up our heads with joy, knowing that our redemption draweth nigh; and say with the church, Lo! this is our

God, we have waited for Him, He will save us:
this is the Lord, we waited for Him we will rejoice and be glad in his salvation.

Make thy ministers wise, and zealous, and successful, in the dispensation of thy word; and let
signs and wonders be done, in the name of thy
holy child Jesus.

We are a sinful people, but Thou hast not dealt
with us after our desert; and Thou hast not left us
without witness; Thou hast, in the midst of us, a
people for thy name; and we pray, that our beloved country, may be a growing part of the empire of the Prince of Peace.

May the root of Jesse stand for an ensign to the
people; to it may the Gentiles seek; and let his
rest be glorious. May he come down like rain
upon the mown grass, as showers that water the
earth. In his days may the righteous flourish, and
abundance of peace, so long as the moon endureth.
Let all nations be blessed in Him; all generations
call Him blessed.

And blessed be his glorious name for ever, and
let the whole earth be filled with his glory. Amen.

LAST EVENING OF THE OLD YEAR.

O God, Thou hast been our refuge and dwelling
place in all generations; before the mountains
were brought forth, or ever Thou hadst formed
the earth and the world, even from everlasting to
everlasting, Thou art God   And a thousand years
in thy sight, are but as yesterday when it is past,
and as a watch in the night. But as for man, his
days are as grass; as a flower of the field so he
flourisheth; for the wind passeth over it, and it is
gone, and the place thereof knoweth it no more.

We appear before Thee, to close in thy presence, another of the revolutions of our fleeting

existence : earnestly praying, that the season may
not pass away, without suitable and serious reflections.   O, let us not imagine—in spite of Scripture, and observation, and reason, and feeling, that
we have many of these periods left to notice ; but
say with Job, when a few years are come, I shall
go the way whence I shall not return.—It may be
only a few months, or weeks, or days,—or hours,—
for we know not at what *hour* the Son of man
cometh.   But we know that our life is a vapour,
that appeareth for a little time, and then vanisheth
away ; we know the frailty of our frame : and the
numberless diseases and disasters to which we are
exposed—so teach us to number our days, that we
may apply our hearts unto wisdom.

What numbers of our fellow-creatures, and many
of them much more likely to have continued than
their survivors, have, during the past year, been
carried down to their long home—but we have been
preserved ; and are the living to praise Thee this
day.   Blessed be the God of salvation, to whom
belong the issues from death, that we are yet in
the regions of hope, that we have yet an accepted
time, and a day of salvation ; and that our opportunities of doing good, as well as of gaining good,
are still prolonged.   Yet are they all diminished
by another irreparable loss ; and the reduced remainder, with every trembling uncertainty attached
to it, calls upon us to say with growing seriousness
and zeal, I must work the works of Him that sent
me while it is day, the night cometh, wherein no
man can work.

Thou hast commanded us to remember all the
way, which thou hast led us in the wilderness.   The
scene of our journeying has indeed been a wilderness ; but the hand that has conducted us is divine ;
and a thousand privileges, not derivable from our
condition, have been experienced in it.

Thou hast corrected us, but it is of the Lord's
mercies we are not consumed.

We have had our afflictions, but how few have they been in number; how short in continuance; how alleviated in degree; how merciful in design; how instructive and useful in their results.

With regard to our severest exercises, we are compelled to acknowledge, Thou hast not dealt with us after our sins, neither hast Thou rewarded us according to our iniquities. It is good for me that I have been afflicted.

But O, what a series of bounties and blessings, present themselves to our minds, when we look back upon the year through which we have passed: and to what, but to thine unmerited goodness in the Son of thy love, are we indebted for all. Health, strength, food, raiment, residence, friends, relations, comfort, pleasure, hope, usefulness,—all our benefits have dropped from thy gracious hand: and there has not been a day, or an hour, or a moment, but has published thy kindness and thy care.

Especially would we acknowledge thy goodness, in continuing to us the means of grace. Whatever has been denied us, we have had the provisions of thy house. The toils and trials of the week, have been refreshed and relieved by the delights of the sabbath. Our eyes have seen our teachers. Our ears have heard the joyful sound of the gospel: and our hearts have often said, Lord, it is good for us to be here.

And O, that every moment of the past year could, if called upon—and it will be called upon, bear witness to our gratitude, love and obedience. O, that it was not in its power to convict us, of the most unworthy requitals of thy goodness. To Thee, O Lord, belong glory and honour, but to us shame and confusion of face. O, who can understand his errors. O, how many duties have we neglected or improperly performed. How little have we redeemed our time; or improved our talents. How little have we been alive to thy glory, or sought, or even seized, when presented, opportunities of

serving our generation.   How unprofited have we
been under the richest means of religious prosperity
—and, when for the time we ought to be able to
teach others, we have need to be again taught ourselves, what are the first principles of the oracles of
God.

God be merciful to us sinners.   Pardon our iniquity, for it is great.   Cleanse us from all unrighteousness : and work in us to will and to do of
thy good pleasure.   Let us not carry one of our
old sins with us into the new year—unforgiven—
unrepented of—unbewailed—unabhorred.   With
a new portion of time, may we have new hearts ;
and become new creatures.

If this year we should die—and in the midst of
life we are in death, may death prove our eternal
gain : and if our days are prolonged, may we walk
before the Lord in the land of the living, and show
forth all thy praise.   The number of our months
is with Thee.   In thy hand our breath is, and
thine are all our ways.   Prepare us for all : and
be with us in all : and bring us safely through all,
into the rest that remains for thy people ; for the
sake of our Lord and Saviour ; in whose words we
call Thee, Our Father, &c.   Amen.

FIRST MORNING OF THE NEW-YEAR.

Of old hast Thou laid the foundation of the
earth ; and the heavens are the work of thy hands.
They shall perish but thou shalt endure ; yea, all
of them shall wax old like a garment ; as a vesture
shalt Thou change them, and they shall be changed ; but Thou art the same, and thy years shall
have no end.   Through all the successions of time,
which with us constitute the past, the present, and
the future, I AM is thy name, and this is thy memorial in all generations.   We desire, O God,

with the profoundest reverence to contemplate the
eternity of thy nature. May our minds be filled
with elevation and grandeur, at the thought of a
Being, with whom one day is as a thousand years,
and a thousand years are as one day; a Being,
who amidst all the revolutions of empire, and the
lapse of worlds, feels no variableness nor shadow
of turning. How glorious, with immortality attached to them, are all thy attributes; and how
secure are the hopes and happiness of all those,
who know thy name and put their trust in Thee.

May we rejoice, that while men die, the Lord
liveth; that while all creatures are found broken
reeds and broken cisterns, He is the Rock of ages,
and the Fountain of living waters. O, that we may
turn away our hearts from vanity; and among all
the dissatisfactions and uncertainties of the present
state, look after an interest in that everlasting covenant, which is ordered in all things and sure.
May we seek after a union with thyself, as the
strength of our heart, and our portion for ever,
and be partakers ourselves of the immutability
we adore; for Thou hast assured us, that while
the world passeth away, and the lusts thereof,
he that doeth the will of God, abideth for
ever.

We thank Thee, that Thou hast revealed to us
the way in which a fallen, and perishing sinner
can be eternally united to thyself; and that Jesus
is the way, the truth, and the life. In His name
we come; O, receive us graciously; justify us
freely from all things; renew us in the spirit of
our minds; and bless us with all spiritual blessings
in heavenly places in Christ.

By the lapse of our days, and weeks, and years,
which we are called upon so often to remark, may
we be reminded how short our life is, and how
soon we shall close our eyes on every prospect below the sun; and, O, suffer us not to neglect the
claims of eternity, in the pursuit of the trifles of

time; but knowing how frail we are, may we be wise enough to choose that good part which shall not be taken away from us; and before we leave the present evil world, may we secure an inheritance in another and a better. May thoughts of death and eternity so impress our minds, as to put seriousness into our prayers, and vigour into our resolutions; may they loosen us from an undue attachment to things seen and temporal; so that we may weep as though we wept not; and rejoice as if we rejoiced not.

And remembering that the present life, so short, so uncertain—and so much of which is already vanished, is the only opportunity we shall ever have for usefulness, may we be concerned, with holy avarice, to redeem the time. May we be alive and awake, at every call of charity and piety. May we feed the hungry, and clothe the naked; may we instruct the ignorant; reclaim the vicious; forgive the offending; diffuse the gospel; and consider one another, to provoke one another unto love and good works, not forsaking the assembling ourselves together, as the manner of some is, but exhorting one another, and so much the more as we see the day approaching.

As we have entered on a new period of life, may we faithfully examine ourselves, to see what has been amiss, in our former temper or conduct; and in thy strength, may we resolve to correct it. And may we inquire for the future—with a full determination to reduce our knowledge to practice, Lord, what wilt Thou have me to do?

Prepare us for all the duties of the ensuing year. All the wisdom and strength, necessary for the performance of them, must come from thyself; may we, therefore, live a life of self-distrust, of divine dependence, and of prayer; may we ask and receive, that our joy may be full; may we live in the spirit, and walk in the spirit.

If we are indulged with prosperity, O, let not our prosperity destroy us, or injure us. If we are exercised with adversity, suffer us not to sink in the hour of trouble, or sin against God. May we know how to be abased, without despondence; and to abound, without pride. If our relative comforts are continued to us, may we love them without idolatry, and hold them at thy disposal; and if they are recalled from us, may we be enabled to say, the Lord gave, and the Lord hath taken away; and blessed be the name of the Lord.

Fit us for all events. We know not what a day may bring forth; but we encourage ourselves in the Lord our God, and go forward. Nothing can befall us by chance. Thou hast been thus far our helper; Thou hast promised to be with us in every condition; Thou hast engaged to make all things work together for good; all thy ways are mercy and truth. May we, therefore, be careful for nothing, but in every thing, by prayer and supplication with thanksgiving, may we make known our requests unto God; and may the peace of God that passeth all understanding, keep our hearts and minds, through Christ Jesus.

Bless, O, bless the young; may each of them, this day, hear Thee, saying, my son give me thy heart; and, from this time, may they cry unto Thee, as the guide of their youth. Regard those who have reached the years, wherein they say, we have no pleasure in them. If old in sin, may they be urged to embrace, before it be for ever too late, the things that belong to their peace; and if old in grace, uphold them with thy free Spirit, and help them to remember, that now is their salvation nearer than when they believed.

Bless all the dear connexions attached to us by nature, friendship or religion. Grace be to them; and peace be multiplied.

Let our country share thy protection and smiles. Bless all our rulers and magistrates.

Bless all our churches and congregations. Bless all thy ministers; may thine ordinances in their

17

hand be enlivening and refreshing, and thy word effectual, to wound and to heal.

May this be a year remarkable for the conversion of souls, and the extension of the gospel. Bless all missionary societies ; and let the circling months see the banners of the Redeemer carried forward ; till all nations are subdued to the obedience of faith. Our Father, which art in heaven, hallowed be thy name ; thy kingdom come ; thy will be done on earth as it is in heaven ; give us this day our daily bread ; and forgive us our trespasses as we forgive those that trespass against us ; and lead us not into temptation ; but deliver us from evil ; for thine is the kingdom, the power, and the glory, for ever. Amen.

GOOD FRIDAY.*

MORNING.

O, Thou King eternal, immortal, and invisible. Though Thou art past finding out unto perfection, we rejoice, that we are not called to worship an unknown God. Thou hast not left thyself without witness. We bless Thee for the revelation which Thou hast given us ; and that in thy word we can view Thee, as the Father of mercies, and the God of all grace. All thy works and ways correspond with the names Thou hast assumed, and demand and justify our confidence in Thee. We praise Thee for the displays of thy goodness in the productions of nature, and the bounties of thy providence : but above all, for thine inestimable love, in the redemption of the world, by our Lord Jesus Christ ; for the means of grace, and for the hope of glory.

---

* A day set apart by the church to commemorate our Saviour's sufferings and death.

Herein Thou hast commended thy love towards us, in that while we were yet sinners, Christ died for us.

We find ourselves this morning at the foot of His cross, where angels are desiring to look into these things—And if they who need no repentance, study the sufferings of Christ, and the glory that should follow, O, how much more should we ; to whom they are not only true, and wonderful, and sublime, but all important, and infinitely interesting. Help us, O Lord, to turn aside and see this great sight ; and not suffer a dying Saviour to address us in vain—Is it nothing to you, all ye that pass by ? Behold and see, if ever there was sorrow like unto my sorrow.

Here, may we see the value of our souls, in the price paid for their deliverance ; and instead of neglecting them, or exposing them, for the vanities of time and sense ; may we regard them, according to the estimation in which they were holden by Him, who gave His life a ransom for many. Here, may we contemplate the evil of sin, and abhor it : here, look upon Him whom we have pierced, and mourn for Him. Yet remembering that He was not only slain by us, but for us ; may we rejoice in our tears ; and by believing enter into rest.

With humble and holy confidence may we be enabled to say, surely, He hath borne our griefs, and carried our sorrows ; the chastisement of our peace was upon Him, and by His stripes we are healed.

May we never degrade His death by fearing that it will not be available for guilt, so great and aggravated as ours, even if we depend upon it, and plead it before God ; but be fully persuaded, that His blood cleanseth from all sin ; and that by the one offering up of Himself, He hath perfected for ever them that are sanctified.

Yet, O God, never suffer us to sin that grace may abound. May we never crucify the Saviour afresh and put Him to an open shame. May He never be wounded in the house of His professing friends. Rather may we live only and wholly for Him, who died for us; and adorn the doctrine of God our Saviour, in all things.

May our old man be crucified with Him : and the body of sin be destroyed, that henceforth we may not serve sin. May we be planted together in the likeness of His death. As He suffered for us, caving us an example, that we should follow His steps; may we learn of Him, submission, and meekness, and forgiveness of injuries; when reviled, may we revile not again; when suffering, may we threaten not, but commit ourselves to Him that judgeth righteously.

Like Him in all the afflictions of life, may we look to the hand that prepares and presents them ; and say, the cup which my Father hath given me, shall I not drink it ?

Whatever be the cross we are required to bear, may we look before us, and see *Him* carrying a much heavier; carrying it for us : and carrying it without a murmur—

> Then let our pains be all forgot,
> Our hearts no more repine—
> Our sufferings are not worth a thought,
> When, Lord, compared with Thine.

Convert and pardon all those, who by their lives or doctrine, are the enemies of the cross of Christ. Have mercy upon the descendants of those who shed His blood : and let His dying prayer be answered, Father, forgive them, for they know not what they do.

As Thou hast made His soul an offering for sin, may He see His seed, and prolong His days, and the pleasure of the Lord prosper in His hand. May He see of the travail of His soul and be satisfied : and by His knowledge may He justify many, having borne their iniquities.

Yea, having been lifted up from the earth, may He draw all men unto Him ; may all kings fall down before Him, and all nations serve Him; and in all the earth which He has purchased with His own blood, may there be one Lord, and His name one.

And when He, who made Himself of no reputation, took upon Him the form of a servant, and became obedient unto death, even the death of the cross, shall come in His glory, with all the holy angels, may we be enabled to say, even so, come Lord Jesus; and unite with those, who will be eternally employed in saying—Unto Him that loved us, and washed us from our sins in His own blood, and hath made us kings and priests unto God, and to His Father, be glory and dominion for ever and ever. Amen.

GOOD FRIDAY.

EVENING.

O Thou, whose name alone is Jehovah, the Most High over all the earth; We desire to adore thy perfections, and to admire thy works, which are sought out of all them that have pleasure therein.

Thou art the only wise God. Thy power is Almighty. Whither can we go from thy presence, or whither can we flee from thy Spirit? Thou art holy in all thy ways. And such is thy purity, that even the heavens are not clean in thy sight.

How shall we come before the Lord, or bow before the high God? we have no offering of our own to bring. No man can redeem his brother, or give to God a ransom for him. The blood of bulls and of goats could not take away sin. The law itself made nothing perfect—but the bringing in of a better hope did, by the which we draw nigh to God.

17*

Yes, blessed be thy name, Thou hast shown us what is good; and we behold the Lamb of God, who is the propitiation for our sins, and not for ours only, but also for the sins of the whole world.

Here a foundation is laid for our hope, in connexion with the highest glory of all thy perfections; and we rejoice to think, that while pleading for salvation by the blood of the cross, we ask Thee not to deny thyself, or to trample on thy holy law; for here, thy law is magnified and made honourable; here, all thy attributes are developed and harmonized; mercy and truth meet together; righteousness and peace kiss each other.

Here, weary and heavy laden, may we come for relief, and find rest unto our souls. May we take fresh views of this adorable sacrifice, under a sense of our constant unworthiness and desert; and in all our approaches to Thee, may we have boldness and access with confidence, by the faith of Him.

May we not only rely upon His cross, but glory in it. Yea, may we joy in God through our Lord Jesus Christ, by whom we have now received the atonement. And may we be able, individually, to say, I am crucified with Christ; nevertheless I live, yet not I, but Christ liveth in me; and the life that I now live in the flesh, I live by the faith of the Son of God, who loved me, and gave Himself for me.

We are thankful, that as He atoned for our guilt, so He procured for us the grace of life, that the blessing of Abraham might come on the Gentiles, and that we might receive the promise of the Spirit, through faith. May we never separate the pardon and sanctification which Thou hast joined together. May we prove, that He gave Himself—not only for our sins, but that He might deliver us from the present evil world; yea, that He might redeem us from all iniquity, and purify unto Himself a peculiar people, zealous of good works.

And, O, that in every future moment of our existence, we may be constrained to live, not to ourselves, but to Him that died for us, and rose again. As He so loved us, may we also love one another: and never deem any thing too great to do, or to suffer, while endeavouring to seek and to save that which is lost.

May the hearts which are too hard to be broken by terror, be melted by love, and gained by confidence. May none of those who are desirous of returning to Thee, be discouraged by a fear of rejection: but calling to remembrance and belief, the infinite proof which Thou hast already exhibited of thy benevolence, thus judge—He that spared not his own Son, but delivered Him up for us all, how shall He not, with Him, freely give us all things.

Smile upon our country. Let all the churches of the faithful, be edified and multiplied. Bless all the ministers of the everlasting gospel; and may they increasingly determine to know nothing, save Jesus Christ, and Him crucified.

Increase the number of those who love his salvation; and as He gave himself a ransom for a..., may it be testified in due time, that he may have the heathen for his inheritance, and the uttermost parts of the earth for his possession; and reign King of kings, and Lord of lords.

In his words we conclude our devotions. Our Father, &c. Amen.

EASTER SUNDAY.*

MORNING.

When we consider the heavens, the work of thy fingers, the moon and the stars which Thou

* A day set apart in commemoration of our Saviour's resurrection.

hast ordained; Lord, what is man, that Thou art mindful of him, or the son of man that Thou visitest him. We are not worthy of an audience at thy footstool—we are not worthy of the least of all thy mercies—our sins have even called aloud for vengeance.

But Thou hast not executed upon us the fierceness of thy anger—because Thou art good as well as great; and thy goodness constitutes thy greatness. Thou hast turned our very fall into an occasion of improving our condition, by advancing us to the possession of more and greater blessings than we originally enjoyed; so that we not only have life, but have it more abundantly.

For this purpose the Son of thy love was manifested; and in the fulness of time, we behold Him assuming our nature, and coming into our world, not to be ministered unto, but to minister, and to give his life a ransom for many. We rejoice to see, in his release from the prison of the grave, the evidence of the all-sufficiency and acceptation of the sacrifice He offered on the cross. O, help us to consider Him as a risen Saviour; and may we feel the power of his resurrection, in establishing our faith, enlivening our hope, and securing our sanctification. May we not only believe his resurrection, but partake of it, and resemble it, that like as Christ was raised from the dead by the glory of the Father, even so, we also might walk in newness of life; reckoning ourselves to be dead indeed unto sin, but alive unto God, through Jesus Christ our Lord.

And if risen with Christ, may we give evidence of it, and act becoming it, in seeking those things that are above.

May we never leave our spiritual and everlasting condition, undecided and unknown; may we never be satisfied, till we are able to say, Blessed be the God and Father of our Lord Jesus Christ, who, according to his abundant mercy, hath begotten us again unto a lively hope, by the resurrection of Jesus Christ from the dead ; to an inheritance incorruptible, undefiled, and that fadeth not away, reserved in heaven for us.

In all our difficulties and dangers, may we rejoice that He who was dead, is alive again, to plead for us, to defend us, and to supply, and has the keys of hell and of death.

In all the afflictions of life, in the decay of nature, and when looking into the horrors of the grave, may we with humble and holy confidence be able to say, I know that my Redeemer liveth, and shall stand at the latter day upon the earth ; and though, after my skin, worms destroy this body, yet in my flesh shall I see God.

Are we called to mourn over the loss of our dear and pious connexions ? Let us not sorrow as those who have no hope ; but comfort one another with these words—That Jesus died and rose again, and them that sleep in Jesus will God bring with Him.

We glory in the victory which our risen Saviour has obtained, not only over death and the grave, but the powers of darkness ; we rejoice that he has set judgment in the earth, and that the isles are waiting for his law ; that his word is translating into every language, and his servants entering every clime. We hail what he has done as a pledge of his universal triumph. And though we yet see not all things actually put under him, we see him, for the suffering of death, crowned with glory and honour ; and in possession of all the resources, necessary to accomplish the benevolent designs of his heart ; and he must reign till *all* his enemies are made his footstool.

Through him, as the once suffering but now exalted Saviour, we address Thee, as our Father, &c. Amen.

EASTER SUNDAY.

EVENING.

O, Thou ever blessed God, we rejoice to think, Thou hast determined to get thyself honour, in this apostate part of thy empire; not by the merited infliction of thy justice, but the displays of thy goodness. For Thou hast said, mercy shall be built up for ever, a monument higher than the heavens, more durable than eternity, and inscribed to the praise of the glory of thy grace, wherein Thou hast made us accepted in the beloved.

We bless Thee, for the appointment and revelation, of the one only Mediator between Thee and us; by whose death sinners are reconciled, and by whose life they are saved. Thou hast laid on Him the iniquity of us all. Surely He hath borne our griefs, and carried our sorrows; the chastisement of our peace was upon Him, and with his stripes we are healed.

Establish in our minds a full persuasion, that he was delivered for our offences, and raised again for our justification; and may we, above all things, be concerned to know not only that He is risen again, but that we are quickened together with Christ, and raised up, and made to sit with Him in the heavenly places. May we hold communion with Him, as a living and reigning Saviour; able to carry on our cause, and save unto the uttermost, all that come unto God, by Him.

Is He not head over all things unto his body the church? Is He not exalted to be a Prince and a Saviour? Has He not assured us, that because He lives, we shall live also? May we view Him as the first fruits of them that sleep; and believe, that as in Adam all died, even so in Christ shall all be made alive. May we view his resurrection, not only a the pledge, but the model of our own;

knowing that he shall not only change our vile body, but fashion it like *His* own glorious body, according to the working, whereby He is able to
subdue *all* things unto Himself.

Thou hast appointed a day in which Thou wilt
judge the world in righteousness, by that man
whom Thou hast ordained: and Thou hast given
assurance of it unto all men, in that Thou hast
raised Him from the dead. O, save us from the
wrath of the Lamb. May we tremble at the
thought of appearing before Him, if we have neglected his salvation, despised his precious blood,
and resisted his Holy Spirit.

Let not the head stone of the corner, be a stone
of stumbling and a rock of offence; but as He is
chosen of God, and precious, may He be precious
to us. And while He is living for us in heaven,
may we be living for Him on earth. May we esteem it our highest honour to be like Him; and
feel it our greatest pleasure to serve Him.

And let all the house of *Israel* know assuredly,
that Thou hast made that same Jesus whom their
fathers crucified, both Lord and Christ. May the
veil be taken from their heart; and may they behold, as in a glass, his glory.

As a nation be merciful unto us, and bless us.
May this christian country, be a country of christians: and let all who name the name of Christ,
depart from iniquity.

Bless all those who preach Jesus and the resurrection. May they preach with the Holy Ghost
sent down from heaven. May their sound go into
all the earth; and their words unto the ends of the
world.

As yet, after all we have read, and heard, and
experienced, we know but little of the value of
the gospel; but we know enough to induce us to
be thankful for our religious advantages; to sympathize with those who are without Christ; and to
pray, that in Him all the families of the earth may

be blessed, and all the generations call Him blessed.

Now the God of Peace, that brought again from the dead our Lord Jesus, that great Shepherd of the sheep, through the blood of the everlasting covenant, make us perfect in every good work to do his will, working in us tha. which is well pleasing in his sight, through Jesus Christ ; to whom be glory for ever and ever. Amen.

WHITSUNDAY.*

MORNING.

O God, Thou hast established thy throne in the heavens, and thy kingdom ruleth over all ; and all nations before Thee are as nothing. Yet, blessed be thy name, it is only in comparison with thy infinite greatness, that they are nothing—not in reference to thy condescension, and kindness, and care. Even as individuals we have been the charge of thy providence ; goodness and mercy have always attended us ; and having obtained help of Thee, we continue to this day. Thou hast been mindful of our souls as well as our bodies ; yea Thou wast pleased to form a purpose of grace in our favour ; and devise means the most glorious, to deliver us from the degradation, and misery, and perdition of sin ; and to make us partakers of the hope of eternal life.

We bless Thee for the dispensation of religion, under which it is our exalted privilege to live. How superior are our advantages, to those enjoyed by many of thy people, in earlier ages. The law was given by Moses, but grace and truth came by

---

* A festival observed in remembrance of the descent of the Holy Ghost upon the apostles.— Acts. ii 3

Jesus Christ. Prophets and righteous men desired to see the things which we see, and did not see them; and to hear the things which we hear, and did not hear them; but blessed are our eyes for they see and our ears for they hear. Instead of a portion of revelation, we have the sacred Scriptures complete. Instead of the blackness, and darkness, and tempest, of Sinai, we have the milder glories, and the small still voice of Zion. We have not received the spirit of bondage again to fear; but the spirit of adoption, whereby we cry, Abba, Father.

We praise Thee for the establishment of the glorious gospel, which at the first began to be spoken by the Lord, and was confirmed unto us by them that heard Him; God also bearing them witness, with signs and wonders, and with divers miracles and gifts of the Holy Ghost, according to His own will. We rejoice, that though His supernatural agency has ceased, with its necessity, the ministry of the Spirit continues, and that His saving influences are confined to no period of the church. All that have been enlightened and renewed since the fall, have been the subjects of His operation; and with Thee is the residue of the Spirit.

We rejoice, that as there is no blessing we so much need, so there is no blessing we are so much encouraged to implore: for thy truth has said, if ye, being evil, know how to give good gifts unto your children, how much more shall your Father which is in heaven, give His Holy Spirit unto them that ask Him.

O Thou God of all grace, fulfil the word unto thy servants, upon which Thou hast caused us to hope. Impart unto us thy Holy Spirit, to open the eyes of our understanding, to sanctify our affections, to comfort our hearts, to glorify Christ, by taking of the things of Christ, and showing them to us

19

May we never commit the sin against the Holy Ghost. Never quench the Spirit. Never resist the Holy Ghost. Never grieve the Holy Spirit But may we pray in the Holy Ghost; and worship God in the Spirit; and be lead by the Spirit; and be filled with the Spirit.

May we always view the commands in connexion with thy promises; our duties and trials, in connexion with our resources. Great is our work; great is our warfare; and far greater than we ever yet felt it to be, is our weakness. But our sufficiency is of God; and Thou hast said, I will never leave thee, nor forsake thee—not by might nor by power, but by my Spirit saith the Lord.

Let the goings of our God and our King, be seen in the sanctuary; and when thy truth is dispensed, let it come to those who hear it, not in word only, but in power, and in the Holy Ghost, and with much assurance.

And bless, not only the gates of Zion, but all the dwelling places of Jacob. May every family contain a church in the house. Pour thy blessing upon our seed, and thy Spirit upon our offspring; and may the rising race grow up, the ornaments, examples, and benefactors, of their day and generation.

To Thee we commend all who have the rule over us; we implore thy favourable regards to the privileged country in which we live. Humble us before Thee for our sins, especially our neglect and abuse of our religious advantages. Withdraw not from us the blessings we have forfeited; and inflict not upon us the judgments we have deserved. But spare us according to the greatness of thy mercy.

And from our land of vision, may the light break forth upon all those who are in darkness, and the region of the shadow of death.

Bless all missionary exertions. Let the various societies employed in this work of faith, and la-

bour of love, view each other with pleasure, and
rejoice in each other's success; and if not in immediate and personal co-operation, yet in accord-
ance, and tendency, and design, may they stand
fast in one spirit, with one mind, striving together
for the faith of the gospel. Let those who remain
at home, hold forth the word of life in their own
circles, and be concerned to evangelize the dis-
tricts in which they reside. But O, let there not
be a deficiency of those, who offer themselves to
the help of the Lord, among the heathen, and say,
Lord, send me. Let it be said, as it was in the
beginning of the gospel—The Lord gave the word,
great was the company of them that published it.

And be with those that are already engaged.
We know that Paul can only plant, and Apollos
water; but Thou canst give the increase.

Pour thy Spirit from on high, and the wilderness
shall become a fruitful field. Our Father, &c.
Amen.

WHITSUNDAY.

EVENING.

O, Thou Author of peace, and lover of concord,
in knowledge of whom standeth our eternal life;
and whose service is perfect freedom: cleanse
the thoughts of our hearts, by the inspiration of
thy Holy Spirit; and give us grace, whereby we
may serve Thee acceptably, with reverence, and
with godly fear.

We adore Thee as the Creator of all things visible, and invisible. Thou art the Maker of our
earth; and Thou art the Maker of man upon it:
and Thou madest man upright, in the possession
of thy image, and the enjoyment of thy presence.
But man being in honour, abode not. Our first

father sinned ; and we have borne his iniquity. We have gone astray from the womb ; and in numberless instances, have evinced ourselves to be the degenerate offspring, of a fallen original—and there is no health in us. As transgressors of thy law, we are under the curse ; and did our deliverance depend upon ourselves, we must lie down in endless despair. We admit, in all its extent, the testimony of thy word against us ; but admire with gratitude, the developement of a plan of mercy and grace, divinely appropriate to all our wants and woes, and uniting the highest display of thy glory, with the salvation of sinners.

Adored be the benevolence that led the Son of thy love, before the foundation of the world, to say, Lo ! I come to do thy will, O God ; thy law is within my heart. Blessed be the day when the angels saw Him who was rich, for our sakes becoming poor, that we through His poverty, might be rich. Blessed be the hour, when the Prince of Life bore our sins in His own body on the tree ; and having obtained eternal redemption for us, ascended up on high, leading captivity captive, and receiving gifts for men even the rebellious also, that the Lord God might dwell among them. We rejoice, that christianity was originally preached, with the Holy Ghost sent down from heaven : and in the demonstration of the Spirit, was so firmly established, that the gates of hell can never prevail against it. We praise Thee, that the sun of righteousness, in the knowledge of the gospel, has arisen with healing under his wings, upon this distinguished land ; and said, arise, shine, for thy light is come, and the glory of the Lord is risen upon thee. And, O, what reason have we to be thankful, if this gospel has come to us not in word only, but in power, and in the Holy Ghost, and in much assurance.

For we bless Thee, that though miracles have ceased, yet thy Spirit is insured to thy people to the end of the world, as the source of light and life, and peace and joy; giving testimony to the word of thy grace; and working in the souls of men, to will and to do of thy good pleasure.

O, Thou Author of all good, save us, we beseech Thee, by the washing of regeneration, and the renewing of the Holy Ghost. May we be found in the number of those, who are born of the Spirit; and give evidence of it, by our walking after the Spirit, and our minding the things of the Spirit. Instead of judging ourselves by dreams, fancies, and impressions, may we prove what is acceptable unto the Lord; and remember, that the fruit of the Spirit, is in all goodness, and righteousness, and truth.

We desire O God, to acknowledge our entire dependence upon Thee. Whatever time we have been engaged in thy service, we are still in the body, and feel our need of the continuance of those counsels, supports, and consolations, which have ever been afforded us. Cast us not away from thy presence, and take not thy Holy Spirit from us.

In all the dangers to which we are exposed, uphold us by thy free Spirit; and may we not think it enough to be preserved from falling; but may we go forward, and be always abounding in the work of the Lord. Strengthen us with might by thy Spirit in the inner man, for every purpose of the Christian life; and may we be satisfied with no attainment, till we are filled with all the fulness of God.

Awaken the careless; convince of their error and guilt, all those who deny, or vilify the work of thy grace; and plant in their consciences the conviction, that if any man have not the Spirit of Christ, he is none of His.

Pour the spirit of grace and of supplication upon all our congregations. Bless the ministry of the gospel, and make it the ministration of the Spirit, and the power of God to salvation to every one that believeth.

But how can they believe in Him of whom they have not heard ? And how can they hear without a preacher ? How many are there, who, by the wretchedness of their condition, if not by their actual desire, are saying, Come over and help us.

Hast Thou not commanded us to pray, that thy kingdom may come ? Hast not Thou promised, that the earth shall be full of the knowledge of the Lord, as the waters cover the seas ?

May we encourage our expectation, by reviewing what Thou hast already accomplished; and remembering, that Thou art a God of truth, and— the Almighty. May we, therefore, realize in our minds, the delightful period, when the heathen shall cast their idols to the moles and to the bats ; when Mahometanism and anti-christ shall perish ; when the Jews shall look upon Him whom they have pierced, and mourn ; and among protestants, every plant which our heavenly Father hath not planted, shall be rooted up.

But why are thy chariot wheels so long in coming ? Why does the whole creation groan and travel in pain together until now ? How many would say, Lord, now lettest Thou thy servant depart in peace, according to thy word—could their eyes see thy salvation, which Thou hast prepared before the face of all people ; a light to lighten the Gentiles, and the glory of thy people Israel.

While using the means, may we trust in thy wisdom, as well as thy faithfulness ; and hear the voice saying, I the Lord will hasten it—in his time.

And to God, the Father, the Word, and the Holy Ghost, he ascribed the kingdom, power, and glory, both now and for ever. Amen.

THE EVENING AFTER A FUNERAL.

O THOU Father of mercies, and God of all comfort. Thou hast often invited us to thyself, by a profusion of kindnesses ; and it manifests our depravity, that we think of Thee so little in the hour of ease and prosperity. But we are now before Thee, in affliction and distress. Yet we rejoice, to know, that Thou art a very present, and an all-sufficient help in trouble.

Thou takest away and who can hinder Thee, or say unto Thee, What doest Thou? Thou hast a right do what thou wilt with thine own. Thou art a sovereign, and the reasons of thy conduct are often far above, out of our sight ; but thy work is perfect, thy ways are judgment. All thy dispensations are wise, and righteous, and kind—kind, even when they seem to be severe.

May we hear thy voice in thy rod, as well as in thy word : and gathering from the corrections with which we are exercised, the peaceable fruit of righteousness, be able to acknowledge, with all our suffering brethren before us, It is good for me that I have been afflicted.

It is not the Scripture only, that reminds us of our living in a dying world, but all observation, and experience. Man is continually going to his long home, and the mourners daily go about the streets. And we are all accomplishing, as an hireling, our day, and in a little time, our neighbours, friends and relations, will seek us—and we shall not be. Our days are swifter than a weaver's shuttle, and are spent without hope. Thou hast made our days as an hand's breadth, and our age is as nothing before Thee : verily every man at his best state is altogether vanity. For our days are not only few, but full of evil. Anxieties perplex us ; dangers alarm us ; infirmities oppress us ; disappointments afflict us ; losses impoverish us—

we are consumed by thine anger, and by thy wrath
are we troubled—O, shut not thy merciful ear to
our prayers ; but spare us, O Lord, most holy : O
God, most mighty : O holy and most merciful Saviour : Thou most worthy Judge eternal, suffer us
not, at our last hour, for any bitter pains of death,
to fall from Thee.

We acknowledge, O God, with shame and sor
row, that the state of degradation and mortality, in
which we groan, was not our original condition.
Thou madest man upright ; but he sought out
many inventions.   Our first father sinned, and we
have borne his iniquity.   By one man, sin entered
into the world, and death by sin ; and so death
hath passed upon all men, for that all have sinned.

And we bless Thee, that this is not our final
state.   By the discoveries of faith, we see new
heavens, and a new earth, wherein dwelleth righteousness.   We see the spirits of just men made
perfect.   We see our vile bodies changed, and
fashioned like the Saviour's own glorious body ;
and man, the sinner, raised above the angels, who
never sinned.

We bless Thee for this purpose of grace, formed
before the world began, and accomplished in the
fulness of time, by the Son of thy love, who hath
abolished death, and brought life and immortality
to light by the gospel : and who, among the rava-
ges of the grave, says, I am the resurrection, and
the life ; He that believeth in me, though he were
dead, yet shall he live ; and whosoever liveth and
believeth in me shall never die.

May it be our immediate and supreme concern
to win Christ, and be found in Him ; knowing that
there is no condemnation to them that are in Christ
Jesus ; and that blessed are the dead that die in
the Lord.

So teach us to number our days that we may
apply our hearts unto wisdom—that wisdom which

will lead us to prefer the soul to the body, and
eternity to time ; that wisdom which will lead us
to secure an interest in a better world, before we
are removed from this.

O, let not the trifles of time induce us to neglect
the one thing needful. While each of us is compelled to say, I know Thou wilt bring me to death,
and to the house appointed for all living, may we
be enabled also to say, I know whom I have believed, and am persuaded that He is able to keep
that which I have committed to Him, against that
day.

And, O, let not the solemnities we have this day
witnessed, be ever forgotten ; for often, our most
serious impressions have worn off, and our goodness has been as the morning cloud and early dew,
that soon passeth away.

Thou hast permitted death to invade our circle,
and hast turned our dwelling into a house of mourning. May we find that it is better to be in the
house of mourning, than in the house of mirth. By
the sadness of the countenance, may the heart be
made better, more serious to reflect, and more
softened to take impression.

With the feelings of the creature, may we blend
the views and the hopes of the christian. May we
remember that Thou hast bereaved us, not as an
aggressor, but as a proprietor ; resuming what was
lent us for a season, but never ceased to be thine
own. May we, therefore, be dumb, and open not
our mouth, because Thou hast done it ; or if we
speak, may it be to acknowledge and pray—I
know, O Lord, that thy judgments are right, and
that Thou in faithfulness hast afflicted me ; let thy
loving-kindness be for my comfort, according to thy
word unto thy servant.

We bless Thee for thy goodness to the deceased,
and that we are not called to sorrow, as those who
have no hope. We ascribe whatever excellency
was found in them to thy grace ; and desire to be

followers of them, as far as they also were of Christ.

Forgive us in whatever instances we failed in our duty towards them. Let the prayers they offered for us while on earth be answered; may we hold communion with them in our living Redeemer; and look forward to a period of renewed and improved intercourse, in which we shall be for ever with each other, and for ever with the Lord.

Now unto him that is able to keep us from falling, and to present us faultless before the presence of his glory, with exceeding joy. To the only wise God our Saviour, be glory and majesty, dominion and power, both now and ever. Amen.

FAST DAY.*

MORNING.

Holy, holy, holy, is the Lord of hosts, the whole earth is full of thy glory. O, for such an impression of thy holiness as Isaiah had, when penetrated with a sense of his own sin, and the sin of the nation, he exclaimed, Wo is me, for I am a man of unclean lips, and I dwell among a people of unclean lips. Banish all insensibility and indifference from our minds, and unite our hearts to fear thy name.

We lament that the world in which we live, formed to show forth thy praise, was so early defiled by sin; that all flesh corrupted its way before God, and every imagination of the thoughts of the heart, was only evil continually. We adore

---

* The two following prayers are particularly adapted to a fast appointed on account of some great calamity, but with slight alterations may be used on ordinary fast days.

thy awful but righteous displeasure, in bringing the flood upon the world of the ungodly, and taking them all away.

Yet even this tremendous desolation, did not hinder the renewed human race from rebelling against Thee; and a long succession of private and public calamities, proclaims the desperate depravity of our nature, and the evil of sin. Our world is the empire of death, a vale of tears; and tempests and earthquakes, and war, and pestilence, and famine, scatter the tokens of thy wrath, for Thou distributest sorrows in thine anger.

Thy judgments are now abroad in the earth—may the inhabitants thereof learn righteousness. They have reached and invaded us—may we lay them to heart, and be suitably impressed, with the afflicted circumstances of the country to which we belong.

We have been equally distinguished by privileges and guilt; and it is impossible for us to review the one, without being reminded of the other. An innumerable multitude of natural, providential, and religious benefits, has distinguished our portion. The lines have fallen to us in pleasant places, yea, we have a goodly heritage. At an early period the gospel visited our shores, and has continued in the midst of us to this hour. We have lived under the administration of laws, just, mild, and beneficent. We have enjoyed civil and religious freedom. The Scriptures have not been withholden from us, nor have our teachers been removed into a corner—but our eyes have seen our teacher; and sitting under our own vine and fig-tree, none have dared to make us afraid. In our dangers, Thou hast appointed salvation for walls and bulwarks; the earth has yielded to us her increase; and God, even our own God, has blessed us.

It is impossible for us to express, or conceive,

the obligations we are under to love and serve
Thee.

But we know—and, O, help us to feel, how un-
worthily and ungratefully we have behaved ourselves, towards our adorable Benefactor. We are
a sinful nation, a seed of evil-doers ; children that
are corrupters. The whole head is sick, and the
whole heart is faint : from the crown of the head,
even to the sole of the foot, there is no soundness,
but wounds, and bruises, and putrifying sores. O
Lord, righteousness belongeth unto Thee, but unto
us confusion of faces, as at this day, to our rulers.

But Thou art the Almighty. Thou hast all
hearts in thy hand, and all events at thy disposal.

And we have heard, that to the Lord our God
belong mercies and forgivenesses, though we have
rebelled against Him. We are proofs ourselves,
that thy compassions fail not—hence though corrected, we are not consumed ; and though guilty,
we are yet allowed and invited to enter thy presence.

With deep humiliation, not unmingled with hope,
may we approach the throne of thy grace, at this
time of need. O, be merciful unto us, and bless us,
and cause thy face to shine upon us, that we may
be saved. For the sake of thy dear Son, who
died, the just for the unjust, by whose name we are
called—behold a country prostrate at thy footstool;
and hear the voice, which will issue to-day, from
so many temples and closets, saying, Spare thy
people, O Lord, and give not thine heritage to reproach.

Remove, if it please Thee, the blow of thy heavy
hand, in the calamity which we are deploring ; and
after giving such a deliverance as this, may we no
more break thy commandments. Or if Thou hast
determined to continue the correction, O, correct
us, but with judgment, not in thine anger, lest
Thou bring us to nothing.

Aid thy people in the private and public devotions of the day. Pour out a spirit of grace and of supplication, that we may sorrow after a godly sort. May thy ministers be faithful and fearless; may they cry aloud, and spare not; but lift up their voice like a trumpet, and show thy people their transgression, and the house of Jacob their sin.

And let the word that is to be spoken, be quick and powerful, sharper than any two edged sword, piercing even to the dividing asunder of soul and spirit, and of the joints and marrow, and be a discerner of the thoughts and intents of the heart.

Our Father, &c. Amen.

FAST DAY.

EVENING.

O GOD, Thou hast established thy throne in the heavens, and thy kingdom ruleth over all. We prostrate ourselves before Thee, deeply impressed with a sense of the vastness of thy agency and dominion. Thou changest the times and the seasons; Thou removest kings, and settest up kings. Empires rise and fall, and fade and flourish, at thy bidding; and all nations are in thy hand, but as clay in the hand of the potter.

But none of thy dispensations are arbitrary. Whatever Thou doest, is done, because O Father. it seemeth good in thy sight; and thy judgment is always according to truth. Thou art holy in all thy ways, and righteous in all thy works—and Thou art good: even in wrath Thou rememberest mercy, and dost not afflict willingly, nor grieve the children of men.

Therefore it is, that we have been this day humbling ourselves in thy presence.

For we acknowledge that we have been deeply guilty. Thou hast nourished and brought up children, but we have rebelled against Thee. The ox knoweth his owner, and the ass his master's crib ; but we have not known, we have not considered. Thou hast given us our corn, and wine, and oil, and multiplied our silver and gold ; and we have prepared them for Baal. Because of swearing, the land has mourned. Pride has com passed us about as a chain. Discontent has rebelled against thine appointments. How has the love of money, which is the root of all evil, abounded among us. How have thy sabbaths been profaned, and thy ordinances disregarded. How has the gospel been undervalued, neglected, despised.

And all our transgressions have been more aggravated than those of any other people, because Thou hast favoured us unspeakably more than all the families of the earth.

Therefore, Thou couldst easily and justly have destroyed us ; but Thou hast not stirred up all thy wrath. In all that has come upon us, for our evil deeds, Thou hast punished us less than our iniquities deserve. Yet Thou hast testified thy displeasure, and visited us with thy judgments ; so that when we looked for light and peace, we have seen darkness and trouble.

O, let us not be inattentive to the design of thy dealings, or insensible under thy rebukes. O, let it not be said of us, as it was of the Jews, The harp, and the viol, and the tabret, and pipe, and wine are in their feasts, but they regard not the work of the Lord, neither consider the operation of his hand. Thou hast striken them, but they have not grieved ; Thou hast consumed them, but they have refused to receive correction ; they have made their faces harder than the rock ; they have refused to return.

In the way of thy judgments, O Lord, may we wait for Thee. Thou hast said, Is any afflicted? let him pray. Call upon me in the day of trouble, and I will deliver thee, and thou shalt glorify me. Fulfil the word unto thy servants, upon which Thou hast caused us to hope. And O, let not the calamity be removed only, but above all, sanctified : let it appear that we have heard the rod, and Him that appointeth it : and be able to say, It is good for us that we have been afflicted.

For which purpose, bless, we beseech Thee, the word of thy grace, which has been spoken : and grant that the professed humiliation of the day, may be real—for Thou lookest to the heart. And let it also be universal : may it extend from the highest to the lowest : may it pervade every part of our country : may it enter every church, and every family—let none of us lose sight of ourselves, in the public calamity. May each individual retire and ask, What have I done ?—and what wilt Thou have me to do ? And though other lords have had dominion over us, henceforth, by Thee only, may we make mention of thy name.

Regard the government under which we live ; and the magistracy of the land—may all be wise in counsel, exemplary in conduct, and faithful to their trust.

And thus may we be reformed, and not destroyed. Thus may we be a holy, that we may be a happy people, whose God is the Lord. Return O Lord, how long? and let it repent Thee concerning thy servants. O, satisfy us early with thy mercy, that we may rejoice and be glad all our days. Make us glad, according to the days wherein Thou hast afflicted us, and the years wherein we have seen evil. Let thy work appear unto thy servants, and thy glory unto their children. And let the beauty of the Lord our God be upon us ; and establish Thou the work of our hands upon us , yea, the work of our hands, establish Thou i·

And to the Father, the Son, and the Holy Spirit,
be rendered the kingdom, power, and glory, for
ever and ever.   Amen.

FOR A DAY OF THANKSGIVING

MORNING.

O God, Thou art very great, Thou art clothed
with honour and majesty ; Thou coverest thyself
with light as with a garment ; Thou walkest upon
the wings of the wind.   When we reflect on the
glory of thy majesty, we are filled with wonder at
the vastness of thy condescension.   For Thou condescendest even to behold things that are in heaven.   What then is man, that Thou art mindful of
him, or the son of man, that Thou visitest him.

We rejoice, that we are under the governance
of a Being, who is not only Almighty, but perfectly righteous, and wise, and good ; that all things,
in our world, are appointed and arranged by thy
paternal agency ; that thy providence numbers the
very hairs of our head, and that a sparrow falleth
not to the ground, without our heavenly Father.

Hitherto hath the Lord helped us.   We bless
Thee for personal mercies,   If we are called, it
is by thy word.   If we are renewed, it is by thy
Spirit.   If we are justified, it is freely by thy
grace through the redemption that is in Christ Jesus.   It is in Thee we live, and move, and have
our being.   Thy goodness has been always near
us, to hear our complaints, to sooth our sorrow, and
to command deliverance for us.   And numberless
are the instances of loving-kindness, that now,
from ignorance, or inattention, elude our notice ;
the discovery of which will awaken our songs,
when we mingle with those who dwell in thy house
above, and are still praising Thee.

We thank Thee for relative benefits ; for blessings on our families, blessings on our churches, and blessings on our country. We confess that we are not worthy of the least of all thy mercies, and of all the truth which Thou hast showed unto thy servants. Sins of every kind and of every degree, have reigned among us ; have spread through all ranks and orders ; and continued, notwithstanding all warnings and corrections ; and if Thou hadst dealt with us, after our sins, or rewarded us according to our iniquities, we should long ago, have had no name, nor place, among the nations of the globe.

But to the Lord, our God, belong mercies and forgivenesses, though we have rebelled against Him All thy dispensations towards us have said, with a tenderness that ought to penetrate our hearts—How shall I give Thee up ' Our privileges, never properly improved, and forfeited times without number, have been continued. We still behold our sabbaths, and our ears still hear the joyful sound. Our constitution, liberties, and laws, have not been subverted, or impaired. Thou hast given us rains, and fruitful seasons ; Thou hast filled us with the finest of the wheat ; our garners have been affording all manner of store ; our oxen have been strong to labour ; our sheep have brought forth thousands and ten thousands in our streets. Thou hast spread thy wing, and sheltered us from the pestilence that walketh in darkness, and the destruction that wasteth at noon-day. Civil discord has not raged in our land ; our shores have not been invaded ; we have not heard the confused noise of warriors, nor seen garments rolled in blood—it has not come nigh us. Our enemies have often threatened to swallow us up, but the Lord has been on our side, and they have not prevailed against us. We are this day called upon to acknowledge thy goodness in (——)*

God is the Lord who hath showed us light ; bind the sacrifice with cords, even to the horns of the altar. May we never convert our blessings into instruments of provocation, by making them the means of nourishing pride and presumption, wantonness and intemperance ; and compel Thee to complain—Do ye thus requite the Lord, O foolish people, and unwise ? Is not He thy Father, that hath bought thee ? Hath He not made thee, and established thee ?

For this purpose meet with us in thy house ; and may the goings of our God and our King be seen in the sanctuary. Be with the preacher, and with the hearers ; and let the words of his mouth, and the meditation of their hearts be acceptable in thy sight, O Lord, our strength, and our Redeemer. May public instruction awaken the ardour of our feelings ; may our gratitude not only be lively, but practical and permanent. And by all thy mercies, may we present our bodies a living sacrifice, holy and acceptable unto Thee, which is our reasonable service.

Bless the Lord, ye His angels, that excel in strength, that do His commandments, hearkening unto the voice of His word. Bless ye the Lord, all ye His hosts : ye ministers of His, that do His pleasure. Bless the Lord, all His works, in all places of His dominion ; bless the Lord, O my soul. Amen.

---

* Here let the particular causes for thankfulness be expressed.

FOR A DAY OF THANKSGIVING.

EVENING.

O God, Thou art good, and Thou doest good. Thou art good to all, and thy tender mercies are over all thy works.'

We have thought of thy loving kindness this day, in the midst of thy temple ; and are again surrounding this domestic altar, to exclaim, O that men would praise the Lord for His goodness, and for His wonderful works to the children of men.

We lament to think, that a world so filled with thy bounty, should be so alienated from thy service and glory. We mourn over the vileness of our ingratitude, and abhor ourselves, repenting in dust and ashes.

O Thou God of all grace, make us more thankful. In order that we may be more thankful, may we be more humble ; impress us with a deep sense of our unworthiness, arising from the depravity of our nature, and countless instances of unimproved advantages, omitted duties, and violated commands. May we compare our condition with our desert, and with the far less indulged circumstances of others. May we never be inattentive to any of thy interpositions on our behalf; but be wise, and observe these things, that we may understand the loving-kindness of the Lord.

How many blessings, temporal and spiritual, public and private, hast Thou conferred upon us. Thy mercies have been new every morning, and every moment.

Our afflictions have been few and alleviated, often short in their continuance, and always founded in a regard to our profit. Thy secret has been upon our tabernacle ; and we have known Thee in thy palaces for a refuge. The lines have indeed fallen to us in pleasant places, yea, we have a goodly heritage. Thou hast not dealt so with any people. It is a good land, which the Lord our God has given us—a land distinguished by knowledge; dignified as the abode of civil and religious freedom; endeared by the patriot's zeal, and the ashes of our forefathers; a land the Lord careth for, and upon which His eye has been from the beginning even to the end of the year.

Thou hast been a wall of fire round about us, by thy providential protection, and the glory in the midst of us, by the gospel of our salvation, the ordinances of religion, and the presence of thy Holy Spirit.

What shall we render unto the Lord, for all His benefits towards us? Because Thou hast been our help, therefore under the shadow of thy wing may we rejoice. Because Thou hast heard our voice and our supplication, therefore may we call upon Thee as long as we live; and in every future difficulty and distress, make Thee our refuge and our portion.

Enable us to bless Thee at all times; may thy praise continually be in our mouth; and may we show forth thy praise, not only with our lips, but in our lives.

Being delivered from the peril and calamity (of ——) with which we have been exercised, may we serve Thee without fear, in holiness and righteousness all the days of our lives.

We dare not trust our own hearts. We have often resembled thy people of old, who, in the hour of deliverance and indulgence, sang thy praise, and said—All that the Lord commandeth us, will we do: but soon forgot His works and the wonders which He had showed them. Keep these things for ever in the imagination of our hearts; and not only draw us, but bind us to thyself, with the cords of love, and the bonds of a man.

And with all our calls to gratitude and joy, may we remember that we have also reason for sorrow and humiliation.   O, give us that repentance which is unto life.   Reform, as well as indulge us ; and pardon, as well as spare.   Let not our prosperity destroy us, nor our table become a snare.   Let us not by our perverse returns, provoke Thee to visit us with heavier afflictions ; and turn the rod into a scorpion.   May our ways please the Lord, that we may hope for a continuance of thy favour, and know that all things shall work together for our good.

Do good in thy good pleasure unto Zion.   Build Thou the walls of Jerusalem.   And as the churches have rest, may they walk in the fear of the Lord, and in the comforts of the Holy Ghost, and be multipled.

Preside over our national councils ; impart wisdom to those who conduct our public affairs ; and may all the various classes in the community, pursue that righteousness which exalteth a nation, and forsake that sin which is a reproach to any people.

Regard the services in which we have been engaged with the thousands of our Israel ; accept of the poor and imperfect thanksgivings we have offered ;   and let thy word, which has been dispensed, in aid of the devotion of the day, accomplish all the good pleasure of thy goodness— through Jesus the Lord, our righteousness and strength ; and in whose words we address Thee as

Our Father which art in heaven, hallowed be thy name ; thy kingdom come ;   thy will be done on earth as it is in heaven ; give us this day our daily bread ; and forgive us our trespasses as we forgive those that trespass against us, and lead us not into temptation ; but deliver us from evil ; for thine is the kingdom, the power, and the glory, for ever.   Amen.

PETITIONS

PARTICULAR OCCASIONS.

FOR RAIN

ARE there any of the vanities of the Gentiles that can cause rain? Or can the heavens give showers? Art not Thou he, O Lord, our God? Therefore will we wait upon Thee, for Thou hast made all these things.

Thou visitest the earth, and waterest it: Thou greatly enrichest it, with the river of God, which is full of water. Thou makest it soft with showers; Thou blessest the springs thereof. Thy paths drop fatness. They drop upon the pastures of the wilderness; and the little hills rejoice on every side.

We have been made to feel the worth of this blessing, by the want of it: and it would be easy for Thee to continue the privation, till the heavens over us were brass, and the earth under us iron: and the husbandman be ashamed for the wheat, and for the barley, because the harvest of the field is perished, and because joy is withered away from the sons of men.

But, O deal not with us after our desert. Turn not a fruitful land into barrenness. Command thy rain to descend; cause the grass to grow for the cattle, and herbs for the service of man; that he may bring forth food out of the earth.

FOR FAIR WEATHER.

How numberless are our wants and dangers! Our hopes are destroyed, not only by the deficiency, but the excess of our supplies. Stop, we pray Thee, the bottles of heaven, which have so long been pouring down water upon us; and cause thy sun not only to rise, but to shine—give us the clear shining after rain, that the earth may yield her increase, in maturity; and opportunity be afforded for the wholesome ingathering of grass for the cattle, and grain for the use of man: that there may be no complaining in our streets; but that we may eat in plenty, and be satisfied, and praise the Lord.

And O let us not forget our souls in our mindfulness of the body; nor expend all our concern upon the meat that perisheth—but be, above all things, anxious to secure that meat which endureth unto everlasting life, and which the Son of man will give; for him hath God the Father sealed.

IN VIEW OF JOURNEYING

O God, Thou hast called thyself the Preserver of men, and the Length of our days. We are therefore encouraged to commit ourselves to thy guardian care, in the journey before us.

Many have parted with their friends, with the hope of soon embracing each other again, but in-

stead of returning to their own dwelling, have been
conveyed to the house appointed for all living.
We pray, with submission to thy pleasure, that
this may not be our experience. Give thine angels charge concerning us, to keep us in all our
ways. Let no evil befall our persons, and no
plague come nigh our dwelling. May we know
also that our tabernacle is in peace, and visit our
habitation, and not sin.

Yet, uncertain what a day may bring forth, may.
we be prepared for every event of thy providence;
and wherever, in dying, we go *from*, may it be our
happiness to know where we are going *to*—and rejoice in the prospect, that when all our wanderings
and partings are ended, we shall unite in our
heavenly Father's house, and be for ever with the
Lord.

FOR A NEW MARRIED PARTY.

BLESS those who have just entered a state honourable in all. May they remember the vows
they have left at the altar; and in the discharge
of their personal and relative duty, may they make
thy word their rule, that mercy and peace may be
upon them. May the husband love his wife even
as himself; and the wife see that she reverence
her husband; and both walk together, as heirs of
the grace of life, that their prayers be not hindered.

Preserve them from the evils which destroy or
diminish the welfare and comfort of the condition
in which Thou hast placed them; and may they
enjoy all the happiness, derivable from prudence,
temper, accommodation, real godliness, and the
divine blessing.

May they expect to discern infirmities in one another; but may they be always most deeply conscious of their own. And let them not look for unattainable, by looking for unmingled bliss on earth: but remember that this is not our rest; and be prepared for difficulties, trials, changes, and final separation.

FOR A WOMAN APPROACHING THE TIME OF TRAVAIL

REGARD thine handmaid who is looking forward to an important hour. Be not Thou far from her when trouble is near. May her mind be kept in perfect peace, being stayed upon the God of her salvation. Bring to the birth, and give strength to bring forth. Soften the pains of labour, as well as command deliverance; and in due time, may she remember no more her anguish, for joy that a child is born into the world. And may the root and the branch, abide under the shade of the Almighty.

FOR ONE UNDER SICKNESS.

THINK, O God, for good upon the afflicted; especially him (*or her*) whom we now commend to thy compassionate regard. Comfort him upon the bed of languishing, and make all his bed in his sickness.

If the sickness be unto death, prepare him for the solemn event, and be with him in it. But we are allowed to implore deliverance, with submission; nothing is too hard for the Lord; Thou canst heal as well as wound—we therefore pray, if it be thy good pleasure, that Thou wilt put efficacy into the means ; rebuke the disorder ; renew the strength ; and prolong the days of thy servant.

Above all, let the dispensation be sanctified to the sufferer, and his connexions ; and may all have reason to acknowledge, in the review, It is good for me that I have been afflicted.

FOR A YOUTH GOING FROM HOME.
(*If with a View to Business.*)

O God, Thou appointest the bounds of our habitations ; and arrangest all our individual concerns; and it is thy pleasure, not only that we should part at death, but often separate in life. When absent from each other in body, may we be present in spirit ; and may our natural affection be strengthened and sanctified by inquiry, and correspondence, and divine remembrance at the throne of grace.

Regard the member of our family, who is now leaving the parental roof, and the parental wing. In all his ways may he acknowledge Thee ; and be Thou the guide and the guard of his youth. Secure him from the paths of the destroyer, and the evils of the world. May uprightness preserve him. In the situation he will be called to fill, may he be dutiful, and obliging, and diligent, and faithful : may he always remember, that the eye of God is upon him ; and be not only amiable, but pious ; and in favour with God, as well as man.

(*If with a View to School.*)

O thou God of providence and grace, we commend to thy care the dear child, about to leave our abode for a season, in order to receive needful instruction. Let his (*or her*) life be precious in thy sight. May he redeem his time, and acquire the improvement that will fit him for usefulness, in his day and generation. And O, let him be made wise unto salvation ; and let the beauty of the Lord our God be upon him ; that he may be a useful and ornamental member in thy church below, and hereafter a pillar in thy temple above, never more to go out.

FOR CHILDREN IN ORDINARY CIRCUMSTANCES.

(All the Petitions need not be used at the same time.)

O GOD, Thou art the lovely Father of all mankind ; Thou hast implanted in us the parental instincts ; and commanded us to train up our children in the nurture and admonition of the Lord--- we feel our awful responsibility, and often exclaim, Who is sufficient for these things ? But Thou givest wisdom to the ignorant, and power to the faint. Aid, O aid us, in discharging the duties we owe to those whom thou hast given us, and continued to us.

We give them up to Thee, who art able to fulfil all our petitions. Rescue them from the numberless accidents and diseases to which they are exposed. Let their tempers be lovely, and meek, and kind. Let their manners be simple and engaging. May they be respectful towards their superiors ; obliging towards their equals ; and condescending towards their inferiors.

Let not envy, and pride, and censoriousness, render them disdainful to others, and wretched in themselves. May they speak evil of no one--- but upon their tongue, may there dwell the law of kindness. May they hate and abhor lying---with all deceit and hypocrisy.

May they be always willing to receive instruction ; and be diligent in acquiring all the knowledge and improvement, that may render them the blessings and ornaments of society.

Keep them from evil company. If sinners entice them, may they never consent; but early may they take hold of the skirt of him that is a Jew. saying, I will go with you, for I have heard that God is with you.

We seek not great things for them as to this world—but O, let them live in thy sight; let them be numbered with thy saints in glory everlasting: let them be blessed with all spiritual blessings, in heavenly places in Christ.

Instead of multiplying riches, and leaving them incentives to pride, and vanity, and idleness, and sensuality; and augmenting a thousand fold all the difficulties of their salvation—May we lay up for them treasure in heaven; may we be concerned to leave behind us, a large inheritance of prayers and instructions, and examples—with the blessing of God, that maketh rich. and addeth no sorrow with it.

If their parents should be taken away from them, when father and mother forsake them, may the Lord take them up. If they should be deprived of their father—be Thou the Father of the fatherless; or, should they be deprived of their mother—as one whom his mother comforteth, so do Thou comfort them.

Should they be removed from us, in early life, may the heavenly shepherd gather the lambs with His arm, and carry them in His bosom; and may we be prepared to resign them. And, if, as we submissively implore, their lives should be prolonged—may they grow up, and prove our comfort and honour; serve thy generation according to thy will; and walk before Thee in the land of the living.

FOR CRIMINALS IN PRISON.

BEHOLD, in the greatness of thy mercy, those who are bound in affliction and iron, because they rebelled against the word of God. May they be led to reflect upon the evil of sin, in the degradation, and misery to which it has reduced them. Give them repentance unto life, that they may acknowledge that Thou art just in all that is brought upon them, and be more concerned to obtain deliverance from the wrath to come, than exemption from the hand of civil justice. If, after lengthened confinement, they should be released, let them be rescued from the bondage of corruption, and partake of the glorious liberty of the sons of God ; and if appointed unto death, O, hear the sighing of the prisoner, and though the flesh be destroyed, let the spirit be saved in the day of the Lord Jesus.

While we feel an abhorrence of sin, may we always display compassion for sinners ; and be thankful that we have been exempted, by the favourableness of our condition in life, by pious relations, by education, by thy restraining and thy sanctifying grace, from so many temptations by which we might have been conquered. Who made us to differ from another; and what have we that we did not receive ?

21*

ADDRESSES

PARTICULAR SEASONS.

SPRING.

Thou art the fountain of life ; in Thee we live, move, and have our being—and the prerogative of that being is, that we are able to contemplate thy perfections, and rise from thy works—to thyself.

Thou sendest forth thy Spirit ; and renewest the face of the earth ; and, from apparent death, all nature starts into re-animated vigour and joy. In what myriads of productions art Thou displaying afresh, the wonders of thy wisdom, power, and goodness—the whole earth is full of thy riches.

While we partake of the general sympathy and delight, may we join with all thy works to praise Thee. And, O Thou God of all grace, bless us with the renewing of the Holy Ghost, in all the powers of our souls. May old things pass away, and all become new in Christ : may the beauty of the Lord be upon us ; and the joy of the Lord be our strength.

May the young remember, that they are now in the spring of life ; and that *this* spring, once gone, returns no more. May they, therefore, eagerly seize, and zealously improve, the short, but all important season, for the cultivation of their minds, the formation of their habits, the correction of their tempers, their preparation for future usefulness, and their gaining that good part which shall not be taken away from them.

SUMMER.

We hail Thee in the varying aspects of the year, and bless Thee for all their appropriate influences and advantages. O, let us not view them and enjoy them as men only, but as christians also; and ever connect with them, the better blessings of thy grace.

How wise, and useful, and necessary, are these intermingled rains and sunbeams—may Jesus, as the Sun of righteousness, arise upon us, with healing under his wings; and may he come down as rain upon the mown grass, and as showers that water the earth.

When we walk by the cooling brook—may we think of that river, the streams whereof make glad the city of God.

When we retire from the scorching warmth of the day, into the inviting shade—may we be thankful for a rest at noon, a shelter from the heat, the shadow of a great rock in a weary land.

May thy servants behold the moral fields, that are already white unto harvest, and be all anxiety to save the multitudes, that are perishing for lack of knowledge.

The harvest truly is great, but the labourers are few; we therefore pray, that Thou wilt send forth labourers into thy harvest.

He that gathereth in summer, is a wise son; he that sleepeth in harvest, is a son that causeth shame. Now is our accepted time, now is our day of salvation. O, let us not waste our precious privileges, and in a dying hour exclaim—The harvest is past, the summer is ended, and we are not saved.

AUTUMN.

How fleeting as well as varying, are the seasons of the year. How insensibly have the months of spring and summer vanished; and nature has no sooner attained its maturities, than we behold its declension and decay. The fields are now shorn of their produce; the beauties of the garden are withered; the woods are changing their verdure, and the trees shedding their foliage—we also never continue in one stay. Many of our connexions and comforts have already dropped away from us; and the remaining are holden by a slender tenure; while we ourselves, do all fade as a leaf, and in a little time, our places will know us no more.

Blessed be the God and Father of our Lord Jesus Christ, for the announcement of an inheritance that fadeth not away. O for a hope full of immortality; for a possession of that good part, which shall not be taken away from us

WINTER.

Ο Thou God of nature and providence; manifold are thy works; in wisdom Thou hast made them all; and all are full of thy goodness. The welfare of thy creatures, requires the severity of winter, as well as the pleasures of spring. We adore thy hand in all. Thou givest snow like

wool; Thou scatterest the hoar frost like ashes.
Thou sendest abroad thine ice like morsels, who
can stand before thy cold?

But we bless Thee, for a house to shelter us;
for raiment to cover us; for fuel to warm us; and
for all the accommodations, that render life even
at this inclement season, not only tolerable, but
full of comfort.

> Not more than others we deserve,
> Yet God has given us more.

May we be grateful; and may we be pitiful.
May we reflect on the condition of those, who are
the victims of every kind of privation and distress—and waste nothing; hoard nothing; but hast-
en to be ministers of mercy, and the disciples of
Him, who went about doing good.

O, let the rich, *now*, deservedly prize their
wealth, and use it as the instrument of usefulness.
May they be willing to communicate, and ready to
distribute; and enjoy the blessing of him that is
ready to perish; and make the widow's heart to
sing for joy.

A TIME OF THUNDER AND LIGHTNING.

WITH Thee is terrible majesty. Thou lookest
on the earth, and it melteth; Thou touchest the
mountains and they smoke. Thou thunderest in
the heavens, and all nature shudders at thy voice.
How vain now is the help of man! Who can resis
thy will! We feel ourselves to be nothing, less
than nothing, and vanity. Our very houses are n
protection now. O Thou, to whom belong the issues from death, defend our persons and our dwelling. May we always stand in awe of Thee, and
sin not. May we know that this awful God is ours,
our Father and our Friend; and may we have

boldness in that day, when the heavens being on
fire shall be dissolved, and the elements melt with
fervent heat, and the earth also, and all the works
that are therein, shall be burnt up.

THANKSGIVINGS

FOR

Particular Events.

FOR RAIN AFTER A LONG DROUGHT.

Thou hast never left thyself without witness, but hast been continually doing good, even to the unthankful and unworthy, in giving them rain from heaven, and fruitful seasons, and filling their hearts with joy and gladness. We acknowledge, that the heavens over us might have been brass, and the earth under us iron. We have justly deserved the calamity; and thy power, without a miracle, could have inflicted it; but though Thou hast tried our patience, and awakened our fears, Thou hast not forgotten to be gracious. We praise Thee for sending us the seasonable and plentiful rain, by which Thou hast refreshed and revived the drooping fields, so that the earth promises to yield her increase.

FOR FAIR WEATHER AFTER MUCH RAIN.

O God, Thou art good, and doest good. Thou hast again surpassed our deserts, and been better to us than our fears. Thou hast caused the clear shining after rain ; so that in the meadows the hay appeareth ; and in the fields Thou art preparing of thy goodness for the poor. Thou preservest man and beast. May we feel our entire dependence upon Thee ; and by prayer and praise, give Thee the glory that is due unto thy holy name.

FOR A GOOD HARVEST.

Again Thou hast crowned the year with thy goodness. The grain might have perished in the earth, or have failed of maturity, for want of the showers, and of the sunshine ; but Thou wast pleased to bless the springing thereof ; and we saw first the blade, then the ear, and after that the full corn in the ear. We hailed the valleys standing thick with corn, and heard the little hills rejoicing on every side. In due time the mower filled his hands, and the binder of sheaves his bosom ; and the appointed weeks of harvest have been afforded us, to gather in the precious produce. O that men would praise the Lord for his goodness, and for his wonderful works to the children of men ! For he satisfieth the longing soul, and filleth the hungry soul with goodness.

We have again witnessed thy faithfulness and truth in the promise—while the earth remaineth, seed time and harvest, and cold and heat, and summer and winter, and day and night, shall not cease---May we learn to trust Thee in all thy engagements.

And make us thankful, that as we have no famine of bread, so we have no famine of hearing the word of the Lord. With regard to the soul, as well as to the body. Thou fillest us with the finest of the wheat.

FOR PEACE.

O Thou that stillest the noise of the seas, the noise of their waves, and the tumult of the people ; we bless Thee, that Thou hast made peace in our borders, and called us to adore Thee, as the repairer of the breach, the restorer of paths to dwell in.

We lament the evils of war, both natural and moral : and confess with shame, that ever since man became an apostate from Thee, he has been an enemy to his brother ; and that from the death of Abel, our earth has been a field of blood. O, let thy word be speedily accomplished. Let the nations learn war no more, but beat their swords into ploughshares, and their spears into pruning-hooks ; and only emulate each other in husbandry, and commerce, and science, and religion.

O, Thou Prince of Peace, preside in every coun cil. May all public teachers recommend peace. In private life, may we follow peace with all men ; and cherish the principles and the dispositions, which will prepare us for that world, where we shall enter nto peace and the sound of war will be heard .o more.

FOR A SAFE RETURN FROM A JOURNEY

As the keeper of Israel Thou hast been with us, not only in the house, but by the way. We might have been injured by wicked and unreasona ble men. We might have been left groaning under the pain of bruised or fractured limbs. Our lives might have been spilt, like water on the ground, which cannot be gathered up again ; and the first tidings that reached our friends, might have plunged them into anguish.

But all our bones can say, Who is a God like unto Thee ? Thy secret too, in our absence, has been upon our tabernacle, and secured it from all evil—O that it may be the tabernacle of the righteous ; and be ever filled, not only with the voice of rejoicing, but of praise.

And be with us in all the future journey of life ; guide us by thy counsel, uphold us by thy power ; and supply all our wants till we come to our Father's house in peace.

FOR RECOVERY FROM SICKNESS.

ALL our times are in thy hand. All diseases come at thy call, and go at thy bidding. Thou redeemest our life from destruction, and crownest us with loving kindness and tender mercies. We bless Thee, that Thou hast heard our prayer, and commanded deliverance for our friend and thy servant, who has been under thine afflicting hand. He (or she) was brought low, but Thou hast helped him : Thou hast chastened him sore, but not delivered him over unto death. May he not only live, but declare the works of the Lord.

As Thou hast delivered his eyes from tears, his feet from falling, and his soul from death, may he daily inquire, What shall I render unto the Lord for all his benefits towards me ? and resolve to offer unto Thee, the sacrifices of thanksgiving, and to call upon the name of the Lord.

And may we ever remember, that a recovery is only a reprieve; that the sentence which dooms us to the dust is only suspended; and, that at most, when a few years are come, we shall go the way whence we shall not return. May we therefore secure the one thing needful; and live with eternity in view.

FOR SAFE DELIVERY IN CHILD BIRTH.

WE bless Thee on the behalf of thine hand-maid, who is now saying, I love the Lord, because he hath heard my voice, and my supplication. Thou hast been with her in the hour of pain and peril, and made her the joyful mother of a living and well formed infant. Complete thy goodness by the renewal of her strength, and her ability to appear again in all the duties of her important station.

Let the impressions produced by recent mercies, be rendered as durable as they are lively : may she remember, and pay Thee the vows, which her soul made when in trouble.

May the life spared, and the life given, be dear in thy sight, and devoted to thy glory ; and may every addition made to the world of creatures, be found an accession to the church of the living God.

TO BE USED AS SOON AS CONVENIENT AFTER SAFE DELIVERY.

I LOVE the Lord, because He hath heard my voice, and my supplication. Consider, O my soul, how greatly thou art indebted to the divine goodness. Look back, and reflect on thy former fears and anxieties ; look up and bless God that they are gone, and that their cause is removed. I found trouble and sorrow. Then called I upon the name of the Lord, and said, O Lord, I beseech Thee, deliver my soul. Gracious is the Lord, and righteous; yea, our God is merciful. I was brought low, and He helped me. Return unto the rest, O my soul, for the Lord hath dealt bountifully with thee.

O, my God, I sincerely thank thee for thy great goodness to me and mine. By supporting me in the hour of pain, by granting me proper assistance, by blessing the means which thy providence afforded me, by making me the living mother of a living child, by strengthening me thus far, and by giving me the prospect of speedy recovery and confirmed health, Thou hast dissipated our fears, calmed our minds, gladdened our hearts, and made a family happy. Thou hast exchanged our face of care for a bosom full of joy, and turned our earnest cries into hymns of ardent praise. Bless the Lord, O my soul, and forget not all His benefits. Who forgiveth all thine iniquities; who healeth all thy diseases. Who redeemeth thy life from destruction; who crowneth thee with loving kindness and tender mercies.

What shall I render unto the Lord for all His benefits towards me? I will take the cup of salvation, and call upon the name of the Lord.

I will cheerfully devote myself, and all I have, unto the God of my life. Oh! never may I forget the mercies I have received. Never may I be unthankful for them. May a lively sense of them dwell on my mind, and be ever visible in my actions; may it be my daily care to pay unto God those vows which I made when my soul was in trouble. I hope my goodness will not be as a morning cloud, and go away as the early dew. But, by the grace of God. I trust I shall continue in faith and charity, and holiness with sobriety. Because he hath inclined His ear unto me, there fore will I call upon Him as long as I live, I will walk before the Lord in the land of the living.

O Thou whose goodness to them that fear Thee knows no bounds, with my whole heart I praise Thee for thy loving-kindness unto me, thine unworthy creature. Thou hast delivered my soul from death, mine eyes from tears, and my feet from falling. To Thee I owe myself, and every blessing I possess. To Thee I dedicate this infant. Lord take it for thine own. On the soul of this dear child draw thine holy image, and keep it for ever from the pollutions of this wicked world. Give me and its father grace to set it a constant, good example, and may we bring it up in the nurture and admonition of the Lord. While we pray that its life may be spared, we also pray for entire resignation to thy blessed will ; but, shouldest Thou, as we hope, be pleased to allot it to the years of man, we earnestly beseech Thee to make it a pillar in thy church, a blessing to the world, and a lasting comfort to its parents. Give them, O God, a heart to love and fear Thee at all times, and may all their future days be spent with the greatest sincerity and faithfulness in thy service, and to thine honour, through faith in Jesus Christ, for whom may their souls most ardently thank Thee. To Him with thy blessed self, O Father, and the Holy Spirit, I desire to ascribe everlasting praises. Amen.

This prayer supposes all things to succeed well; but in different circumstances, different expressions will naturally be adopted. Should it please God to bless this little piece to the good of souls, and should the favour of the public call for a new edition; possibly a meditation ‑ ‑ ‑ ‑ particular cases may be adde

A MORNING PRAYER TO BE PUBLICLY
READ IN SCHOOLS.

O LORD, Thou who hast safely brought us to the beginning of this day! defend us in the same by thy mighty power, and grant that this day we fall into no sin, neither run into any kind of danger; but that all our doings may be ordered by thy governance, to do always that which is righteous in thy sight.

Particularly we beg thy blessing upon our present undertakings. Prevent us, O Lord, in all our doings with thy most gracious favour, and further us with thy continual help; that in these and all our works begun, continued, and ended in Thee, we may glorify thy holy name, and finally, by thy mercy, obtain everlasting life.

We humbly acknowledge, O Lord, our errors and misdeeds; that we are unable to keep ourselves, and unworthy of thy assistance; but we beseech Thee, through thy great goodness, to pardon our offences, to enlighten our understandings, to strengthen our memories, to sanctify our hearts, and to guide our lives. Help us, we pray Thee, to learn and to practise those things which are good, that we may become serious christians, and useful in the world; to the glory of thy great name, and our present and future well-being. These prayers, both for them and ourselves, we humbly offer up in the name of thy Son Jesus Christ our Redeemer; concluding in His perfect form of words:

Our Father which art in heaven, hallowed be thy name; thy kingdom come; thy will be done on earth, as it is in heaven. Give us this day our daily bread; and forgive us our trespasses, as we forgive them that trespass against us. And lead us not into temptation, but deliver us from evil; for thine is the kingdom, the power and the glory, for ever and ever. Amen.

AN EVENING PRAYER TO BE PUBLICLY READ IN SCHOOLS.

ACCEPT, we beseech Thee, O Lord, our evening sacrifice of praise and thanksgiving, for all thy goodness and loving-kindness to us, particularly for tne blessings of this day ; for thy gracious protection and preservation ; for the opportunities we have enjoyed for the instruction and improvement of our minds ; for all the comforts of this life ; and the hope of life everlasting, as declared unto us by Jesus Christ our Redeemer.

Forgive, most merciful Father, we humbly pray Thee, all the errors and transgressions which Thou hast beheld in us the day past ; and help us to express our unfeigned sorrow for what has been amiss, by our care to amend it.

What we know not, do Thou teach us; instruct us in all the particulars of our duty, both towards Thee and towards men ; and give us grace always to do those things which are good and well-pleasing in thy sight.

Whatsoever good instructions have been here given this day, grant that they may be carefully remembered, and duly followed. And whatsoever good desires Thou hast put into any of our hearts, grant that, by the assistance of thy grace, they may be brought to good effect : that thy name may have the honour ; and we, with those who are assistant to us in this our work of instruction. may have comfort at the day of account.

Lighten our darkness, we beseech Thee, O Lord and by thy great mercy defend us from all perils and dangers of this night. Continue to us the blessings we enjoy ; and help us to testify our thankfulness for them, by a due use and improvement of them.

Bless all those in authority, together with all our friends and benefactors, particularly the conductors of this school, for whom we are bound in an especial manner to pray. Bless this and all other seminaries for religious and truly christian education; and direct and prosper all pious endeavours for making mankind good and holy.

These praises and prayers we humbly offer up to thy divine Majesty, in the name, and as the disciple of thy Son Jesus Christ our Lord; in whose words we sum up all our desires.

Our Father, &c.

A MORNING PRAYER TO BE USED BY A CHILD AT HOME.

GLORY to Thee, O Lord, who hast preserved me from the perils of the night past, who hast refreshed me with sleep, and raised me up again to praise thy holy name.

Incline my heart to all that is good; that I may be modest and humble, true and just, temperate and diligent, respectful and obedient to my superiors; that I may fear and love Thee above all things; that I may love my neighbour as myself, and do to every one as I would they should do unto me.

Bless me, I pray Thee, in my learning; and help me daily to increase in knowledge, and wisdom, and all virtue.

I humbly beg thy blessing upon all our spiritual pastors and masters, all my relations and friends, [*particularly my father and mother, my brothers and sisters, and every one in this house.*] Grant them whatsoever may be good for them in this life, and guide them to life everlasting.

I humbly commit myself to Thee, O Lord, in the name of Jesus Christ my Saviour, and in the words which He Himself hath taught me:

Our Father, &c.

AN EVENING PRAYER TO BE USED BY A CHILD AT HOME.

GLORY be to Thee, O Lord, who hast preserved me the day past, who hast defended me from all the evils to which I am constantly exposed in this uncertain life, who hast continued my health, who hast bestowed upon me all things necessary for life and godliness.

I humbly beseech Thee, O heavenly Father! to pardon whatsoever Thou hast seen amiss in me this day, in my thoughts, words or actions. Bless to me, I pray Thee, whatsoever good instructions have been given me this day; help me carefully to remember them, and duly to improve them; that I may be ever growing in knowledge, and wisdom, and goodness.

I humbly beg thy blessing also upon all our spiritual pastors and masters, all my relations and friends [*particularly my father and mother, my brothers and sisters, and every one in this house.*] Let it please Thee to guide us all in this life present, and to conduct us to thy heavenly kingdom.

I humbly commit my soul and body to thy care this night; begging thy gracious protection and blessing, through Jesus Christ our only Lord and Saviour; in whose words I conclude my prayer.

Our Father, &c.

A SHORT PRAYER ON FIRST GOING INTO THE SEAT AT CHURCH.

LORD, I am now in thy house: assist, I pray Thee, and accept of my services. Let thy Holy Spirit help mine infirmities; disposing my heart to seriousness, attention, and devotion; to the honour of thy holy name, and the benefit of my soul, through Jesus Christ our Saviour. Amen.

BEFORE LEAVING THE SEAT.

Blessed be thy name, O Lord! for this opportunity of attending Thee in thy house and service. Make me, I pray Thee, a doer of thy word, not a hearer only. Accept both us and our services, through our only Mediator, Jesus Christ our Lord. Amen.

PRAYERS AT TABLE.

BEFORE MEAT.

ALMIGHTY God! the eyes of all wait on Thee, and Thou givest them their meat in due season. Bless, we beseech Thee, the provisions of thine earthly bounty, which are now before us ;---and let them nourish and strengthen our frail bodies, that we may the better serve Thee, through Jesus Christ. Amen.

or thus:

BOUNTIFUL giver of every good and perfect gift! Thou art never weary of supplying our returning wants,---Grant, we pray Thee, that the food of which we are about to partake, may contribute to the comfort and support of our bodies,---and enable us to engage with more zeal in thy service ; which we ask for Jesus Christ's sake. Amen.

or thus:

LET thy blessing, Almighty God, descend on this portion of thy bounty, and on us, thy unworthy servants, through Jesus Christ our Lord.

or thus:

ALMIGHTY God, we beseech Thee to pardon our sins, to bless the refreshment now before us, to our use, and us to thy service, through Jesus Christ.

FATHER of Lights, from wnom cometn down every good and perfect gift, enable us to receive these fruits of thy bounty with humility and gratitude, and give us grace, that, whether we eat or drink or whatever we do, we may do all to thy glory, and be accepted to the great Redeemer.

or tnus:

BOUNTEOUS God, we acknowledge our dependence on Thee, and our unworthiness of thy benefits. We pray Thee to forgive our sins; to bless us in the reception of this food, and enable us to improve the strength we may derive from it to thy glory, for Christ's sake.

or thus:

SANCTIFY, O Lord, we beseech Thee, these thy productions to our use, and us to thy service, through Jesus Christ our Lord. Amen.

AFTER MEAT.

WE thank Thee, O God, our heavenly Father! for the innumerable good gifts of thy providence. Especially do we thank Thee for the rich provision Thou hast made for our souls— Accept our grateful acknowledgments for the food we have now received: and enable us to prove our sincerity by the holiness and obedience of our lives, for the sake of our Lord and Saviour, Jesus Christ. Amen.

or thus :

WHAT shall we render to Thee, O God, for all thy benefits ? Every day of our lives we are receiving fresh tokens of thy favour. O, let thy goodness lead us to repentance. And if we can do no more than express our gratitude---help us to do that in the sincerity of our souls---and thine shall be the glory, for ever, through Jesus Christ. Amen.

or thus

ACCEPT, heavenly Father, our humble thanks for this, and for all thy blessings, through Jesus Christ.

or thus :

WE thank Thee, our heavenly Father, for tne rich provision Thou hast made for our temporal and eternal welfare ; especially for the food we have now received. May thy goodness lead us to repentance, and thy grace prepare us for heavenly entertainments, through Jesus Christ our Lord.

or thus :

WE praise Thee, O Lord, for the provisions of thy providence and grace, and in particular for this renewed token of thy favour. May we feel our increased obligations to be thine, and be fitted at length, to eat bread in thy heavenly kingdom, through our Lord Jesus Christ.

or thus :

WE bless Thee, O Lord, for this kind refreshment. Be pleased to continue thy favours and feed us with the bread of life. Supply the wants of the

23

needy, and enable us, while we live on thy bounty
to live to thy glory, for Christ's sake.　Amen.

or thus :

BLESSED and praised be thy holy name, O Lord,
for this and all thy other blessings bestowed upon
us, through Jesus Christ our Lord.　Amen.

FINIS.

www.ingramcontent.com/pod-product-compliance
Lightning Source LLC
Chambersburg PA
CBHW020351030726

47496CB00007B/2105